Federal Britain

In *Federal Britain*, John Kendle explores and analyses the British engagement with the federal idea from the early 1600s to the present day. The United Kingdom is faced with two major federal constitutional debates. The first is about the nations which comprise the British state and, hence, the division of power between Westminster and regional parliaments. The second surrounds the United Kingdom and the European Union. John Kendle sets these contemporary discussions in context in this book and provides valuable insights into their origins.

John Kendle argues that the federal idea has been a consistent feature of constitutional debate in the British Isles since the union of the crowns. In *Federal Britain* he examines the break-up of the first British empire and the development of modern federalism. As well as discussing the Anglo–Irish relationship and the United Kingdom's relationship to Europe, the author focuses on other contemporary issues such as the world order, imperial federation and decolonization. He considers the possibility of a rearrangement of constitutional relations within the United Kingdom.

Federal Britain outlines arguments for and against the adoption of the federal idea as a solution to either domestic or world problems. It is a timely addition to British constitutional thought and a thorough survey which will appeal to all historians and political scientists concerned with what offers the best potential government for a state.

John Kendle is Professor of History and Chair of History, University of Manitoba, Canada.

Federal Britain

A history

John Kendle

London and New York

First published 1997
by Routledge
11 New Fetter Lane, London EC4P 4EE

Simultaneously published in the USA and Canada
by Routledge
29 West 35th Street, New York, NY 10001

© 1997 John Kendle

Typeset in Times by Routledge
Printed and bound in Great Britain by TJ International,
Padstow, Cornwall

British Library Cataloguing in Publication Data
A catalogue record for this book is available from the British Library

Library of Congress Cataloguing in Publication Data
Kendle, John, 1937–
Federal Britain : a history / John Kendle.
Includes bibliographical references and index.
1. Federal government–Great Britain. 2. Central-local government
relations–Great Britain. 3 European Union–Great Britain.
I. Title.
JN297.F43K46 1997
320.8′0941–dc20   96–44155
                                                       CIP

ISBN 0–415–15862–1 (hbk)
ISBN 0–415–15863–x (pbk)

To the memory of G.S. Graham and W.L. Morton

Contents

Preface

This book explores and analyses the British engagement with the federal idea from the early 1600s to the present day. From the union of the crowns at the beginning of the seventeenth century the federal idea has consistently been recognized and often resorted to by Britons and their government as a solution to complex domestic, imperial and foreign problems. As the twenty-first century rapidly approaches the United Kingdom is again confronted with two major constitutional issues. The first is the interrelationship of the nations comprising the British state and the division of powers between the central parliament located at Westminster and various regional or provincial parliaments established to handle the affairs of those nations. The second, and at present the most contentious, is the relationship of the United Kingdom to the European Union. In both instances, the federal idea is at the centre of debate.

The purpose of this book is to set these contemporary discussions in context and to demonstrate that far from the federal idea being an alien concept to the British, it has in fact been a consistent feature of constitutional debate in the British Isles and has been rigorously explored at various moments of domestic crisis, extensively implemented in the empire as a means of resolving complex ethnic, linguistic, religious and territorial problems and consistently suggested as a means of establishing greater order and stability in the wider world. This exploration of the federal idea by various Britons at various times has resulted in extensive archival material and a rich pamphlet, article and monographic literature that has all too often been neglected or summarily shunted aside by both historians and political scientists. Given current circumstances it would seem appropriate to examine the reactions of Britons over time to an idea which reflects a desire for more plural constitutional arrangements than those made possible within a state where the concept of undivided sovereignty remains sacrosanct. In exploring that reaction it is necessary to examine why the British, particularly the English, remained attached to the idea of undivided sovereignty for so long in the domestic sphere while willingly experimenting with it from the 1840s in their empire and especially during the years of rapid decolonization after 1945.

The federal idea has often elicited a harsh reaction within the United Kingdom but all too often that reaction has either been the result of a misconception about the nature of 'true federalism' or a defensive stance by an elite unwilling to contemplate a sharing or transfer of power. Since the late seventeenth century the British, particularly the English, have been anxious to preserve the stability of the state. The most obvious way to do that was to preserve a highly centralized government at Westminster with minimal latitude for independent action in the various nations and regions. As a consequence sovereignty was said to lie with a central parliament, i.e. king, lords and commons, and was indivisible. This line of constitutional argument was beaten into a dogma by the nineteenth century and further enshrined by such constitutional pundits as Edward Freeman and A.V. Dicey. It was widely accepted and rarely questioned and is still pervasive today. This has often made it exceedingly difficult for the proponents of the federal idea to gain a wide hearing amongst the general public or to generate consistent support in the upper echelons in Whitehall and Westminster.

In the nineteenth century the greatest fear of Unionists such as Dicey and of mainline politicians was the weakening of the British state. To their minds, the adoption of a federal system of government would have that result. It would divide sovereignty between the centre and the regions and thus lessen the authority of Westminster at home and abroad. But as anyone knowledgeable could attest this was to misunderstand completely the federal idea. Admittedly, its essence is an agreed division of powers between a central government and regional or provincial governments, but in a 'true' federation each government remains sovereign in its particular sphere. Therefore, a central government responsible for defence and foreign affairs would not have its international authority diminished one iota under a federal system nor would its authority be lessened in those areas where it was responsible for domestic matters of concern to the country as a whole. Similarly, the regional parliaments are sovereign within their defined juris-dictions. In essence, a federal system of government is the reconciliation of central control and local self-government. It enables each level of govern-ment to operate without interference from the other. Within a federation sovereignty is divided but coordinated and can be wielded cooperatively. It is the ideal form of government for preserving or creating unity while protecting diversity.

These positive attributes of the federal idea were not lost on all nineteenth-century observers. Baron Acton recognized, as Dicey apparently did not, that undivided sovereignty could lead to centralization and abso-lutism. For him liberty by definition meant diversity and in turn diversity preserved liberty. This fitted in with the essence of modern federalism as devised by the Americans in the 1780s. Under such a system there was not only a division of sovereignty between central and regional governments within which each was sovereign, but the regions were also involved in the decision-making at the centre by means of a second chamber, the Senate.

Moreover, and perhaps of most significance, both the central and regional governments were dependent on the citizenry. In fact, it could be argued that since popular sovereignty was the underpinning of the authority of both the central and the regional governments that sovereignty was always intact. Certainly, Henry Sidgwick, the late nineteenth-century constitutional observer, was struck by these positive features of federal government. To him a federal state was more democratic than a unitary one and he believed it was only a matter of time before it was realized that the federal form of government offered the best means of maintaining liberty with order. This is how many of the ardent advocates of the federal idea viewed the situation and the literature is replete with their passionate conviction that only by adapting federalism at home and abroad could the United Kingdom become properly democratic and the world a safer place.

But to emphasize only the zeal and idealism that lay at the heart of such groups as the Round Table movement and Federal Union would be to distort the full range of motives underlying the British involvement with the federal idea. At crucial moments a federal system of government seemed to offer the only possible solution to complex political problems. This was especially so in the late nineteenth and early twentieth centuries when the question of the relationship of Ireland to the United Kingdom was a constant concern. On the one hand, it appeared to offer a means of maintaining the unity of the British state while preserving the multiple loyalties and distinctive ethos of each of its four nations. Initially, the term 'federal' was loosely used to mean no more than home rule all round or 'federal devolution', but gradually even died-in-the-wool Unionists such as Lord Selborne and Walter Long concluded that only 'true' federalism offered any real hope of preserving unity while protecting diversity. Walter Long was instrumental in keeping the federal idea alive in discussions at the most senior levels of the Lloyd George coalition and in ensuring that the Government of Ireland Act of 1920 was based on federal principles. Unfortunately, when it failed the six north-eastern counties of Ireland were left entombed in the constitutional straitjacket of devolution with restricted political and financial powers and at the mercy of Westminster, a reality startlingly demonstrated in 1972 with the abolition of the Stormont parliament. While the province of Northern Ireland was a unique constitutional feature in the United Kingdom landscape, owing its genesis to the pragmatic adoption of the federal idea by English Unionists, it was not a valid example of 'true federalism'. Nevertheless, the constitutional debate stretching from the 1870s to 1921 over the Anglo-Irish relationship was critical to the future of the British state and highly revealing of attitudes towards the relationship of the state and the 'nation' and of the state and the individual. At the heart of that debate was the federal idea.

Similarly, but for a somewhat longer spell, the federal concept was central to the discussions about the relationship of the United Kingdom to its empire. Again, the impetus was the protection of the United Kingdom's stature and status in a world of emergent rivals, gathering friction and intense economic and strategic competition. In the latter decades of the nineteenth century and well into the 1920s the possibility of imperial federation was constantly explored, debated and advocated by publicists, theorists and politicians as a means of preserving the integrity of the empire. Very often the possibility of imperial federation could not be separated from the discussions surrounding a federal United Kingdom and this not only enriched the debate but obliged politicians of all parties to become familiar with at least the essence of the federal idea. It is during those years straddling the nineteenth and twentieth centuries that the influence of Dicey and Freeman was most manifest. Dicey, in particular, was a passionate defender of undivided sovereignty and thus of the Union and an apparently devastating critic of the federal idea. The fact that he misrepresented the issue of the sovereignty of parliament and was misleading about the strengths and weaknesses of federalism was not obvious to most of his readers or political allies, the majority of whom could not contemplate a fragmenting of either the United Kingdom or the empire and were only too happy to have their predisposition backed by constitutional 'expertise'. As a result, the federal idea received a rough ride from many sides but its advocates persisted and its merits as a system of government were widely canvassed.

By the 1920s the British government and its civil service were actively exploring the federal idea as a potential solution to difficult regional, economic, political, ethnic and religious problems in the West Indies and East Africa and by the early 1930s had begun the process of devising a federal governmental structure for India. This adoption of the federal idea in the imperial arena in the twentieth century was not entirely surprising in that the British had been willing since the 1840s to use it as a means of ensuring economic, strategic and political stability in the white settlement colonies of British North America, New Zealand, Australia and South Africa. This had not been a position quickly arrived at but the merits of adopting the American federal system became increasingly obvious to many empire watchers and Colonial Office officials such that by the 1860s they were encouraging the British North Americans to unite in a federation. The Dominion of Canada became the first federation within the empire in 1867 and was followed in 1901 by the Commonwealth of Australia.

The obvious question to ask in this context is why did the British readily adopt the federal idea in the empire but not at home? The answer would seem to lie in a reluctance of the political elite to share power – to divide sovereignty – within the United Kingdom. The sovereignty of the Westminster parliament would not be challenged by the creation of federal structures at the periphery of empire. The ties of such newly created polities would still be with Westminster and Whitehall. The British therefore proceeded with impunity to 'invent' federal structures abroad but to spurn the concept at home.

The attractions of the federal idea as a solution to complex colonial problems only increased after 1945 as British power waned, its internal and external problems mounted and the pressure from the colonies for self-government and independence intensified. Federations seemed to offer not only a quick route to independence for the colonists but also a handy means of launching reasonably reliable political and economic unions. The federal idea offered British governments an attractive constitutional means of extricating themselves from both the difficulties associated with maintaining an empire and the opprobrium that would follow from releasing a number of small states onto the world stage. The intensive discussions of the federal idea by Federal Union in the late 1930s and early 1940s had proved an enormous boon. It had, among other things, led to the first full-ranging discussion of the application of the federal idea in a colonial context and from those debates had emerged some first-rate British writing on federalism by men such as Kenneth Wheare and Ivor Jennings who were soon called upon to advise on the application of the federal idea during the intensive decolonizing process of the 1950s and 1960s.

Thus by the time the debates over the United Kingdom's internal and external constitutional futures were joined in the 1960s there existed an extensive body of home-grown literature on the federal idea, increasingly detached, analytic and persuasive and free of the vague shibboleths of the past. That material has not received extensive analysis nor have the arguments for and against the adoption of the federal idea by the British as a solution to either domestic or imperial or world problems. It is the purpose of this book to examine these debates and arguments over the last four centuries and thereby to contribute to an understanding of an idea central to the reformulation of the British state and the relationship of that state to Europe. In doing so I hope to fill a significant gap in the literature on British constitutional thought and practice at home and in the empire, to suggest that indivisible sovereignty is a constitutional concept without much contemporary substance and to point out that contrary to a widely held belief the federal idea in its 'true' form offers the best potential government for a state concerned above all else with both liberty and order.

Acknowledgements

For help in preparing this book I am grateful to the staff of the following institutions: the British Library; the Public Record Office; the House of Lords Record Office; the Institute of Historical Research; the British Library of Political and Economic Science; the University of London Library; the Bodleian Library; Cambridge University Library; the National Library of Ireland; the National Library of Wales; the National Library of Scotland; the Scottish Record Office; the University of Minnesota Library; the Manitoba Provincial Library; the University of Manitoba Library; and St John's College Library, University of Manitoba.

This project has been generously supported by the Social Sciences and Humanities Research Council of Canada which by awarding me a three-year research grant greatly facilitated the completion of the project. A six-month research/study leave from the University of Manitoba gave me a period of time uninterrupted by other commitments and enabled me to write the first draft of this book. I am particularly grateful to Heather McCallum and her colleagues at Routledge for their excellent advice and to Lynn Woycheshen of St John's College, University of Manitoba, for so rapidly and efficiently typing my drafts. A special thanks to Judy for her support, understanding and advice.

1 Indivisible sovereignty

It is natural to begin an examination of the 'federal idea' in the United Kingdom with the seventeenth century. At the beginning of the century James VI of Scotland became James I of England. This resulted in a major debate over the nature of the union. It was clear the English, as the stronger 'imperial' power, preferred a complete union while the Scots wanted a union that reflected the equality of the two kingdoms. The questions surrounding the relationship of this new union to the kingdom of Ireland rarely arose, and the subservience of Wales to England was taken for granted. The multiple kingdoms of the British Isles had no ready examples to turn to nor any prevailing theories to assist them in their constitutional dilemma.

No one, certainly not the English and the Scots, had developed a theory or concept of federalism by the beginning of the seventeenth century that might have helped clarify possibilities nor had they fully elaborated the concept of sovereignty. As Jenny Wormald has pointed out, there were no historical or contemporary European models that might have provided guidance and insight. Those states which historians and students of politics have sometimes referred to as federal examples, such as the unions of Norway and Sweden, Castile and Aragon, and Poland and Lithuania, were no more than unstable composite kingships and certainly a far cry from any arrangement that could later be construed as federal.[1] Anyway, the English were convinced of their superiority to the Welsh and the Irish and viewed with suspicion a close relationship with the Scots. On their side, the Scots had no intention of surrendering their religious, legal and educational systems to a cross-border unity. Neither the English nor the Scots were prepared in the early seventeenth century to explore more subtle resolutions to the problem. As Wormald succinctly states, 'there was very little interest indeed in consolidating and integrating the kingdoms of Britain into a British kingdom. The main parties were almost entirely indifferent, except on [those] rare occasions when the security of both was threatened at the same time; and then, like a seismic shock, there was a British Problem.'[2]

Thus when James VI of Scotland became James I of England on the death of Elizabeth in 1603 commentators and political analysts had no precedents or well-developed political theories on which to draw for either context or analysis. James was prepared to move quickly beyond a 'union of the Crowns' to a complete union, 'a perfect union', by uniting England and Scotland. This would have involved uniting their parliaments, administrations and legal systems; in other words, uniting into one British state the two states of England and Scotland. Such a union would not have made provision for the distinct English and Scottish legal systems nor their different religious structures. It would definitely have united the two economies. There was a logic in James's approach. The two countries shared a common language as well as similar cultural, religious and ethnic characteristics, and, of course, they were contiguous which would facilitate amalgamation. James's plan did not, however, appeal to either the Scots or the English. The former feared a loss of sovereignty and the latter were suspicious of Scottish intentions.[3] By 1608 James's efforts had been thwarted and a full-scale discussion of union set aside.

During the debate a number of tracts had been published by both Scots and English exploring the implications of union. One, 'A Breif Consideracion of the Unyon of Twoe Kingedomes in the Handes of One Kinge', written in 1604 by John Doddridge, a lawyer, MP for Horsham, Sussex, and an ardent supporter of the King, raised not only the important question of equal representation in any unified parliament but also suggested a way by which Scotland and England could retain their own parliaments while achieving parliamentary union. Doddridge argued that

> there cann bee no perfect unyon of twoe kingdomes except there bee
> established a meetinge of bothe states and, as it were, a common parlia-
> ment for bothe kingdomes, for the generall causes which shall equallie
> concerne bothe people. Suche a parliament or assemblie have all the
> cantons or confederat states of the Helvetions and Swisors for theire
> generall causes, althoughe every estate perticulerlie have nevertheless his
> proper and peculiar parliament. [In constituting of which general parlia-
> ment] and assembly of bothe nacions in any unyon to be made, great care
> and vigilancy is to bee used in appoytinge what persons shal bee called
> together of those estates, least the one exceede the other in nomber of
> sufferage or voice . . . [4]

This is one of the earliest references to what might be called a federal arrangement although Doddridge did not elaborate any further. While it is clear he wished to devise a means of preventing the domination of the Scots by the English, it is equally clear that he had not thought through all the implications of such an arrangement because his concern for equal representation avoided the problems posed by the disproportionate populations and tax bases of the two kingdoms. Doddridge's joint parliament more closely resembled a senate in a two-tiered parliament of a later day.

In addition to this fleeting reference in 1604 there is only one other consideration of what might be called a federal idea before the late seventeenth century. That occurs in an anonymous pamphlet entitled 'The Devine

Providence in the Misticall and Real Union of England and Scotland' located in the Papers on Scotch Affairs at Beaulieu Palace House. According to Brian Levack, the pamphlet contains 'a more complete constitutional proposal' than Doddridge's. It called

> not only for the perpetuation of 'national parliaments' but also for the establishment of a 'general' parliament to handle matters of common concern. All legal matters would be restricted to the national assemblies, unless there was a conflict between them, in which case the general parliament would settle the matter. Individuals born in one country who possessed land or dignities in the other would be entitled to sit in the national parliament of the other.[5]

While venturing in the direction of a division of powers and, therefore, presumably, a divided sovereignty, there was no elaboration and no theoretical reflection. No consideration was given, for example, to the fundamental issue of the distribution of taxing powers. It should be noted, however, that another 1604 tract by John Russell, 'A Treatise of the Happie and Blissed Unioun', clearly outlined the Scottish determination to avoid losing control over its own affairs. This concern for Scottish sovereignty, although not referred to as such, was to surface continuously in any discussion over union and eventually led the Scots to advocate a 'federal' solution.[6]

During the upheavals of mid-century there was much discussion about a religious union of the two countries but the secular or constitutional dimensions of the relationship rarely surfaced. That did not occur until after 1670 and only received concentrated attention in the early 1700s when discussions over union reached a peak.[7] Similarly, while the Cromwellian union of England, Wales, Ireland and Scotland was a political and administrative union it did not lead to an appraisal of a more flexible, less 'imperial', integration and, of course, it collapsed with the end of the Protectorate. It had reflected neither the existence of a 'British' caste of mind nor an interest in a union that would protect each nation's autonomy within the borders of a single state. Nevertheless, it was obvious that whenever the issue of union was seriously addressed the desire of the Scots to protect their sovereignty was fundamental.

The Scots were understandably concerned about being subsumed politically within an English-dominated union. As the 1670 negotiations revealed, the Scots were concerned to protect the identity of their parliament while creating a body for common concerns. This had also been at the heart of the covenanters' loose union proposals of the 1630s and 1640s. While these proposals have been referred to as 'federal' by recent commentators it should be understood that 'federal' in the seventeenth and early eighteenth centuries meant no more than a covenant, or a compact, or a treaty, or an alliance. It did not mean a union of states involving a division of sovereignty. The Scots did not envision such a division but even if they had the English would not have been interested. The size and resources of the two states were so disparate that, for the English, there was no possibility of an equal union. To them the 'federal' arrangement that lay at the heart of both the covenanters' proposals and the Scottish schemes of the early eighteenth century would simply provide a recognized means for the Scots to interfere in English affairs. This was not an irrational reaction. The degree to which the 'regions' should be represented in a central 'federal' parliament has lain at the heart of the debate over federalism since the late eighteenth century. It is easy to understand, given the prevailing notions of 'federalism' and 'sovereignty' in the early eighteenth century, why the English insisted on a complete, incorporating union or no union at all.[8]

The debate that occurred at the beginning of the eighteenth century was not over whether union would or should occur but whether it would be a 'federal' or 'incorporating' union, with the Scots favouring federation and the English incorporation. The English government had been reluctant to consider union and it was only when it seemed the Scots might decide to choose their own monarch, distinct from an English one, on the death of Queen Anne, plus the exigencies of the War of Spanish Succession, that the English made every effort to secure a continuation of the regal union but this time in a more all-inclusive form. Given that the English had a low opinion of the Scots there was little question of allowing them any political parity. The Scots, in the main, resented such assumptions and engaged in a vigorous effort to promote a union, oftimes referred to as 'federal', that would preserve autonomy while providing a means for cooperation in areas of mutual interest. There was no suggestion on either side that what was being forged was a 'British' nation; a state perhaps, but not a nation. Both the Scots and the English were fiercely protective of their own cultural forms and a wider patriotism was not yet an attraction.[9]

The Scottish concept of a 'federal' union was vague. To the degree that the various pamphleteers and discussants used other models, the constitution of the United Provinces – the Netherlands – seems to have proved attractive, but overall the Scottish perception of a 'federal' union was fuzzy and certainly added up to no more than a treaty or confederal relationship. Of prime concern was a desire to retain legal, religious and educational autonomy, preferably within an autonomous political unit but otherwise within a wider political and economic union. Certainly, the Scots Commissioners were neither attracted to a 'federal' solution nor repelled by an 'incorporating' union. Their feeling was that equality of trade and, particularly, access to colonial trade would be a great boon for Scotland. Moreover, an unwillingness to accept such an arrangement might well mean war, an English invasion, humiliating defeat and the loss of all control over the vital religious, legal and educational fields.[10]

Again it has to be remembered that the concept of federalism as developed in the late eighteenth century and adopted widely in the nineteenth and twentieth centuries was unknown at the end of the seventeenth. The 'federal' cry at the beginning of the eighteenth century was a reflection of Scottish dismay at the proposed abolition of their parliament and the consequent loss of individuality and autonomy that would entail. While some pamphleteers of the late seventeenth century were attempting to unravel the degree of sovereignty the parliaments of England, Scotland and Ireland might have within an 'empire', speculation about the powers of an 'imperial' parliament had not fully begun. The actions and activities of colonial assemblies were not yet readily seen as a form of *de facto* federalism. All powers of such assemblies were assumed to originate in the 'sovereign' parliament at Westminster.[11] The exploration of a division of powers or a division of sovereignty was undertaken cautiously and with limited sophistication and insight. Given the recent civil war in the British Isles and the reaffirmation by the English in 1688 of the power of parliament it is not surprising that this should be so. Even though the full-blown concept of the indivisible sovereignty of parliament was not to be either fully developed or explored until the mid-eighteenth century, it was patently obvious by the early 1700s that the English were already acting as if it were so, either out of arrogance or conviction.

The Country Party in Scotland wanted to protect Scotland's national existence while resolving its considerable economic problems. It wanted a federal rather than an incorporating union but, as James Mackinnon later pointed out, 'England was not prepared to negotiate for any measure short of incorporation'. For the English, incorporation was 'the price of free trade'.[12] To them federalism, as they understood it from the example of the Netherlands, was a weak form of government. They believed 'that a federal solution would not give England the required guarantee of security'. On 11 April 1706 the Duke of Portland wrote, 'an entire union is contemplated . . . I do not comprehend the material benefit of a federal union, nor the means of arriving at it'.[13]

By the time the commissioners opened negotiations in 1703 the Scots had begun to mount a campaign on behalf of a 'federal' constitution and various schemes and ideas, some of them no more than assertions, were circulating. The most elaborate and well thought out was contained in a pamphlet by James Hodges published in 1703.[14] Hodges argued that the word 'union' could be reduced to two principal kinds: incorporating union and federal union. Incorporating meant 'whereby distinct and independent Kingdoms and Dominions parting with their distinction, and Independency do so unite themselves with another Kingdom, as to be embodied with it, and to become a particular Part, Province, or District of the Kingdom with which they do unite, being subject to the laws and government thereof'.[15] Hodges went on to point out,

> That having thereby resigned their liberties, and independency, as free states, they, being once incorporated, are wholly diverted of all separate claims of right, and can never plead any distinct immunities or privileges, contrary to the will, resolutions, and free determinations of the one

government, to which they have subjected themselves and all their public affairs, by the irrevocable consent of an incorporating union, depriving them of all capacity to contradict the governing power, to which they have effectually submitted all those their separate rights, without reserve.[16]

On the other hand, Hodges argued, 'A Confederate or Federal Union is that, whereby distinct, free, and independent kingdoms, dominions or states, do unite their separate interests into one common interest, for the mutual benefit of both, so far as relates to certain conditions and articles agreed upon betwixt them, retaining in the meantime their several independencies, national distinctions, and the different laws, customs and government of each.' Hodges believed that 'the word Union in this Federal Sense, is a general term of a very large comprehension, tho' restrained to the amicable compacts, relations and obligations of kingdoms and states to one another. Being applicable to all the various Treaties of Alliance, Agreements, Confederations, and Settlements of mutual interest, which their joint concerns, in an indeterminable multitude of contingencies, may happen to incline or oblige them to.' Hodges referred to Holland, the Swiss Cantons and ancient Greece as examples of what he had in mind.[17]

In attempting to be more specific, Hodges continued, 'Now, when I speak of a Federal Union, in distinction from an Union by Incorporation, I do not mean such an Union, as consisting barely in articles of Confederacy betwixt the two Kingdoms, otherwise altogether disunited; but an Union of a close nature, whereby both Kingdoms are to be united under one common Monarch of both.' Also the 'Federal Union' he had in mind should

be such, as shall infer no other alteration in the proper Constitutions of either Kingdom, but that each, notwithstanding the said Federal Settlement, are to retain their National Distinction, to enjoy their particular liberties, privileges, and independency, and to hold their different governments in Church and State, with the Laws, Customs and several rights of each, after the same manner, as they did before the Union; except as to amendments agreed upon for rectifying innovations and abuses in the government on either side.

Hodges argued that such a federal union would be much more agreeable to the interests of both nations and it would not be possible to consult the true interest of either nation by an incorporating union.[18]

This was an interesting idea but like so many of the so-called 'federal' ideas of the time it was rather vague in crucial areas. Hodges did not outline a constitution nor a plan nor a scheme, and he did not address the issue of sovereignty in either a theoretical or a political way. He did not tackle the problems associated with shared areas of concern, a common parliament and representation. Three years later, in 1706, in his *Essay Upon the Union*, Hodges argued that 'the best security against encroachments on both sides is to have separate Parliaments with an express proviso, that no laws about trade, or the common concerns of the United Nations shall be of force, unless agreed to by both Parliaments'.[19]

Hodges did not provide a systematic treatment of sovereignty but it is clear that his primary concern was the protection of Scottish sovereignty. He realized that an 'incorporating union' would mean the end of Scotland as he knew it, for Scotland was weaker than England in almost all respects. Despite the arguments of Jean Bodin in the sixteenth century and those of John Locke and Hugo Grotius in the late seventeenth century, the concept of sovereignty was still not fully understood. Sir Robert Filmer and Thomas Hobbes had argued that it was located in the monarch and that it was absolute. Others, including John Locke in his *Second Treatise of Government* published in 1690, argued that it was the legislature that was supreme. The idea of the sovereignty of parliament did not go unchallenged in the late seventeenth century and throughout the eighteenth century. Nevertheless, as H.T. Dickinson points out, it was 'increasingly realized that the sovereignty of parliament could both limit the power of the crown and protect the propertied élite from any threat from the lower orders of society'.[20] While references might occasionally be made to the possibility of 'divided sovereignty', nothing came of them in Great Britain.[21] It is therefore hardly surprising that Hodges wished to protect the sovereignty of Scotland and its parliament but that he did not offer an acceptable way of doing this within his 'Federal Union'.

Sir John Clerk of Penicuik was one of the Scottish commissioners who negotiated the Union. He favoured the Union and opposed those who favoured a 'federal' solution. In his journal he made it clear that

> The first grand point debated by the Commissioners for Scotland amongst themselves was whether they should propose to the English a Federal Union between the two nations, or an Incorporating union. The first was favoured by the people of Scotland, but all the Scots Commissioners, to a Man, considered it ridiculous and impracticable, for that in all the Federal unions there behoved to be a supreme power lodged some where, and whenever this was lodged it henceforth became the States General, or, in our way of speaking, the Parliament of Great Britain, under the same royal power and authority as the two nations are at present. And in things of the greatest consequence to the two nations, as in Councils relating to peace and war and subsidies, it was impossible that the Representatives or their suffrages in both nations cou'd be equal but must be regulated in proportion to the power and riches of the several publick burdens or Taxations that cou'd affect them; in a word, the Scots Commissioners saw that no Union cou'd subsist between the two nations but an incorporating perpetuate one. But after all the trouble we gave ourselves to please the people of Scotland, we knew at the time that it was but losing our labour, for the English Commissioners were positively

resolved to treat on no kind of union with us but what was to be incorporating and perpetual.[22]

In the end, of course, the Scots Commissioners accepted the English
insistence on an 'incorporating union' 'as the only way to establish the
lasting peace and prosperity of both nations'.[23] As Mr Seton of Pitmeddon
had pointed out in the 1706 debate in Scotland, a close examination of
existing 'federal unions' would reveal that they were 'impracticable, or of
very little use to us'. He asked,

> whether a federal union be practicable betwixt two nations accustomed to
> monarchical government? Whether there can be any sure guaranty
> projected for the observance of the articles of a federal compact, stipu-
> lated betwixt two nations, whereof the one is much superior to the other
> in riches, numbers of people, and an extended commerce? Whether the
> advantages of a federal union do balance its disadvantages? Whether the
> English will accept a federal union, supposing it to be for the true interest
> of both nations? Whether any federal compact betwixt Scotland and
> England, is sufficient to secure the peace of this island, or fortify it
> against the intrigues and invasions of its foreign enemies? And, whether
> England, in prudence, ought to communicate its trade and protection to
> this nation, till both kingdoms are incorporated into one?[24]

This was a perceptive comment and underscored one of the insuperable
problems to the achievement or realization of a federal union in the British
Isles – the preponderating size, power and prosperity of England. How
would that be circumvented? It was not obvious in 1706 and remained a
puzzle nearly 300 years later.

One who advocated a federal union at that time was Andrew Fletcher of
Saltoun, a member of the Scots Parliament and a leading spokesman for the
Scottish Country Party. In fact, he was the champion of a federation as
opposed to an incorporating union but he did not offer many details. He
simply and continuously asserted that Scotland would suffer economically
within an incorporating union.[25] Fletcher argued that 'if in the union of
several countries under one government, the prosperity and happiness of the
different nations are not considered, as well as of the whole united body,
those that are more remote from the seat of the government will be only
made subservient to the interest of others, and their condition very miser-
able'. Fletcher suggested the diverse sovereignties unite in common defence.
If Scotland, England (Wales) and Ireland united it would obviate the necessity of making conquests abroad, especially in Europe. Fletcher seemed to
be talking about a form of regional government and a lessening of the
power of London: 'For all the same offices that belong to a great kingdom,
must be in each of them.' Fletcher reasoned that if Scotland separated from
England there would be perpetual war, but if they united Scotland would
suffer from a remote seat of government. He asked:

and pray where lies the prejudice, if the three kingdoms were united on so equal a foot, as for ever to take away all suspicion and jealousy of separation? that virtue and industry might be universally encouraged, and every part contribute cheerfully and in due proportion to the security and defence of this union, which will preserve us so effectually from those two great calamities, war and the corruption of manners. This is the only just and rational kind of union. All other coalitions are but the unjust subjection of one people to another.[26]

Despite Fletcher's arguments in 1706 in favour of either a separate Scottish parliament or 'a Union of equality, but with separate parliaments, with England',[27] it was Sir John Clerk of Penicuik and others like him who carried the day, pointing out the weaknesses inherent in continuing with a scheme that maintained the parliaments in both kingdoms with the same powers. England was so dominant that it would virtually dictate Scottish legislation, so that would not work. Similarly, if both kingdoms retained their parliaments but transferred to the monarch, assisted by persons chosen equally from both kingdoms, under the name of the Parliament of Great Britain, all things relating to public laws, taxes, trade, peace and war, and leagues and alliances, it would emasculate the power of the English parliament and would never be acceptable. And if a third option were tried whereby both parliaments retained their existing powers but a common representation was chosen by both kingdoms to determine differences between parliaments a thousand difficulties over management would result. England would never agree to any of these unions. Only an incorporating union would be acceptable and it would, in fact, benefit Scotland. Penicuik also explored the problem of representation in a joint parliament. He cited the example of Middlesex which currently had eighty representatives in parliament while Scotland under an incorporating union would receive forty-five. Middlesex had almost the same population as Scotland, was vastly richer and paid at least ten times more taxes than Scotland. How could that disparity be resolved in a federal union?[28] These were perceptive criticisms, and ones fairly easy to make. The intriguing thing is that the Scottish proponents of 'federal union' made no effort to counter them with schemes that would have incorporated strategies and/or devices to mitigate problems. The 'federalists' were not acting in concert, did not fully understand their brief and were not blessed with a background in constitutional law; nor did they have the fire of revolution driving them as did the delegates to the convention in America in 1787.

Many commentators in revisiting the Act of Union of 1707 and in exploring its impact have tended to emphasize the 'federal' or 'quasi-federal' feature of the new union. While recognizing that the Union had resulted in the full political incorporation of Scotland with England and the loss of a separate parliament, many writers have been persuaded that Scottish retention of separate legal, banking and educational systems along with the continuation of two separate churches resulted in a 'federal' arrangement because a good deal of power lay outside parliament and the political area. To a degree this was so, but it must equally be recognized that the new parliament was considered sovereign and there could indeed be changes wrought in all areas. What came into being was patently a unitary state with parliamentary sovereignty firmly anchored at Westminster. There was no devolution or derogation of powers under the Act of Union. Admittedly, legal, banking, ecclesiastical and cultural organizations differed but so do they in many states, both unitary and federal. Such differences do not make a state federal although they could make it pluralist. They may not even make it pluralist if it is accepted that to be plural there must be some division of *political* sovereignty. Since the Scottish decision-making body and its control over foreign and domestic policy had been absorbed in a 'continuing union', the new polity was unitary and therefore neither federal nor quasi-federal. There was no division of political power as in a federal state. The concept of divided parliamentary sovereignty and the concept of popular sovereignty, both of which are at the front of the modern concept of federalism, had not yet been systematically explored or fully formulated and therefore could not be brought to bear on the Union of 1707.[29]

On looking at the aftermath of Union it is quickly apparent that the Scots were absorbed into an essentially English parliament. They had only forty-five seats in the Commons while the English had 513, and only sixteen of the existing 160 Scottish peers joined the 180 from England in the new House of Lords. This was patently not a British nation and arguably not a British state either given the predominance of the English factor. That dominance did not, of course, lessen with time and Scotland was soon fully drawn into an essentially English state and empire. On the surface the Scots were more distinct within that state and empire than the Welsh but no more politically viable in any autonomous sense. The Scots were quick to take advantage of the new relationship, prospering in the new trade environment, flocking to London and to the colonies for advancement and settlement, and into a variety of state and state-protected positions in England and overseas. The Union was good for both Scotland and the Scots but it was not a federal arrangement. That possibility was not to be fully re-explored or exploited until a much later date.[30]

The discussions over the constitutional reorganization of Anglo-Scottish-Welsh relations in the late seventeenth and early eighteenth centuries had focused almost exclusively on internal relationships within the British Isles. Fletcher of Saltoun had made a deliberate effort to envision a new set of European relationships within which both Scotland and England would independently play a part but neither he nor, apparently, anyone else had viewed the matter in an imperial context or taken any inspiration from examples drawn from imperial experience. This was not particularly surprising because there was no clearly delineated structural organization of the empire and no obvious sharing or distribution of power between the imperial centre and the colonial periphery that could be copied or emulated at home. Neither the New England Federation, founded in 1643, nor the Leeward Islands 'federation' of the years 1674 to 1711 were pointed to as models or seen as practical examples of how 'definite conflict of interests or some other problem in the organization of government' might be resolved.[31]

Even if these models had been used by the 'federalists' it would have been to no avail. The English had no interest in anything but an incorporating union and the majority of those Scots in positions of power, or in a position to decide matters, shared that view. As many writers have pointed out, the union of Scotland with England and Wales was a political decision brought about by fear, intimidation and greed. Any schemes which had at their heart the protection – to any degree – of Scottish political sovereignty were simply not acceptable. The brute reality was that the English had no interest in sharing political power. If the Scots wanted to keep their cultural forms intact that was acceptable, if not entirely agreeable, because the English recognized that key decisions involving key economic and political issues would be made in the seemingly 'British' but still patently English-dominated parliament. Many Scots were willing to see their parliamentary, and thus political, sovereignty vanish because they thought it would free them from the dominance of the Scottish peers, little appreciating that the new 'British' parliament would further marginalize them.[32] In this atmosphere 'federal' ideas, however construed, had no hope of acceptance and no impact whatsoever on the Union of 1707. They were an interesting set of schemes and ideas, reflecting current thinking and knowledge about sovereignty and the division of powers, but they had no short- or long-term impact on constitutional discussions either on the domestic or external fronts over the next 175 years. It was only with the growth of Scottish nationalism in the late nineteenth and the early twentieth centuries that the Scottish writers of the late seventeenth and the early eighteenth centuries were recalled and their ideas resurrected and published.

The constitution of the British Isles was patently a unitary one by the early eighteenth century. Even if one draws the Irish and their parliament into the analysis the conclusion is not significantly altered. The Irish parliament was little more than a window box for the Anglo-Irish, and all its actions had to be reviewed and approved by Westminster. Even if one argues that Ireland was a colony, analogous to those in America, one is struck by the limitations placed on Irish power and flexibility by the island's strategic significance. While the English might be prepared to allow the American colonies to go their own way for decades, even if it meant continuous frontier clashes with their arch-rival France, they were not prepared to give the Irish the same latitude. They simply could not. While the Irish might have the appurtenances of power and of 'nationhood', it was a sham quickly revealed in the matrix of war and revolution at the end of the century. There were no lessons to be learned from the Irish experience other than the obvious ones. The English-dominated parliament believed itself to be sovereign and when challenged was prepared to uphold its views rather than rethink or reevaluate them.

The next opportunity for a sustained analysis of the problems associated with sharing, dividing or transferring power did not occur until the 1760s and 1770s when in the aftermath of their stupendous victories and consequent expanded responsibilities of the Seven Years' War the British (or rather the English) attempted to implement empire-wide controls from the imperial centre. This set of actions, enshrined in the so-called Intolerable Acts, precipitated an indignant and ultimately violent response in the American colonies where there had developed a vastly different set of assumptions about the imperial relationship, and thus about sovereignty, than existed in London. This had, in part at least, come about as the result of the emergence of a constitution for the empire vastly different from that which existed within the British Isles. The fact that it owed its particular nature to decades of neglect by London in no way diminished its validity or credibility for the Americans.

The imperial constitution which existed as of the 1760s, while not written down, had evolved via custom and precedent from the time of first settlement in the Americas in the early seventeenth century. It was clearly not a unitary constitution like that which existed in the British Isles. It was a unique quasi-federal arrangement whereby the internal affairs of the individual colonies were handled by local assemblies and external matters by the king, lords and commons in London. It is very clear that while the British empire was unitary in theory and the parliament sovereign in theory, in practice it was otherwise. Before 1763 the British had made no real effort to control the internal affairs of the colonies and as a consequence the assemblies had grown in strength and stature. That the British did not think they had grown in status, i.e. constitutionally, was obvious after 1763 when the British parliament decided to exercise its long dormant powers and legislate for the empire. The colonies bridled, primarily on two grounds: custom and natural rights. They argued that no legislature or parliament had authority unless given it by the people. Moreover, the Americans argued that the people had taken their rights with them when they had emigrated and that over the decades the exercise of those rights had become customary and, since unchallenged, accepted.

The British had an entirely different attitude and by the mid-eighteenth century they firmly believed in the supremacy of the British parliament. To them sovereignty was indivisible and was located only in the tripartite king, lords and commons. The definitive statement of parliamentary supremacy was provided by Sir William Blackstone in 1765. In his view, 'what the parliament doth, no authority upon earth can undo . . . the power of parliament is absolute and without control'.[33] There could be no deviation from this credo. The realities of the imperial relationship went unacknowledged by the majority of politicians and publicists of the imperial capital. They were purblind to the quasi-federal nature of their empire and few engaged in a discussion of the sharing, demission or division of powers and authority. Not so the American colonists who, especially in the 1760s and 1770s, grappled assiduously with that problem and concluded that British efforts to lay claim to authority in both internal and external spheres was illegal; that custom had rooted rights in colonial assemblies and the British parliament could not transgress them. They argued, perceptively, that not only was there a jurisdictional case but that their democratic rights, their natural-born rights as Englishmen, to be consulted in matters affecting them was being sullied by the British attempts to raise taxes in the colonies for imperial purposes. In other words, sovereign power did not reside in the legislature but in the people.

The British simply could not, or would not, accept this proposition. Parliamentary supremacy had been hard won in the seventeenth century and it reflected a desire for stability which could only be effected by a strong central government. The devolution or division of power would endanger that stability. Given the recent Jacobite threat and the continuous and draining warfare with France it seemed only logical that central authority should be preserved. The possibility that strength could be maintained, even furthered, by providing for diversity within unity was not seriously considered. It seemed ludicrous to question the supremacy of parliamentary sovereignty.[34]

In a famous essay written in 1918, Andrew C. McLaughlin of the University of Chicago contended that 'the essential qualities of American federal organization were largely the product of the practices of the old British empire as it existed before 1764'.[35] He argued that the central problem in the discussions of the 1760s and 1770s was that of imperial organization and that the crux of that problem was 'the difficulty of recognizing federalism; and, though there was great difficulty in grasping the principle, the idea of federalism went over from the old empire, through discussion into the Constitution of the United States'. By federalism, McLaughlin meant 'that system of political order in which powers of government are separated and distinguished and in which these powers are distributed among governments, each government having its quota of authority and each its distinct sphere of activity'.

McLaughlin pointed out that the central authority in London had charge of such imperial matters as foreign affairs, the army and navy, and war and peace but that it rarely legislated for strictly local internal affairs of the colonies. On the other hand, the colonial representative assemblies handled local police and militia, levied taxes for local purposes, voluntarily contributed to the defence of the empire, managed local trade and handled the myriad of things that concerned colonial daily life. 'Any one even slightly familiar with [the] American constitutional system', asserted McLaughlin, 'will see at once that to a very marked degree we have here the distribution of powers characteristic of American federalism.' He therefore concluded that 'Britain had a working federal empire by the middle of the eighteenth century . . . her imperial history had selected and set apart the particular and the general. . . . On that general scheme of distribution the Constitution of the United States was founded.'

McLaughlin argued that by 1760 imperial practice had outstripped contemporary English thinking which was a 'largely insular argument, based on insular experience and founded on insular history'. The unwritten constitution of the empire was 'the other way, and that is just what the men, especially the Englishmen, of a hundred and fifty years ago could not see. They could not think and talk imperially, when it came to a matter of constitutional law.'

> If the practical working empire of 1760 had been frozen into recognizable legal shape, the right to tax the colonies would not have been within the legal competence of Parliament, even as an imperial legislature. And because the Englishmen did not think imperially, because they did not realize that time had wrought out for them a composite federal empire, because they insisted on the principle of centralization in theory, they failed patiently to set about the task of determining some way by which, while recognizing federalism and colonial integrity, they could on a basis of justice and consent obtain authoritatively an acknowledged legal right to tax for strictly imperial purposes. Men that could not comprehend federalism, who denied the possibility of its existence, were incapable of dealing with a crisis of an imperial system in which federalism already existed.

Admittedly, said McLaughlin, the idea was hard to grasp for both colonists and Englishmen and it would take protracted discussions to define, but once defined it turned out to be 'the old scheme only in part modified, representing in its method of distributing powers the familiar practices of the empire'.

This idea that 'the empire before 1763 . . . was federal in practice, though not in form',[36] while still widely accepted, has been recently challenged by Robert Tucker and David Hendrickson.[37] Tucker and Hendrickson point out, rightly, that McLaughlin's definition of a federal system of government is faulty. In essence it does not go far enough. It could just as easily be a definition of a devolutionary system. Tucker and Hendrickson agree with K.C. Wheare, the acknowledged expert on federalism, that a system in which the central government is dependent on the regional governments is at best confederal. In that light, argue Tucker and Hendrickson, 'it is evident that the constitution of the First British Empire was neither federal in principle nor federal in practice'. Nevertheless, they do agree it had 'federal features' and was 'federal in spirit' in that a central parliament did primarily concern itself with matters beyond the power of the various colonial assemblies while the latter were able to exercise considerable discretion. It was also true that the colonists were quick to make the distinction between imperial and local concerns – in other words, to fasten on the federal features of the system – even if the politicians and civil servants at the imperial centre were not. Tucker and Hendrickson contend, however, that the assertion of central powers after 1763, 'far from representing a departure from federal practices', as McLaughlin would have it, was rather 'the institution – or reaffirmation – of federal practices'. This does seem to over-stretch their argument for, as even they have to admit, it was clear the Grenville ministry was more concerned with reaffirming the supremacy of parliament than with reasserting 'federal practices'. The British were obdurate about parliamentary supremacy because they feared the consequences of a divided sovereignty. They did not wish to lose control of their colonies. The American colonists, of course, were fearful of losing the powers they currently exercised.

Before the outbreak of the Seven Years' War, the American colonies and their relationship with the mother country attracted little sustained attention in England either from the general public or the press. Individuals such as Thomas Crowley and Joshua Steele who in their writings foreshadowed a 'federal' arrangement for the empire were very much the exception.[38] The majority of those who did give the matter some thought were believers in the legislative supremacy of the parliament at Westminster. With the passage of the so-called Intolerable Acts, however, more individuals were prepared to recognize that a problem existed and undertook to find a means of reconciling both parties. None of the resulting schemes, however, contained a full-scale 'federal' solution. A.L. Burt would appear to be correct to assert that while vague suggestions were made no proposals similar to nineteenth-century imperial federation plans surfaced before American independence.[39] As H.T. Dickinson has concluded, 'Fear of anarchy and dread of civil war made the acceptance of parliamentary sovereignty appear to be a political necessity.' The concept of divided sovereignty was alien to those in power in Britain and they therefore were constrained in their approach to the problem of imperial government and imperial reorganization.[40]

By 1783 there had been no resolution of the problem of imperial organization either from a British or a colonial perspective and clearly no willingness at that moment to establish anything more than a confederal arrangement between the former colonies. That confederal arrangement proved inoperable. Its weak centre and lack of any concentrated authority in the key areas of taxation and defence obliged the Americans to pursue other alternatives. That process of discussion, primarily occurring in 1787–8, led to the adoption of what is now accepted as the classic form of modern federalism. At the heart of the task confronting the Americans were the twin concerns of utility and liberty.[41] They had to devise a system of government that not only recognized the individuality and integrity of the former thirteen colonies but also rested on the popular support of the people of the new United States. It was therefore essential to have the central government and the state governments equally answerable to the citizenry. Moreover, given the recent experience with king, lords and commons, it was equally important to separate the legislative, executive and judicial powers. This resulted in both a horizontal and a vertical division of sovereignty. As Dickinson puts it, the Americans

> divided sovereignty between executive, legislative and judiciary, and between federal and state governments. They also defined the people's rights in a written constitution and established a system of judicial review to defend this constitution. Furthermore, in the last analysis, they acknowledged the sovereignty of the people. The critics of parliamentary sovereignty in eighteenth century Britain never developed, and only rarely suggested, such effective restraints.[42]

The Americans, of course, also protected the state's rights at the centre by creating a bicameral legislature, in the upper chamber of which, the Senate, each state would have two representatives. Thus proper due was given to territory at the same time that appropriate provision was made in the House of Representatives for the representation of the people.

The British conviction about the indivisibility of sovereignty is summed up particularly well by Akhil Reed Amar:

> The conventional British position understood 'Sovereignty' as that indivisible, final, unlimited power that necessarily had to exist somewhere in every political society. A single nation could not operate with two sovereigns any more than a single person could operate with two heads; some single supreme political will had to prevail, and the only limitations on that sovereign will were those that the sovereign itself voluntarily chose to observe. To try to divide or limit sovereignty in any way was to create the 'political monster' or 'hydra' of 'imperium in imperio' – 'the greatest of all political solecisms'.[43]

The British, of course, continued to have difficulty accepting the concept of 'two masters' through to the 1840s when they finally acknowledged that the theory of responsible government had colonial application. Until that time on the imperial stage, and certainly in the domestic sphere, the concept of the balanced constitution of king, lords and commons, representative of the one, the few and the many, continued to hold sway.

The heart of the American solution to the problem of sovereignty was to argue that absolute sovereignty lay with the people and that they could divide it between different levels of government (central and regional, federal and state) and between different agents of the people (the executive, the legislature, the judiciary). These vertical and horizontal divisions of power would be enshrined in a written constitution, subject to amendment and judicial review. By moving absolute power from parliament and transferring it to the people and ensuring that the people retained residual powers the delegates of the twelve colonies at Philadelphia in 1787 made it possible for a number of independent states to merge and yet to retain their particular individuality while at the same time protecting the rights of the people at both levels of government through directly elected representative legislatures. The needs of both utility and liberty had been met.

As Amar points out, 'the problem of allocating power vertically between central and local officials [was] the problem of federalism. The issue was notoriously difficult. In the mid-1770s, it had cracked open the British Empire'.[44] The British reaction had been simply 'like sovereignty, the Empire was legally an all or nothing concept. Take it or leave it.' The confederal model had initially been tried by the Americans but it failed to provide sufficient power or support at and for the centre. Only by vesting sovereignty in the people as a whole had a solution to the problem of sovereignty been found. The federal and state governments would both be agents of the people. Power had been conquered by dividing it.[45] Or, as Jack Greene puts it, the 'framers of the Constitution had invented a radical new scheme of governance whereby the basic powers of sovereignty could be divided without dividing sovereignty itself'; sovereignty, of course, being popular and not parliamentary.[46]

The American Revolution and the creation of a new form of government in the United States did not force the British to revise their thinking about how the government of Great Britain or the empire might be restructured. If anything, their recent experiences convinced them of the need to reemphasize central control. Despite the modest gains of Grattan's parliament in 1782–1800 these were not gains by the Irish people, particularly the Catholics, so when the Protestant elite was threatened by the 1798 rising it was quick to accept incorporation and, hopefully, protection and security in a union with Scotland, England and Wales – the United Kingdom. Federal ideas played no part in a resolution of that relationship nor did they as the British grappled in those years with a variety of imperial exigencies. In fact, the development of the crown colony system and the reassertion of the concept of the balanced constitution in the Canadas in 1791 reflected the state of British thinking. In their estimation, the sovereignty of parliament was sacrosanct and its power indivisible. As a consequence, federalism, which rested on the alternative premise that sovereignty was divisible, did not attract them. Nevertheless, the debates over the relationship of Scotland and England and of the imperial centre to its colonies had touched on all the key ideas underpinning the federal concept. Those ideas would prove increasingly attractive to a wide range of politicians, civil servants and theorists grappling with the complexities of a plural society and its multiple loyalties, and with a fragmenting empire.

2 Nineteenth-century practice and theory

The American federal system devised in the 1780s was born out of practical necessity and did not rest on any full-blown federal theory. The practical scheme that emerged was founded, however, on basic principles of Anglo-American constitutional thought. The first was 'natural rights' and the second was popular sovereignty – a republican idea promulgated by James Harrington in the seventeenth century but owing a good deal also to John Locke. The British consciously contributed nothing to federal theory but their manner of managing their empire had led to the *de facto* practice of allowing considerable latitude to colonial assemblies over a wide range of essentially local issues. This apparent division of powers was less real than it seemed, as was shown by the British reassertion of central authority in the 1760s, but it allowed the Americans to assume that such a division should be a part of generally accepted constitutional practice. The federal arrangement of the 1780s incorporated such a division as a central feature.

The federal idea received only intermittent attention from the British in the forty years following the American Revolution. The protracted struggles with revolutionary France and the consequent dramatic changes in imperial and domestic circumstances did not provide many opportunities for a major rethinking of constitutional verities. The influx of loyalists into Quebec during and after the American Revolution led directly to the passage of the Constitutional Act of 1791 but the British government was not adventurous in its thinking on that occasion. Quite the reverse, in fact. Recognizing that stability on the colonial frontier was essential at a time of crisis, the British readily accepted the division of Quebec into Upper (English dominated) and Lower (French dominated) Canada and ensured that the governments of both colonies would conform to the ideal of the balanced constitution. The democratic element, the assembly, was circumscribed by the powers granted to the legislative council and the governor. No consideration was given to federal forms of government for these two inland colonies nor for the cluster of colonies on the Atlantic seaboard of British North America. It is true that William Smith had passed around his ideas related to a form of federal government modelled to some degree on the earlier suggestions of Joseph Galloway, but these had not met with any support in British government circles and were allowed to languish until picked up and reformulated by later advocates of federation in British North America.

The Irish crisis of the late 1790s led the British government not towards consideration of some federal management to accommodate Irish aspirations within a continuing union but to opt emphatically for an incorporating union similar to that adopted for Scotland in 1707. This time, however, there was no full-blooded discussion paralleling that which had occurred in the early 1700s. The British government acted preemptively and decisively. As of 1801, Ireland was a part of the United Kingdom with 100 (later raised to 105) MPs in the Westminster parliament and without a parliament of its own. Nothing could have as dramatically or as plainly underscored the 'colonial' status of Ireland in English eyes as the manner of its incorporation. Nor did its future administration soften that condition. Ireland was administered as a separate unit within the United Kingdom – quite unlike Scotland and Wales – with a lord lieutenant and a chief secretary as heads, respectively, of government and administration. This structure was unique in the empire. Nowhere else was a province or a territory or a colony represented in the imperial parliament nor was any other part of the British Isles administered in so obviously a colonial style. This novel arrangement reflected Ireland's particular status. Sitting as close as it did to British shores, it represented a strategic threat to the safety of the larger island containing England, Scotland and Wales. The British government simply could not contemplate the possibility of a self-governing, and therefore unpredictable, Ireland. For safety's sake, if for nothing else, it had to be brought under central control – under the supreme authority of the Westminster parliament. Such thinking did not allow federal ideas to take more than very shallow root but there is little evidence to suggest that the federal idea was much more than mooted let alone explored seriously.

This lack of any interest in the federal idea at the centre of British imperial and domestic life prevailed until the 1830s and 1840s when a crisis in British North America, mounting agitation in Ireland for a change in the constitutional arrangement of 1801, and a desire to unify the disparate Australian colonies raised the possibility of a federal solution to these various problems. The continuing political difficulties in Canada in the 1850s sustained interest in the idea, and when in the 1860s the various colonies in British North America decided to explore the possibilities of a federal union the British were finally prepared to accept it.

Thus from the 1830s to the 1860s the federal idea was a constant if minor thread in political and constitutional discussions in the domestic and, particularly, in the imperial arenas. It was brushed aside by the British government as a solution to the problems of the Union and as quickly dropped by Daniel O'Connell in the face of Young Ireland's objections, but it prevailed as a more serious factor in discussions related to Australian and British North American issues and increasingly was suggested as a means of maintaining the unity of the empire as a whole. Throughout there were repeated references to the American example. It offered a model for all interested in finding a solution to the problem of recognizing diversity while maintaining unity and of transferring or dividing or sharing power.

The imperial arena provided the opportunity for the most sustained reflection on federalism and this was natural enough. Most of the white settlement colonies in British North America, Australia, New Zealand and South Africa were by mid-century either in possession of responsible government or close to attaining it and all were anxious to acquire a greater degree of self-government. These pressures – violent in the Canadas in 1837–8 but more subtle elsewhere over the next twenty years – prompted a few politicians at Westminster, some Colonial Office officials and a number of concerned observers of the imperial drama to consider a federal solution to the various problems. Proposals for a federal union of the Canadas, or of the Canadas with the Maritimes colonies, surfaced in London in the late 1830s and remained a constant thread in discussions related to the future of the British North American colonies down to the 1860s. Similarly, suggestions for the federation of the New Zealand and then the Australian and South African colonies surfaced in the 1840s and 1850s, again initiated in London. The proposals were rebuffed and dropped in both New Zealand and Australia and did not really get off the ground in South Africa. Nevertheless, it is clear that the federal idea was by mid-century a serious option for all concerned with resolving the problems connected with granting self-government while maintaining a wide-flung imperial union.

The majority of the schemes that surfaced, of course, were not truly federal. They did not conform to the American model. They were at best efforts to ensure cooperation between disparate polities which might well benefit from a closer relationship. These schemes and the accompanying rationales revealed how shallow was the grasp of 'true federalism' in the United Kingdom and how reluctant most advocates of change were to contemplate a division of sovereignty – the only real indicator of a truly federal solution. On the other hand, it was clear that some of those who raised or advocated the federal idea fully understood the essence of the American example. One of them was the third Earl Grey who was Colonial Secretary 1846–52 and a keen supporter of a federal solution to the problems of government in British North America, New Zealand and Australia from the 1830s.

The idea of a federal union of the British North American colonies had been suggested in various forms since the 1780s. It usually had a two-fold purpose. First, to neutralize the French Canadians in a majority of English-speakers and, second, to provide a larger polity for the display and development of political and economic talent. By the mid-nineteenth century, of course, a third and even more compelling reason had emerged – the need to provide a cohesive British North American defensive alternative to the omnipresent United States. The British were finally drawn by this gathering concern to throw their weight behind the idea. It would relieve them of a heavy defensive burden and it would compel the British North Americans both to examine potentially provocative policies and attitudes and to assume a major share of the defence burden.

William Smith in the 1780s, Jonathan Sewell in the early 1800s and John Beverley Robinson in the 1820s all broached plans for consolidating the British North American colonies designed to strengthen them both internally and externally. Sewell, for one, made no secret that his intention, at least in part, was to circumscribe the democratic element – the colonial assemblies – and to place primary power in the hands of a united parliament chosen not by the electorate at large but by the respective assemblies. These various schemes were not federal but rather confederal or colonial in nature. There was a recognition by each man that certain powers affecting the union as a whole should be assigned to a central parliament and that the colonial or provincial assemblies should be responsible for essentially local matters. Not one of the schemes was sufficiently detailed to enable firm conclusions to be drawn about the division of sovereignty, but since the primary purpose behind them was either defence or containment of the French-Canadians or restriction of the democratic element it is doubtful if divided sovereignty was seriously considered by Smith, Sewell and Robinson. What is clear is that none of these schemes made much of an impact in the British Isles although Sewell, in his later capacity as Chief Justice of Lower Canada, did pass on his ideas to Lord Durham.[1]

Federal ideas were first seriously considered by the British in the late 1830s in the aftermath of the rebellion in the Canadas. Lord Durham was sent out to British North America to advise the British government about changes that might be constructively made in the imperial relationship. Durham was a member of a small group in British political life known as the Colonial Reformers who under the inspiration of Edward Gibbon Wakefield were taking a critical look at the land-granting, emigration and political policies of the British insofar as they affected the overseas white settlement colonies. Their reflections had led them by the late 1830s to argue that Englishmen abroad should be given the power to run as much of their own affairs as possible. In their estimation this would ensure that the newly settled overseas colonies in Australia and also the more established ones in British North America would remain loyal to the British connection.

Durham was in sympathy with these ideas and also sensitive to the need to protect British interests in North America. He made every effort to push the federal idea but finally had to accept that any such scheme was premature and that a union of Upper and Lower Canada would have to be a preliminary step. Such a union would be essential to hasten the assimilation of the French-Canadians. Without assimilation a wide union, even a federal one, might be endangered. Durham was aware that in April 1837 James Roebuck, the MP for Bath, had recommended the creation of a northern federal republic to offset US interests. Moreover, on the day of Durham's appointment, Lord Glenelg, the Secretary of State for War and the

Colonies, had suggested that some form of 'joint legislative authority' might resolve the problems in the Canadas. Durham arranged to meet Roebuck and the latter provided him with a memorandum on the colonial problem which was eventually published in 1849 under the title *The Colonies of England: A Plan for the Government of Some Portion of our Colonial Possessions*. Durham used Roebuck's ideas as a base for his discussions in British North America.[2]

It is clear that Durham wished to maintain Britain's supremacy but at the same time wanted to enable each colony to manage its own 'peculiar affairs'. The scheme he outlined was clearly federal in nature. While the provincial governments would control local affairs there would also be 'such a general government for all the Provinces in British North America present or future as will control and regulate all such matters as may be common to all, or to some two or more of them'. In his view, the scheme should apply initially to the Canadas and then to the Maritime colonies at a time of their choosing. The provincial legislatures were to have residual powers, i.e. control of all matters not specifically conferred on the central government. Since the provincial governors were to correspond directly with London it was clear that neither the governor of the new British North American union nor the central legislature would have any control over provincial authority. There was to be a clear separation – division – of powers between the two levels of government. In recommending direct contact with the imperial government, however, Durham obviously wanted to preserve 'the supremacy of the Crown of England as inviolate at present'.

Durham's ideas received a mixed reaction. New Brunswick, in particular, disliked the notion of union with the French Canadians, and many in the Canadas to whom he showed the idea had various objections. Moreover, the vast distances separating the small concentrations of population, the unwillingness of the Maritime colonies to surrender any of their own identity, and the deeply rooted suspicions of the French-Canadians were insuperable problems at that moment. Although it is likely that he had not entirely abandoned the federal idea at the time of his departure from North America on 1 November 1838, the report published in January 1839 recommended neither a federal union of the British North American colonies nor of the Canadas but a legislative union of the Canadas accompanied by a grant of responsible government. Nevertheless, he did look ahead to the other colonies eventually joining the Canadas in a wider union. He recognized that for the time being such a union would have to wait upon the completion of a railway link between the Maritimes and the Canadas and the development of common interests. Union would, in the long run, be necessary to offset the growing might of the US and to provide a larger forum for the development of colonial interests.

Two men who had also raised the possibility in the late 1830s of a federal union for not only British North America but for colonies in general were the Permanent Under-secretary for the Colonies, James Stephen, and the

Parliamentary Under-secretary for the Colonies, Lord Howick, later better known as the third Earl Grey. Both men, as Ged Martin has pointed out, preferred 'schemes of evolutionary federation' to ones of legislative union. The latter might lead to a rapid assimilation of the French Canadians but it might also be disruptive. The two men wanted, if possible, to conciliate the French and provide a united front to the United States. The American model was clearly favoured by the 'federalists' but it did pose problems in an imperial setting for it would result in 'a mezzanine tier of government between the colonial assemblies and Westminster'. This would leave the regional federation with little to do, or so it seemed, since much that was 'external' would still be the responsibility of the London government while 'internal' matters would ideally remain at the provincial level.

Both Stephen and Howick were averse to the idea that the use of force in the Canadas would resolve the basic constitutional and ethnic problems. There had to be another way. Lower Canada was the primary problem and Stephen was firm in his belief that a convention of the five colonies, meeting with a larger union in mind, would be a positive step in resolving North American difficulties while maintaining the unity of the empire. Howick was more specific than Stephen in envisaging a 'Federal body' which would 'supply that bond of connection between the different provinces . . . and would thus enable the Home Government gradually to relax the reins of its authority and to substitute a system of ruling by influence for one of direct control'. In this statement, Howick revealed his reformist tendencies and his sympathies with the position of the Colonial Reformers. In the end, neither Stephen's nor Howick's promotion of the federal idea gained much support and Durham, of course, finally decided to push for legislative union; a solution that, as Martin argues, 'appeared to combine the maximum of British control with the minimum of French assertiveness'. Federal schemes would require 'a measure of trust in a rebellious Lower Canadian population'. There were other compelling reasons for setting aside the federal idea at that time; three of the more substantive were the difficulties of communication, parliamentary supremacy and the problem of autonomy for French Canada in a federal system. The irony, of course, was that during the 1840s the legislative union in the Canadas increasingly operated as a quasi-federal one, and understandably by the end of the decade full federation of all the British North American colonies was again being mooted. By this time so was a federation for New Zealand and for the Australian colonies.[3]

By mid-century Howick had inherited the title and was now the third Earl Grey. Between 1846 and 1852 he was the primary promoter within the British government of federations in New Zealand, Australia, South Africa and British North America.[4] Grey was an ardent free-trader and his promotion of colonial federations was directly linked to his concern for both administrative convenience and commercial advantage. He believed, as did James Stephen and Lord Elgin, the Governor-General of Canada in the late 1840s, that the problems of government in large colonial areas where the population was small and scattered and communications were poor could be resolved by a combination of municipal, provincial and federal institutions. His ideas were based on convenience and efficiency and not upon any ideas of nationalism or even ethnicity. The various schemes that he suggested for New Zealand, Australia, South Africa and British North America were based on federal ideas but the proposals were vague. They were above all managerial exercises such as would be devised in a later age by cost-conscious efficiency experts or systems analysts. They had no real philosophical underpinnings and minimal support in the colonies themselves. Grey was obliged to abandon his scheme in New Zealand as unworkable and to drop the federal portions of his Australian legislation due to opposition and indifference both in the colonies and at Westminster.

It is obvious that Grey was not a systematic thinker. While he undoubtedly believed that federal union would ensure freer trade he was not a student of federalism in any sustained or trained sense and his ideas were not always in tune with anything more than generalities. This was not unusual but it did blunt his effectiveness. What is apparent, however, is that Grey's desire to ensure a free trade area led him to advocate federation of the Australian colonies in particular as a *centralizing* device. It was seen by him as a system of government that allowed the central authorities to avoid or by-pass the particularistic interests of the individual colonies. The fact that the colonists disliked or were confused by the federal idea should not blind us to the fact that federations were often viewed by its advocates in London as a means of suborning diversity, not protecting it. Grey's efforts to ensure the maintenance and extension of the representative principle was in tune with his reformist instincts but the adoption of such a principle did strengthen the centre vis-à-vis the individual states or provinces. The failure of Grey's schemes and initiatives was due to many factors but one was common to all four settings. The colonists had not initiated the idea. They were not prepared to accept constitution-mongering on that scale from the imperial centre. Until they were ready to accept the logic of a wider union there was little the British government could do at a time when self-government was increasingly accepted as the working shibboleth of empire. The fact that Grey, Stephen and Elgin, all supporters to one degree or another of the federal idea, were prepared to push from the centre reflected the essentially paternalistic and patronizing essence of imperial management.

This point was underlined, in fact, by Stephen himself who in a minute on Canadian affairs of 30 April 1836 reasoned that the British North American colonies were already assuming

> a distinct national character; and the day cannot be very remote when an Independence, first real, and then avowed, will take the place of the present subjection of these Provinces to the British Crown. . . . A forecasting Policy would appear to suggest that provision should be deliberately, though of course, unavowedly, made for the peaceful and

honourable abdication of a power, which ere long it will be impossible to retain; and for raising upon the North American Continent a counter-poise to the United States. . . . After all, the authority of the Mother Country rests altogether upon the respect and voluntary obedience of her Colonial subjects.[5]

Lord John Russell, the Home Secretary, was also leery of a federal solution because of the inherent difficulties associated with the division of powers between the two levels of government. He shrewdly added, 'Nor will the creation of a federal body by the Crown satisfy the representatives of the people against whom a decision may be made.'[6]

By the late 1840s Russell's fears were not widely shared by most of those men who dealt with colonial affairs on a regular basis. It was clear from their letters and discussions that the concept of divided sovereignty was understood and accepted. But what did puzzle them, particularly Elgin, was what would be the role of a federal government in a colonial setting. As he shrewdly put it in 1847:

if an attempt were made to create a federal system on a more extended basis after the model of the United States, the central Body having no foreign Policy army and navy to manage, will either occupy itself in doing mischief, or in the discharge of duties which now devolve on the Provincial legislatures – In other words a federal can hardly fail to become either a nuisance or a legislative Union.[7]

By 'nuisance' Elgin apparently meant 'an invasion of the imperial sphere' by the colonial federal government. Increasingly, the concern about what a 'federal' government in a colonial setting would occupy itself with dimin-ished as government became more complex in the nineteenth and twentieth centuries but the same issue surfaced in the 1930s to 1950s, especially in India and the British West Indies. The question then was what did the central government in a colonial federation do if that federation was not fully autonomous but was a dependency of the United Kingdom. This was a particularly knotty constitutional problem and one unique to the British experience. It was not an issue that had had to concern the authors of *The Federalist* nor was it an issue that received much attention from the various theorists of the eighteenth and nineteenth centuries. It was essentially a problem of practical day-to-day politics but it had considerable constitu-tional implications.[8]

What is of particular significance is the stance adopted by Lord John Russell towards the federal idea. In the 1840s he adamantly opposed Daniel O'Connell's efforts to promote a federal solution to the Anglo-Irish problem at the same time that he finally lent his support to Grey's efforts to create federations in both Australia and British North America. Apparently, Russell was prepared, as were so many British politicians then and later, to experiment with – even to accept – federation on the colonial periphery but would draw his last breath before even considering it as an option for the United Kingdom. There the legislative union was sacrosanct.

Another advocate of federation in the colonial setting in the 1850s was Sir Edmund Head, the Lieutenant-Governor of New Brunswick and subsequently Governor-General of Canada. Head had first outlined his ideas in 1850–51. He had become convinced that the British North American colonies would eventually become either independent or join the United States. He did not believe they would be viable separately and concluded it was the responsibility of the London government

> to foster common interests that would prepare the colonies for independence as a unit; otherwise, instead of balancing the power of the United States, they would fall, one by one, into the neighbouring republic. At the same time, union should be in such a form as to insulate Britain from the troublesome French of Canada East. . . . Everything that concerned imperial matters could best be handled by a federal government where the French power for mischief was effectively nullified by an overall English majority.[9]

But whereas Head favoured a union with a strong link to Britain's monarchical constitution which he believed would offset the popular sovereignty of the American model, the primary interests of those in Britain who came to support such a union were essentially conservative and defensive. They wanted to contain the French-Canadians, ensure better, more efficient government and offset the United States. The last aim was the most important and in the end the most persuasive to both the British and the colonists.[10]

When Head seized the initiative in 1858 and suggested that a conference be held between the Maritime colonies and Canada to discuss the possibility of federation, he did so because he, in the end, believed that the question of federation was 'necessarily one of Imperial character. . . . It is, therefore, one which properly belongs to the Executive Authority of the Empire, and not to that of any separate province, to initiate.'[11] But Head had misread his separate audiences. The Colonial Office, the key government department in London, was offended because Head's call for a conference had breached protocol. In the ensuing huff the federal idea did not receive any sustained examination in Whitehall. When officials did comment they were cautious. The difficulties being experienced at that time in the United States federation were not lost on British civil servants. One, T.F. Elliott of the Colonial Office, doubted the merits of federation. He thought there would be too little for the federal government to do while the provincial assemblies might be reduced in status, and – here he was prescient – 'there were certain to be difficulties in the division of political powers and the apportionment of financial obligations'.[12] A colleague at the Board of Trade shared Elliott's concern. He believed federal structures were cumbersome and, as in the United States version, were at their weakest in enforcing federal resolutions against individual states. But, unwittingly, he went on to make a point which underlined the potential strength rather than weakness of a federal system vis-à-vis a unitary one when he argued, 'The American Union could not last a week if it had not in addition to its federal Legislature its federal Executive and judiciary, if that federal legislature did not represent the principle of population as well as of state sovereignty, and, I may add, if a conflict of laws between Congress and the State Legislatures was not carefully avoided by marking out for each an exclusive field of jurisdiction.'[13] The advocates of the federal ideal, given the opportunity, would have responded, 'But of course, that is how unity can be achieved while protecting and ensuring both diversity and democracy.'

In addition to misjudging his London audience, Head had also missed the change in emphasis in British North America. What he and Elliott and Lord Lytton, the Colonial Secretary, failed to appreciate was that the issue of federation in British North America had moved beyond abstractions. It was now an integral part of the political agenda in the Canadas and increasingly so in the Maritimes. The initiative had clearly passed to the colonists. Although this should have been increasingly obvious it was not a lesson readily absorbed by those in the United Kingdom who had their hearts set on wider goals. Lord Lytton, for one, saw the British North American federation of 1867 as an integral part of a broadened imperial future. Lord Carnarvon who introduced the British North American bill in the House of Lords shared that view. In fact, he took comfort in the claim that Canadian confederation had been brought about by an external authority. He saw in this some security against the conflicts between the centre and the regions which had recently proved so disastrous in the United States. What Carnarvon failed to recognize or chose to ignore was the fact that the impulse and impetus for federation had originated in the colonies and that the Crown's actions only followed on from colonial initiative. To suggest that imperial authority alone could either create a stable federation or resolve inner difficulties was completely misleading. Even when the initiative did lie with the colonies tensions inevitably arose. Such tensions were even more marked if the centre acted imperiously – as Carnarvon was to find out in Southern Africa in the 1870s. These problems associated with the imperial centre and its role were to become particularly obvious in the twentieth century.[14]

By the mid-nineteenth century the federal idea was clearly receiving a good deal of attention, especially in official circles and among empire-minded publicists. Despite this gathering interest there had been surprisingly few sustained analyses of federalism by British writers, theorists or politicians. This state of affairs gradually shifted and a number of significant commentaries were published in the later decades of the century. All of them naturally reflected the time in which they were written but each took the American federal system as the bedrock for analysis. As both the complexities of the Anglo-Irish relationship and questions related to the future of the British empire inexorably forced themselves to the front of the political stage, the commentaries increasingly reflected the need to address these key issues and the ambiguities of purpose each entailed.

The first major work to incorporate a consideration of a federal system was John Austin's *Province of Jurisprudence Determined*, published in 1832, in which Austin discussed the location of sovereignty in a federal system. He clearly understood and accepted the division of powers, and thus the division of sovereignty, that was central to a federal system and he acknowledged that the federal government could not trespass onto the domain of the several states of which it was composed and vice versa. He also pointed out that the courts would of necessity have to monitor actions on both sides of the divide in order to ensure that the application of the two levels of sovereignty was not only protected but consistent. He made a point of distinguishing a federal from a confederal system but patently favoured the compact thesis, i.e. the idea that a federal state resulted from the decision of a number of states to pool certain of their sovereign powers in a common government, and thus he left the door open for the secession of states. Nevertheless, in a true federal system, Austin argued, sovereignty was coordinate and nowhere supreme. Austin was analytically descriptive in his approach rather than judgemental. Unlike A.V. Dicey later in the century, he did not engage in a protracted analysis of the purported weaknesses of the federal system. However, his assertion that a federal structure was a compact hinted at a weakness in that it assumed the right of any party to the compact to withdraw. In this he foreshadowed the states' rights argument in the USA.[15]

H.L.A. Hart, who introduced the 1954 edition of Austin's work, pointed out that when the lectures were published in 1832 no notice was taken of them outside Austin's small circle of friends and they were not reviewed.[16] It would therefore be difficult to contend that his ideas about sovereignty and federalism had much influence on contemporary politicians, civil servants and publicists although they can still be taken as a reflection of contemporary utilitarian assumptions given his close friendship with Jeremy Bentham. It is also apparent from his presentation that Austin would have accepted the concept of 'multiple loyalties' that lies at the heart of a federal structure. 'Joint' sovereignty suggests a capacity for loyalty to more than one level of government and in that recognition he foreshadowed E.A. Freeman and clearly was more astute, or at least more flexible, than A.V. Dicey whose rejection of anything but the supremacy of the Westminster parliament revealed a purblind attitude to the realities of not only Irish, Scottish, Welsh and English but also regional life in the United Kingdom.

Walter Bagehot published his now classic volume *The English Constitution* in 1867 and a second edition in 1872. He did not comment specifically on federalism but he did make slighting remarks about the American system of government and made it clear that he did not approve of the division of powers. In light of the American Civil War, Bagehot concluded that too much power had been conceded to the states and that this had severely weakened the federal government's capacity to address the issue of slavery. He pointed out that under the American system sovereignty was not simply divided between federal and state levels. He contended that sovereignty at the federal level was divided and subdivided between Congress and the president and, in the area of international affairs, between the president and the Senate. Bagehot much preferred 'a single determining energy; a distinct force for each artificial compartment will make but a motley patchwork, if it live long enough to make anything. The excellence of the British Constitution is that it has achieved this unity; that in it the sovereign power is single, possible and good.'[17] The problem with Bagehot's work is that he confined himself to a description of the British constitution; he did not grapple with general principles or theories nor with nuances and therefore failed to appreciate the vagaries and complexities and consequent compromises so necessary in a variety of working constitutions. So compelling was his style and the clarity of his explanation that no commentators have ventured much further than him. Dicey certainly did not and while Freeman gave pure federalism its proper due he had no use for it in either the domestic or imperial sphere.

Edward Freeman was a respected historian and constitutional authority who in 1863 published the first, and, as it proved, the only volume of his *History of Federal Government from the Foundation of the Achaian League to the Disruption of the United States.* His analysis drew essentially on the experiments of the Greeks and carried the investigation formally no further than the Lombard League in Italy, but he did comment directly on the American experiment. Freeman was clearly fully aware of the principles underlying the American experience and he readily asserted that the division of sovereignty between the central and regional governments was central to the federal idea. He recognized that in a modern federal state sovereignty was both divided and coordinated and that federalism was essentially a compromise based on a willingness to cooperate for the greater good of the citizenry. Freeman also believed that a federal system would work best, in fact have most chance of success, if previously separate small states united into a federal state. He did not believe it was possible nor advisable to create a viable federation from an existing unitary state, certainly not from one such as the United Kingdom:

> No one could wish to cut up our United Kingdom into a federation, to invest English Counties with the rights of American States, or even to restore Scotland and Ireland to the quasi-Federal position which they held before their respective Unions. A Federal Union, to be of any value, must arise by the establishment of a closer tie between elements which were before distinct, not by the division of members which have been hitherto more closely united.[18]

Freeman's arguments were, to a degree, in line with Dicey's later ones although he was by no means as vehement in his defence of parliamentary sovereignty. He did recognize the merits and value of the federal system in certain contexts. The United Kingdom was just not an appropriate setting for it, and nor was the British empire.

Another writer who in mid-century offered an analysis of federalism was John Stuart Mill, who included a chapter entitled 'Federal Representative Governments' in *Considerations on Representative Government*, published in 1861. Mill was familiar with *The Federalist*[19] and had obviously remained abreast of the tensions between the central government and the states in the USA, for his remarks reflected a sound understanding of the workings of the modern federal system. He wrote favourably about federal government, recognizing that under certain circumstances it was a preferable constitutional alternative. Far better to have a larger state with a division of sovereignty within it than a number of smaller, factious states whose ongoing tensions created unacceptable levels of instability. He did, however, point out that diversity could be accommodated within a unitary state, particularly if that diversity were of a legal or administrative nature, but he recognized that was a decision best left to the prospective members. He did not suggest that a federal system was inherently weak and he did not argue that a federal state could only result from integrative as opposed to disintegrative forces, as did Freeman and Dicey. His was a dispassionate view. Admittedly, he was no more searching or satisfying in his examination of first principles and nuance than Bagehot or Dicey, and he was equally as pragmatic but much less negative than Bagehot, Freeman, Dicey or James Bryce.[20] It should not go unnoticed that Mill's preference for unitary over federal states, all else being equal, probably owed something to his close acquaintance with Bentham and Austin, both of whom were dubious of a federal solution for interstate or intra-state problems.[21]

Probably the most noted nineteenth-century British commentator on the federal system was Albert Venn Dicey, Vinerian Professor of Law at Oxford, who in an article in the *Contemporary Review* in July 1882 and in his lectures entitled *The Law of the Constitution* published in 1885 tackled the issues of federalism, federal government and sovereignty, particularly as they affected Ireland and the overall United Kingdom. Dicey made no secret of the fact that he thought federalism was not in the interests of the United Kingdom. It would involve a written constitution, a superior court and a distribution of powers, and by providing Ireland with a separate parliament Dicey believed the chances of further conflict between Ireland and Great Britain would be enhanced. For Dicey, the vital essence of the British constitution was 'the absolute omnipotence, the sovereignty of Parliament'. Federation would mean a division of power and a consequent diminution in the omnipotence of parliament. He was appalled by the possibility of federalism for it would 'dislocate every English constitutional arrangement'. He was convinced that federal government was weak government and would enfeeble the British state in its dealings with aggressive foreign powers. Dicey also believed that federalism would result in a division of loyalty and an enhancement of national and local allegiances that would fragment the polity. As he put it in his 1882 article:

[Federalism] revolutionizes the whole constitution of the United Kingdom; by undermining the parliamentary sovereignty, it deprives English institutions of their elasticity, their strength, and their life; it weakens the Executive at home, and lessens the power of the country to resist foreign attack. The revolution which works these changes holds out no hope of conciliation with Ireland. An attempt, in short, to impose on England and Scotland a constitution which they do not want, and which is quite unsuited to the historical traditions and to the genius of Great Britain, offers to Ireland a constitution which Ireland is certain to dislike, which has none of the real or imaginary charms of independence, and ensures none of the solid benefits to be hoped for from a genuine union with England.[22]

In stating his position so firmly, Dicey rejected the analysis of his contemporary Baron Acton. Acton, unlike John Stuart Mill and Dicey, did not believe it was a necessary condition of free institutions that governmental boundaries coincide with nationalities. On the contrary, he reasoned that undivided sovereignty could lead to centralization, corruption and absolutism while the 'presence of different nations under the same sovereignty' could provide against 'the servility which flourishes under the shadow of a single authority, by balancing interests [and] multiplying associations'. 'Liberty', he contended, 'provokes diversity, and diversity preserves liberty by supplying the means of organization. . . . The combination of different nations in one State is as necessary a condition of civilized life as the combination of men in society.' Referring to the United Kingdom, Acton argued that the 'parliamentary system fails to provide for [national claims], as it presupposes the unity of the people. Hence in those countries in which different races dwell together, it has not satisfied their desires, and is regarded as an imperfect form of freedom.' He went on: 'The greatest adversary of the rights of nationality is the modern theory of nationality. By making the State and the nation commensurate with each other in theory, it reduces practically to a subject condition all other nationalities that may be within the boundary.'[23]

While Acton had not specifically addressed the issue of federalism or the division of powers within a state his discussion of the relationship between the nation, the state and nationality was pertinent to an understanding of its nature and ultimate worth. Unfortunately, such an analysis was rare amongst British commentators and one searches in vain for discussions of the difficulties that ethnic, national and religious differences could pose for a unitary state such as the United Kingdom.

Dicey, for one, remained immune to any such reflections and in his 1885 lectures on the law and the constitution he simply reiterated his earlier arguments, especially in the lecture 'Parliamentary Sovereignty and Federalism'. After comparing the British parliamentary system with the United States federal system – which he considered the most advanced form of modern federalism – he rehearsed the essential elements of that system: the supremacy of its written constitution, the division of powers and the authority of the courts in interpreting the constitution. He concluded that because no authority would have supreme, overriding power in a federal system it would always be weaker than a unitary state such as the United Kingdom where the king in parliament, i.e. the king, lords and commons, had 'absolute legislative sovereignty or despotism'. Dicey was also alarmed by the degree to which federalism, at least as practised in the United States, gave such an important role to the judiciary. To him this resulted in 'the prevalence of a spirit of legality among the people'. He did not approve of the apparent shift in power from the legislature to the judiciary.

Dicey's was a most negative reading of federalism. It was clear from his writings that he fully understood the mechanics of federalism. He was a reliable guide as long as he stuck to exposition, but when he came to analysing the implications of the federal system he tended to ignore the flexibility inherent in such a system and to emphasize its rigidity. He also completely misread the strength that a federal system could display in the face of external foes and overemphasized the system's inability to deal with internal pressures. He preferred not to think of federalism as coordinate and a federal system as essentially a compromise. His commitment to the preservation of the Union was such that it blinded him to the merits of a federal system. His particular error was his unwillingness, or inability, to consider the divisibility of parliamentary sovereignty. He obviously had culled no lessons from the debates before and after the American Revolution nor was he sensitive to the changes in the imperial constitution that had been unfolding since the 1830s. His refusal to consider federalism constructively made him a formidable antagonist in the constitutional discussions of the next forty years and his convictions underpinned the arguments of unionists. For Dicey, federalism would weaken both the British state and the British empire. It would inflame national and regional aspirations. It had, therefore, to be fought to the last ditch. Dicey never deviated from his analysis of the 1880s and he wrote and lobbied continuously against both home rule and the federal idea. To him, the latter was not a solution for either the United Kingdom's or the empire's woes.[24]

Dicey believed that a key condition for the formation of a federal state was the presence of 'a body of countries such as the Cantons of Switzerland, the Colonies of America, or the Provinces of Canada, so closely connected by locality, by history, by race, or the like, as to be capable of bearing, in the eyes of their inhabitants, an impress of common nationality'. Moreover, he thought it would in general be found that 'lands which now form part of a federal state were at some stage of their existence bound together by close alliance or by subjection to a common sovereign . . . it is certain that where federalism flourishes it is in general the slowly-matured fruit of some earlier and closer connection'. What is interesting about the earlier part of the statement is Dicey's reference to 'common nationality' and to matters such as race. Did the failure of the British to adopt, or move towards, federalism mean that British nationality not only did not exist but could not? And since the contemporary discussion of federalism was so overwhelmingly legalistic and non-sociological, Dicey's use of the term 'race' is intriguing. Did it mean 'whites' or 'blacks' could happily unite only in their own federal states and that a federal state containing units of different races was impossible? It would seem so. Dicey's second key condition was the desire for union among the inhabitants of the various units proposing to unite. In his words, 'They must desire union, and must not desire unity. If there be no desire to unite, there is clearly no basis for federalism.' The foundation of federalism was a 'combination of union and separation . . . the desire for national unity and the determination to maintain the independence of each man's separate State'.[25]

Two writers who shared Dicey's preference for unitary government but who wrote more favourably about federalism were James Bryce and Henry Sidgwick. Both men wrote at the end of the century at a time of great turmoil in Anglo-Irish and imperial affairs when the federal idea was often broached as a solution to constitutional problems at home and abroad. Bryce was the author of *The American Commonwealth*, published in two volumes in 1888,[26] and therefore an acknowledged expert on federalism. His book, while it was a close analysis of the American federal system, was not philosophic or theoretical in nature being essentially an exposition of the mechanics of American government, an analysis of its day-to-day operations and a personal view of its strengths and weaknesses. Nevertheless, it made a highly useful reference work for all interested in the federal model and it was avidly devoured and constantly consulted before and during the debates that led to the federation of Australia in 1900.

In addition to his analysis of the American constitution, Bryce further explored the federal model in a number of speeches throughout the last twenty years of the nineteenth century. In two lectures given in 1884 he analysed what he referred to as 'flexible and rigid constitutions'.[27] A 'flexible' constitution was unwritten and, like the English constitution, based primarily on precedent and tradition and readily adaptable. A 'rigid' constitution was usually written and often federal in nature with limitations built in as to how change might be effected. Bryce clearly favoured 'flexible' constitutions although he recognized that since the American Revolution and the increasing role played by the 'Many' as opposed to the 'Few' the trend had been toward 'rigid' rather than 'flexible' constitutions, initially to protect the rights and interests of the 'Many' but latterly to protect the rights and interests of the 'Few'. In re-examining the federal option in 1901, Bryce referred to the recent debates over the suggested creation of a federal parliament for the empire and a federal parliament for the United Kingdom. Under either scheme the sovereignty of the British parliament would be reduced and both the imperial and domestic constitutions would become 'rigid'. He concluded, 'The difficulties, both legal and practical, with which these proposals, taken either separately or in conjunction, are surrounded, are greater than those who advocate them have as yet generally perceived.'

Again, in these lectures and reflections, Bryce did not grapple with the philosophic underpinnings of federalism. He saw a federal solution as a compromise between centrifugal and centripetal forces. He accepted the principle of divided sovereignty and, while recognizing the difficulties inherent in any potential move to a federal system at either the imperial or domestic levels, he did not argue, as Dicey did, that a federal system was a naturally weak system. He agreed it was less flexible but then it could be more protective of democracy. However, he did point out that in the late nineteenth century it was apparently seen by the 'Few' as a means of offsetting democratic trends and of entrenching and/or protecting their rights. In other words, federal structures were pragmatic devices born out of certain circumstances for particular reasons which, dependent on the timing of creation, could reflect either democratic or elitist interests or even a mixture of the two.

Henry Sidgwick in *The Elements of Politics*, published in 1891, and *The Development of European Polity*, published in 1903 after his death, looked at both ancient and modern federalism. Sidgwick contended that a 'confederation of states' and a 'federal state' represented 'two stages in the development of federality'.[28] For him, a federal state was 'only one kind of a composite state' but the one more 'in harmony with the ideal of modern democracy than a unitary polity – as a means of realizing the maximum of liberty compatible with order'. Sidgwick held out great hopes for the federal form of government. On the assumption that the 'growth of civilization' would lead to continually larger societies, Sidgwick thought it

> not beyond the limits of a sober forecast to conjecture that some further integration may take place in the West European states: and if it should take place, it seems probable that the example of America will be followed, and that the new political aggregate will be formed on the basis of a federal polity. When we turn our gaze from the past to the future, an extension of federalism seems to me the most probable of the political prophecies relative to the form of government.

Sidgwick was well aware that in forming a polity and considering the distribution of functions, differences in law, customs, race, religion or 'the level of civilization attained' could be key factors in reaching decisions.[29] For Sidgwick federalism was 'a mode of political organization by which a nation may realize the maximum of liberty compatible with order'. However, Sidgwick believed federalism was 'likely to be in many cases a transitional stage through which a composite society passes on its way to a completer union'. On the other hand, he was at pains to point out, 'the development of democratic thought and sentiment, so far as it favours liberty and self-government, tends in favour of federality'.

Sidgwick provided readers with a careful explanation of the circumstances that would naturally tend to the adoption of a federal system. Nevertheless, anyone reading his articles and chapters would have been inclined to come away highly sensitive to the difficulties inherent in working a system based on divided sovereignty. While liberals and home rulers and federalists would certainly have been able to draw succour from Sidgwick, it is also clear that unionists would have equally been able to use his work to seemingly prove the problems inherent in a federal system, particularly for a small and vulnerable polity. Nevertheless, Sidgwick had provided a thoughtful basis for reflection.

On reviewing the works of those nineteenth-century writers who devoted space to the federal model one is struck by how little theoretical material there is. The essays or chapters are primarily a combination of exposition and explanation of the structure or mechanics of the federal system and an analysis of how it worked either in an ideal form or in particular instances. The American model was naturally the one that attracted the most attention and it was used as the benchmark for all other analyses. It was uniformly recognized that federalism in its modern form originated with the American system devised in the 1780s. Most writers had a sound grasp of that system and fully understood the vertical and horizontal divisions of sovereignty it entailed but all of them tended to think it an inappropriate system for either the United Kingdom or for the empire. It was viewed either as too rigid, and therefore lacking the necessary flexibility, or potentially weak in the face of external foes. Also, it was seen as a way-station on the road to greater unity – an integrative force – rather than the reverse. In other words, it was a system based on the need for cooperation by a number of small, roughly equal units and not a means of distributing or sharing or coordinating power by creating a federal state out of a unitary one. While these writers did intellectually accept the division of sovereignty as workable and appropriate in the federal systems that were emerging in the nineteenth century, they still believed the British constitution, unwritten and with sovereignty undivided, provided the ideal form. All were reluctant to consider the federal idea seriously either for the United Kingdom or the empire, even in the face of the Irish problem and the mounting challenges to British economic and political power abroad, but none were as rigid and dogmatic in their hostility as Dicey. Federalism had no champion of stature to offset his arguments. Constitutional musings had not led to any theoretical breakthrough amongst British writers and the nineteenth century was pretty much a wasteland insofar as furthering insight into the options available in the formation of states or in achieving balance between the state and the individual.

The urge and desire for greater control over the political arena by the general populace was but grudgingly recognized and met in the United Kingdom in the nineteenth century, and it was not until the 1840s and 1850s – and later still in many places – that both responsible government and self-government were extended to certain of the 'white settler' colonies. But the acceptance of the principle of home rule in the colonial empire did not result in an adoption of that option in the United Kingdom. The British had had little choice but to accept the concept of a division of sovereignty between the metropole and the colonial periphery if they were to avoid rupture and/or warfare, but at home such a division was seen as potentially divisive and therefore highly dangerous to the security of the state. Power and sovereignty at home had to be supreme and unbridled and undivided even if it could be pragmatically divided within the empire. Even then it was accepted because it was felt to be the only way to ensure the maintenance of the bond between the metropole and the periphery and, therefore, the overall strength and continued unity of the empire. Paradoxically, a relaxation of the tie between London and certain of its colonies was viewed as the only way to ensure that the tie existed at all. Diversity and unity were compatible in a quasi-federal or proto-federal setting within the empire but not at home. At home parliament, i.e. king, lords and commons, was supreme and the differences in religious, legal, administrative and cultural practices and forms between England, Scotland, Wales and Ireland were nothing but necessary glosses on a brute reality. This was a *united* kingdom with one supreme and all-powerful centre in the hands of an elite reluctant to relinquish any portion of that power to provincial or regional centres. The need to protect the British Isles against all comers and to have the means of doing so securely under limited control was paramount. As long as that perceived need existed and so long as regional 'nationalism' remained unfocused or ill-organized or unappealing to the mass then that deep-rooted need to preserve the supremacy of the Westminster parliament would go unchallenged and unsullied.

Federalism was a system of government, at least in its modern form, born of necessity. It was a system based on compromise and cooperation between a number of suspicious but vulnerable rivals whose recognition of their mutual interest and needs finally out-weighed their desire or capacity to function independently. As long as parallel tensions and needs either did not exist or were not widely recognized in all the nations of the national state of the United Kingdom then federalism in its pure form, or even in its attenuated, devolutionary home-rule-all-round form, would not be adopted. Certainly, its attainment was not helped or advanced by the writings and musings of the constitutional experts.

3 'Federation' of the empire

The interest in maintaining the unity of the empire was a continuing one from the late eighteenth through to the mid-twentieth century. It took varying political, economic and defensive forms depending on the nature of domestic and external circumstances. 'Imperial union' or 'closer union of the empire' were umbrella phrases underscoring the goal or aim in mind but they were, and are, of little help in explaining or defining the means of maintaining or achieving union. Similarly, the term 'imperial federation' was loosely used to describe a bewildering variety of schemes and plans for union, most of which had little in common with federation *per se*. More recently, the term 'empire federalism' has been coined to describe the various constitutional devices designed either to preserve the unity of the empire or to at least ensure its better management. Again, the majority of those ideas had little to do with federalism. Only if one defines federalism very loosely to mean any idea that promotes cooperation, whether by federal means or not, does the term have any currency. The various schemes for including colonial MPs in the Westminster parliament and the plethora of proposals for advisory councils, conferences and congresses that surfaced were all interesting, often ingenious, usually impracticable and definitely not federal. Only the schemes establishing an empire-wide parliament, increasingly to the fore in the late nineteenth and early twentieth centuries, were truly federal in nature.[1]

Federal ideas, or proximate suggestions, for the unification of the empire surfaced fitfully from the 1820s but it was not until the early 1850s that the term 'imperial federation' was coined and then only as of the late 1860s that sustained attention was given to the federal idea. In 1852 an anonymous writer in the *Westminster Review* pointed out the need for 'a constitutional arrangement for the public discussion in England of colonial questions, under which, like British questions in the British parliament, they can be opened and debated as of right'. He asked whether the establishment of a 'confederation' for the empire might not only relieve congestion at Westminster but promote the unification of imperial defence. Moreover, such a 'federation' might 'influence the rest of the world for good'. Apart from underscoring a widespread belief in the world-wide merits of English civilization this writer had neither a 'confederation' nor a 'federation' in mind. His real preference was for an advisory body composed of colonial representatives, British ministers and civil servants. Supreme authority would remain with the Crown and with the legislature in Great Britain. Despite his use of the term 'federal' there was no discussion of federation *per se*.[2]

The next year, 1853, another anonymous author, writing this time in the *London Quarterly Review*, argued that the British empire should not dissolve as its members matured. Instead, it would be preferable to ensure continued unity. The writer argued that 'our possessions are not dependencies, to be schooled while weak, and dismissed when strong, but members of one family, to be endeared to us by every tie, considered in every decision, and held in the bonds of perpetual amity'. To the writer, the empire represented freedom and was the only bulwark against abuse of power. He suggested there was a need to lay down the 'organic laws' of the empire and to establish an 'Imperial Senate' for the discussion and approval of imperial questions to which each member state of the 'Imperial Federation' should send representatives. The writer suggested a division of powers between local and imperial legislatures but did not elaborate. He did make it clear, however, that he was referring only to 'the real British provinces' of the empire and not to 'Plantations' such as the West Indies and Mauritius, nor to 'Subject Countries' such as India and Ceylon, nor to 'Stations' such as Gibraltar and St Helena. Unless such far-seeing provisions were made, he claimed the empire would dissolve and England would be left alone, 'a kingdom, with, perhaps, a few dependencies'. He wanted 'the idea of the United Kingdom . . . to merge in the greater and juster idea of the British Empire'. While this was the first time that the term 'imperial federation' appears to have been used, the writer obviously did not have a federal system in mind.[3]

The first substantial analysis of a purely 'federal' issue was provided by Edward Freeman in the October 1865 issue of the *Fortnightly Review*.[4] In assessing 'The Proposed Revision of the Swiss Federal Constitution', Freeman demonstrated a clear understanding of federalism as well as a close acquaintance with the debates and developments in the United States. He acknowledged that it was difficult for the citizen of one nation to understand the constitutional workings of another. For example, the fact that the British constitution was based on convention and was thus unwritten made it difficult for Englishmen to compare their system with those of other nations. Freeman thought Switzerland 'the most perfect federal union which Europe has seen'. Freeman clearly understood the division of powers inherent in a federal system and pointed out that only in 1848 did the Swiss adopt a constitution like that of the United States – thus realizing 'the full perfection of the Federal idea'.

Freeman explained:

In a Federal State a written Constitution seems to be a necessity. It partakes of the nature of a treaty. Certain States, previously independent, either in history or in theory, agree to become one State for certain purposes, while they remain distinct States for certain other purposes. It is the essence of a Federal Union that the several States should surrender some of their powers to a central body, and should retain others in their own hands. If the States retain all their powers, or if they surrender all their powers, they do not form a Federal Union at all. . . . There must be something entrusted to the Federal power which the several States cannot touch, and something left to the several States which the Federal power cannot touch.

This was divided sovereignty and the essence of a federal system. Freeman also pointed out that the states forming a federation had to make provision for the amendment of the constitution, 'otherwise revolution or secession must be the result'.

Freeman observed that in the United Kingdom 'the Crown and Parliament can do anything, because with us Law and Constitution are one' but in a federation the federal constitution was essentially a compact and federal power could only be derived from the constitution; it was not inherent. The federal constitution prescribed 'the limits of Federal and State authority'. Freeman made the important point that 'the revision of a Constitution, Federal or Cantonal, does not convey to a Swiss the same notion of radical and revolutionary change which it does to an Englishman. A revision of the Constitution may be needed to alter some point which, in England, might be settled by an ordinary Act of Parliament, with very little of debate within the Houses or of public excitement out of them.' This stemmed from the habit of incorporating in both the Federal and Cantonal Constitutions many provisions which the British would think a matter for ordinary legislation.

Freeman's article was extremely important and a landmark in the public discussion of the federal idea in nineteenth-century Britain. It provided a primer for the uninitiated and few Britons, having read it, would any longer be able to claim ignorance of the essential principles of a federal system. Its publication was also fortuitous for as of the late 1860s there was an intensification of debate about the future of the empire. To many observers in the United Kingdom and the white settlement colonies, the decision to withdraw troops from those colonies by Gladstone's Liberal administration (1868–74), when coupled with a long-standing unwillingness in the British Treasury to back colonial ventures, had been a further indication that the British government was bent on severing the ties between the self-governing colonies and the mother country. Such was the concern in England, in particular, that in 1868 the Colonial Institute was founded to promote the closer union of the white empire. By the early seventies a debate over the future of the empire was in high gear and during the next decade at least 150 schemes for the consolidation of the empire were published. An increasing number of commentators believed they had found in the federal system a solution to the problem.

The first soundings were tentative. The recent establishment in Canada of the first federal government in the empire prompted Auberon Herbert to consider how the existing government of the United Kingdom might be adapted to involve the white settlement colonies, thereby strengthening the empire. He quickly concluded that colonial representation in the House of Commons would be inadequate but he thought the business of the House could be divided so that foreign affairs, the army and navy, India and the colonies could be handled by a certain number of Westminster MPs plus a just proportion of colonial members sitting in an 'Imperial Chamber' on days when the House of Commons was not. Another alternative would be to have domestic issues considered by a 'Provincial House' and imperial questions by an 'Imperial House', each House being elected by the constituencies of the country. But if the number of English representatives was to be kept small in keeping with the overall size of the House the size of English constituencies might be too large. Here Herbert touched on an important problem that was to persist throughout the discussions of the next hundred years: how to contend with the size and power of England in either a domestic or imperial reconstruction? He recognized that such ideas were controversial and subject to criticism but he reminded his readers, presciently as it turned out, that 'where a national instinct once has begun to touch the minds of men, even if they are only a handful in the crowd, it is too great a power to perish silently either under contempt or criticism'. 'At present,' he concluded, 'those who look forward from the Island to the Empire can afford to wait, feeling confident that a cause which appeals to our widest and noblest patriotism, must eventually triumph over an opposition that finds its stronghold in the instincts of provincial selfishness.'[5]

While Herbert had raised an important issue, he had not fully explored the federal idea. This was left to Arthur Mills who in 1869 examined a number of the schemes designed to maintain the integrity and unity of the empire.[6] One idea he had found rather popular and fashionable was 'Colonial Confederation', although he wondered how it would work. For, as he pointed out, 'even where local and central institutions have been simultaneously created by one and the same legislative Act, and the limits of municipal and federal power have been defined by specific enactments, harmonious action as between the central government and its satellites has proved difficult of attainment'. The diverse interests of nine governments, the difficulties of intercolonial communication and the onerous costs of double government had impeded the New Zealand experiment with the federal concept and similar concerns were preventing any serious consideration of such a system in Australia and South Africa. As for the recent adoption of a federal constitution in British North America, Mills recognized the mutual interests of the various colonies did make it feasible. Nevertheless, the 'real difficulties of the scheme consist in the due adjustment of the three-fold relations between the imperial, federal, and local governments'. Here Mills touched on a key problem that was constantly to bedevil federal constitution makers well into the twentieth century. As long as a federal state was still a dependency within the British empire there would be a problem defining a role, not to say the appropriate powers, for such a federation.

As Mills put it:

What *we* have to fear, and if possible to guard against, is the constant peril of a three-fold conflict of authority, implied in the very existence of a federation of dependencies, retaining, as now proposed, any considerable share of intercolonial independence. We may schedule as we please 'local' and 'general' topics of legislation; we may define with the utmost possible distinctness the limits of each, or the concurrent authority of both governments; we may equitably adjust financial disabilities, and allot to the central and provincial authorities their respective spheres of power over redistributions and rearrangements, but it is on the accuracy and sharpness with which the prerogatives of the federal executive are defined, that the success and permanence of a constitution, necessarily clogged with checks and counterpoises, must eventually depend.

Mills was clearly also leery of coordinate sovereignty. In direct reference to the recent North American federation, he said the vital question was 'how the inherent weakness of all federations can in this instance be cured, and the central government armed with a sovereignty which may be worthy of the name'. It was, he asserted, 'the essence of all good governments to have somewhere a true sovereign power'. In the end, Mills did not push his earlier insight. He concluded that it was 'impossible to regard this federation in any other light than that of a transition stage to eventual independence'. Therefore, the precise form that imperial sovereignty might assume was a matter 'of comparatively secondary importance'.

Mills's comments were perceptive but they also reflected the general suspicion with which the federal idea was greeted. It was so out of tune with the prevailing norms in the United Kingdom that even when its usefulness in certain settings was admitted it was nevertheless considered a tenuous system of government with built-in liabilities. It would be difficult for federal enthusiasts and theorists to counter that prevailing view.

One who was convinced that a closer union of the empire must be achieved was J.A. Froude, but his conviction did not translate into a specific scheme and he seemed airily impervious to the telling observations of Mills. In an article entitled 'England and her Colonies' published in January 1870, Froude pointed out that 'Other nations once less powerful or not more powerful than ourselves, are growing in strength and numbers, and we too must grow if we intend to remain on a level with them.' He argued that Great Britain must encourage emigration to the colonies and build on their desire to be part of a united empire. He countered the scepticism he knew existed by arguing that the legislative union with Scotland was found possible, and there were rather greater difficulties in the way of that than those which obstruct a union with the colonies. The problem then was to reconcile two nations which were hereditary enemies. The problem now is but to reunite the scattered fragments of the same nation, and bridge over the distance which divides them from us. Distance frightens us; but steam and the telegraph have abolished distance.

As for the difficulties in achieving a union and devising a constitution, he argued it would be quickly done if the will were there and if the country's interests required it: 'Neither the terms of the federation, the nature of the imperial council, the functions of the local legislatures, the present debts of the colonies, or the apportionment of taxation, would be found problems hard of solution, if the apostles of *laissez-faire* could believe for once that it was not the last word of political science.'[7]

If anything, Froude's passionate appeal revealed an ignorance of both the strengths and weaknesses of the federal idea and certainly a naively optimistic assessment of the process of constitution-making. One who brought a tougher mind and a broader perspective to bear on the problem was Herman Merivale, a former permanent under-secretary in the Colonial Office and a long-time perceptive commentator on imperial affairs. In an article published in early 1870, Merivale referred to the current feeling that 'something ought to be done' to both arrest the further disintegration of the empire and to give it added vigour and strength. It was clear he had read extensively about federal practice in the United States and that he was fully conversant with its intricacies. It was thus not surprising that he was both more cautious and more practical than Froude. In surveying the various schemes that had been touched on by some, he turned particularly to the possible federation of the empire. While not opposed in theory, Merivale felt obligated to remind his readers that as matters then stood,

> the authority of Parliament is absolute. Although numbers of inferior legislatures, in Australia as elsewhere, have been created by statute or subsist by usage, these are all entirely subordinate. As against Parliament they have no right at all – one might almost say no existence. No definitions, no barriers of any kind, separate matters which are of the cognizance of local legislatures from those which are of Imperial. Such is the British constitution.

Thus, while the federal scheme conformed to sound abstract reasoning and while it might be that due to the press of business parliament might have to define and limit its functions, Merivale believed there was nevertheless something self-contradictory about the idea. As he put it, 'If Parliament be politically omnipotent (as it is) Parliament cannot possibly abdicate its own omnipotence.' Moreover, Merivale thought the federal idea had emerged too late as an option. It might have worked earlier on but now it 'would involve too great a change in our general institutions to be acceptable or practicable'. Merivale was not unsympathetic to federalism but like the majority of his contemporaries he had difficulty grappling with the division of parliamentary sovereignty that would be involved.[8]

The federal idea was examined only sporadically in the 1870s. Given the plethora of schemes and proposals that were given a sounding during these years one might have expected more theorizing than in fact occurred. By this time, of course, the creation of the Dominion of Canada was well known and the British North America Act was readily available; so too were the details of the new German federal constitution of 1871. There was no shortage of federal examples and apparently no lack of interest in them but it was rare to find that interest translated to the British or imperial constitutional arenas.

A rare exception to the general intellectual disengagement were two articles written by Edward Jenkins and published in the *Contemporary Review* in early 1871. Entitled 'Imperial Federalism' and 'An Imperial Confederation', they reflected the current state of knowledge and confusion surrounding federalism.[9] Edward Jenkins bemoaned the drift in the government's colonial policy and called for the unification of the empire. He believed the solution lay in 'Imperial Federalism' which, he argued, had two dimensions. Viewed 'from the observation-point of an organizing power' it was imperial but when seen 'from the local basis of each province or colony' it involved 'in some degree the notion of federalism'. For Jenkins, federalism as an imperial question related to 'the union of the different constituents of the empire for imperial purposes'; as a local question it had to do with 'Imperial union for the advantage of each constituent'. He defined 'Imperial Federalism' to be the

> doctrine of a legislative union, in the form of a confederation, of each subordinate self-governing community which is now included within the British Empire. To preserve that Empire intact, on the ground that such a policy is not only imperial but dictated by the selfish interest of each constituent; to combine in some flexible and comprehensive system the great concourse of subordinate states whereof our empire is composed, for the benefit of all; and lastly, to confirm to every individual member of the imperial community those rights and privileges to which he is born – rights and privileges justly inalienable from himself or his children; these three things must be at once the aim and the reason for Imperial Federalism.

While Jenkins recognized the differing motivations that might lie behind a desire to federate the empire, dependent on whether one viewed change from the vantage point of the metropole or the periphery, he did not appear to be fully familiar with the essence of the federal idea nor altogether comfortable with the necessary division of sovereignty. For example, he continually used 'confederation' and 'federation' as if the two terms meant the same thing and he used 'legislative union' in association with 'confederation'. Jenkins's confusion of terms was not unusual in the late nineteenth century and was, in fact, to bedevil a considered appraisal of the federal idea for decades. Yet it is also clear that he was familiar with the recent developments in Canada and the break in the legislative log-jam that had occurred there as a consequence of federation. He concluded that the adoption of 'Imperial Federalism' would not only result in a general sharing of the mother country's tax and defence burdens but might also be the key to the relief of congestion in the Westminster parliament. He reasoned that 'Imperial Federalism' would give to each province the maximum of independent action, and yet preserve for it and for the empire at large the maximum of mutual aid and benefit. He particularly thought such an arrangement would help resolve Anglo-Irish difficulties. 'Would it not', he asked, be a sensible policy 'to let the Irish people manage their domestic affairs for themselves? Would not the re-establishment of a provincial government, with such limited powers as Federalism must necessarily leave them' be a stimulus to Irish society? Even here, however, Jenkins made a point of referring to the 'limited' powers under federalism, suggesting that he did not grasp the coordinate nature of that constitutional form. Jenkins ended his article by printing Sections 91 and 92 of the British North America Act and used them to demonstrate the advantages of two jurisdictions – again, however, he was careful not to mention divided sovereignties. 'Nothing', he concluded, 'need be added to prove that the Federal principle is capable of embodiment in a form at once promoting unity, protecting personal liberty, and fostering local independence, while in enlarging the scope of imperial splendour it gives strength to the play of imperial loyalty.'

Unlike the majority of his contemporaries, Jenkins did not think it wise to elaborate any specific scheme. He thought the recent efforts to do so would be more likely to injure than advance the cause. 'At present,' he argued, 'it is for the Federalist simply to show his doctrine to be reasonable, his suggestions to be *primâ-facie* practical, his system to be desirable, and to demonstrate that it deserves to be made the subject of a united conference and negotiation.' After familiarizing himself with the debates in British North America in the 1860s and rereading both *The Federalist* and Freeman's recent volume on federal government, Jenkins concluded that

> the leading object of pure Federalism is to secure for each party to the federal compact the utmost independence in its own affairs, while it aims at combining into one central authority such forces as are best adapted to secure the common welfare and common defence. Thus, within the coalition, local life and vigour are not merged in an overpowering and centralized despotism; while externally, and towards all other nations, it presents a single and serried front.

Beyond that broad description, however, Jenkins was not prepared to go.[10]

Amid the speculation of the 1870s about the future development of the colonies a variety of suggestions were made as to how the unity of the empire could be both preserved and strengthened. Most of the proposals were neither grounded in reality nor firmly buttressed by philosophic principles, and, for the most part, they were met with caution and scepticism. Edward Freeman, for one, questioned the wisdom of radical change which broke 'the continuity of institutions'. While he had no quarrel with 'the mere improvement of detail' in any constitution, he referred to 'the inherent evil of an organic change, of the snapping of a link between the past and the present'. He pointed out that the wisdom of the British 'consisted in always making such changes as were needed at any particular time' but 'in not making greater changes than were needed at that particular time'.[11] Lord Blachford was blunter than Freeman. He captured the sceptical mood more explicitly when he suggested that as the colonies developed they must either become separate nations or be given a share in the government of the empire. He sensed that the colonies wished to handle things themselves and he cautioned those who wished to bind them too closely.[12]

Not everyone interested in the empire's future was deflated by such arguments. As one writer pointed out, while the empire had steadily grown its political system had remained stationary and that was clearly unsatisfactory.[13] In his estimation, the

> one great principle which must form the ground-work of the required changes is the separation of local from national or Imperial interests. In a truly unified empire the Imperial Parliament should be entirely superior to the local affairs of any one part of the Empire. The local affairs of Great Britain should have no more place in the Imperial Parliament than have the local affairs of Canada or Australia. The Imperial Parliament should deal only with the affairs of the Empire at large.

The first step in effecting a change would be to separate local from imperial affairs which could only be done by local parliaments for Great Britain and Ireland. Those parliaments would be responsible for all the hundred and one local matters that currently clogged the House of Commons machinery while the imperial parliament would deal with all international, inter-colonial and imperial matters.

These were shrewd comments. Not only had the writer made the telling point that the British had not adapted their imperial political system to reflect the new strength, importance and self-regard of the settler colonies, he had also drawn attention to the increased congestion of parliamentary business and the intensifying demand for Irish home rule. He had concluded, as had so many other observers of the British domestic and imperial scenes, that such fundamental problems could only be resolved by a separation of local, national and imperial affairs by means of a federal system. A division of responsibilities would result in a more efficient and stronger empire.

What form that might ultimately take and how each constituent part might be effectively represented was, however, still clearly a puzzle to him. While wanting to ensure appropriate colonial representation in a new imperial parliament, he still wanted to leave England, Scotland and Ireland with 'a preponderance over the colonial members'. His dilemma was not unique. Even if one readily accepted the division of powers, it was more difficult, first, to resolve the problems associated with the overwhelming demographic advantage of the United Kingdom and, second, to relinquish British control of the actual reins of authority. As long as the United Kingdom was a first-class power and so markedly superior to the self-governing colonies in population and in military and economic strength, it would be difficult to devise a constitution that would at one and the same time observe 'true federalism', ensure equity and acknowledge the realities of Britain's position in the world. As the critics of the federal idea were quick to point out, the mother country would never willingly relinquish control over either its own destiny or that of its empire.

The first major critique of the federal idea as it applied to both the empire and the United Kingdom appeared in the *Contemporary Review* in July 1882. It was written by A.V. Dicey, the constitutional expert, who shared with Edward Freeman an aversion to any abrupt break with tradition.[14] Dicey's appraisal of federalism had been stimulated by a recent rereading of Isaac Butt's pamphlet *Home Government for Ireland, Irish Federalism: Its Meaning, Its Objects, and Its Hopes* which had originally been published in 1870 but was earning fresh attention in the light of both Irish demands for home rule and the debate over imperial federation. It is an important article because, first, it is by Dicey and sets the tone of his response for some forty years; second, it reveals widely held assumptions about both sovereignty and federalism; and, third, it dealt in a major way with the interlocked issues of the future of Ireland, the United Kingdom and the empire.

Dicey agreed with Butt that the English would not accept Irish independence and that federalism would be much less injurious to British interests than Irish separation; however, he thought it fallacious for Butt to go on to conclude that federalism also offered 'to England a fair compromise between the reasonable claim of Englishmen to preserve the prosperity of England and the greatness of the British Empire, and the natural desire of Irishmen for national independence'. Dicey pointed out that the adoption throughout the United Kingdom of a federal system modelled on that of the United States would be a radical departure from British constitutional practice. It would involve a written constitution, a definition of the respective powers of the central and state governments, a supreme court with the authority to decide if the federal pact had been observed, the provision of an amendment process and the establishment of some means by which the principles of the court could be upheld and, if necessary, enforced against the resistance of one or more states. These, argued Dicey, were the essential features of any federal system and all depended on the simple but often overlooked fact that a federal constitution implied 'an elaborate distribution and definition of political powers'; that it was, by its very nature, a compromise.

Dicey did not believe such a system would be beneficial either for the empire or for the United Kingdom. Admittedly, federation might avert disintegration and lessen the outflow of material resources but any such gains would be offset by a number of, as he characteristically put it, 'evils'. First, constitutional powers were difficult to change in a federation, and second, the sovereignty of the centre and the states would be mutually reduced. Dicey here seemed to confuse power with sovereignty. While the powers of the centre and of the states would be respectively limited under a federal system, the sovereignty of each within its own sphere would still be supreme. Dicey seemed not to understand, or was not prepared to accept, this point. He was convinced that a division of sovereignty meant a diminution of sovereignty. This conviction helps explain Dicey's passionate defence of the sovereignty of the British parliament in its existing form. To him, 'Irish Federalism' would in effect be 'British Federalism' and would amount to the most 'revolutionary' change in the British constitution ever proposed.

He contended there would be three disadvantages to any such change. First, all British constitutional arrangements would be 'dislocated' because it would mean the undermining of 'the true source of [the British constitution's] life and growth'. In other words, 'the absolute omnipotence, the sovereignty of Parliament' would be permanently impaired. On reviewing the American federal system, where 'every ordinary authority throughout the Union [was] hampered by constitutional restriction', Dicey was confirmed in his belief that the unwritten British constitution was far superior. Throughout this facet of his appraisal Dicey persistently used the term 'English' rather than 'British' thereby betraying his essential lack of empathy for the other nations within the United Kingdom. What concerned Dicey more than anything was *English* power and *English* sovereignty. Not only did he pass quickly over the heterogeneity of the British state but he paid no heed to the complex regional mix within England.

His second concern related to Britain's standing on the international stage. He was convinced that both federation of the United Kingdom and federation of the empire would diminish the power of the United Kingdom. It would mean that the 'Central Government would . . . merely from that division of powers which forms part of Federalism be as feeble against foreign oppression as against local resistance'. Moreover, in an empire-wide federation the United Kingdom would be but one component state, albeit the preponderant one, and thereby constrained. When confronted with the example of the Canadian federation, Dicey resorted to some highly contentious reasoning and did not fully address the essence of federalism. He dismissed the Canadian experiment with the federal idea by arguing that Canada was simply a colony, that the British parliament was supreme there and thus 'the dangers and difficulties of Federalism are to a brief extent avoided by the supremacy of the British crown'. This was, at best, carelessly misleading and a gloss on the nuanced, and evolving, Anglo-Canadian relationship, but there were few in a position to counter Dicey's broad generalizations.

Finally, Dicey contended, the adoption of the federal system would probably enhance rather than diminish the prospects of further disagreement with Ireland. Since the prospects of imperial union were often seen to rest on the continued union of Ireland with Great Britain, any suggestion that federalism would lead to a weakening of that tie was always taken seriously. By arguing as he did about both the federal idea and about sovereignty, Dicey was deliberately catering to those fears. In the process, he did not give the federal idea its full due nor explore it in a theoretical or philosophic manner. Dicey was a partisan in the domestic and imperial politics of his day and his attitudes coloured his treatment of the federal idea. His reputation was such that his arguments were usually accepted without close scrutiny.[15]

Dicey's discussion of federalism continued through the mid-1880s with the publication of his lectures *The Law of the Constitution*. His ideas and arguments were therefore in wide circulation just at the moment when the imperial union movement in the United Kingdom reached its apogee with the formation of the Imperial Federation League in London in 1884. Created to promote imperial union the League was active during the next decade and a number of branches were established in Great Britain and in the settler colonies of Canada, South Africa, New Zealand and Australia. Despite the flurry of enthusiasm that greeted its appearance, the League failed to achieve the success held out for it. The League harboured within its ranks too many conflicting views. The federationists vied with those wanting a less formal advisory council, and both clashed with the supporters of union for defensive or economic purposes. Federal ideas were vulnerable in this contentious atmosphere and the League rarely discussed federal principles or the associated issue of divided sovereignty. The League proved an ineffective champion of the federation of the empire and it was not altogether a surprise either to its members or to outside observers when it was dissolved in 1893.

Its essential problem lay in the fact that 'federation' was a misnomer. The term reflected neither the functional aim of the League nor its root beliefs. One prominent advocate of closer union, F.P. de Labilliere, was frank enough to state openly that the word 'federation' was used by imperial unionists 'simply because it is the most convenient word we can find to represent the idea we have in view – the idea of some organization which shall efficiently give us that which we want to maintain – the strength and security of the Empire'.[16] Even when an individual advocate made the effort to familiarize himself with federal theory and practice his public comments were not always as helpful or as illuminating as they might have been.

This was demonstrated in an article written by J.N. Dalton for the July

1884 issue of the *Nineteenth Century*, entitled 'The Federal States of the World'. Dalton had obviously done his homework and was familiar with the German, the Austro-Hungarian, the Swiss, the Canadian and the United States constitutions. Certainly, anyone who read his article would have become reasonably well informed about both the principles underpinning those diverse systems and their varied working operations. It was equally apparent that Dalton recognized the need to separate local, national and imperial affairs. A federal parliament for the empire would deal only with imperial questions, 'that is with the supreme questions of peace and war, foreign relations, diplomacy and consular agencies, the defence of the whole against all external foes (army and navy, forts, garrisons, arsenals, naval stations and dockyards), India and the crown colonies, foreign and inter-colonial trade, postal and telegraphic communication, with everything, in fact, affecting the interests of the whole, as a whole'. It was imperative that the self-governing colonies be involved. It irked Dalton that 'in relation to all such great, national, and fundamental subjects, the colonists of our own race, lineage and language, living on British soil and under the British flag, remain to this day as unrepresented as if they were aliens'.[17]

This line of argument foreshadowed the substance of the case to be made by the Round Table movement some twenty-five years later and demonstrated that Dalton was sensitive to the gathering conundra associated with the interconnection of nationalism and imperialism at the periphery of empire. What would have confused most of his readers, however, and led some to doubt Dalton's grasp of 'true federalism', was his surprising assertion that England and Scotland had been federally united from 1607 to 1707, as had Great Britain and Ireland from 1782 to 1800. This, of course, was simply not true, as any constitutional expert would have been quick to point out. It was remarks of this nature that underlined how difficult it was for the 'federal idea' to receive an objective hearing in the United Kingdom of the late nineteenth century. It was not a natural British constitutional construct and even its advocates could prove to be its worst enemies.

This was certainly the conclusion reached by another contemporary observer.[18] In a speech entitled 'National Unity' at the Royal Colonial Institute, George Baden-Powell argued that 'the Federal principle does not take root in British soil' for, in his estimation, the tendency in the islands was 'towards national unity'. As for the British empire, he did not believe 'the literal Federal idea' was likely to take root there either. There were no independent sovereignties to be dealt with. It was true every province, every settlement, every individual, enjoyed certain rights and liberties which it would be the height of injustice and folly to impair or ignore. But, Baden-Powell suggested, those very rights were in 'the jealous care of the national sovereignty'; they lived and had their being 'in an old established national unity'.

He concluded that the 'tendency and spirit of British developments is thus seen to be fully in accord with the development of national as opposed to Federal union. This is the more cheering, seeing that history tells us there is a completeness and finality in National unions, but that Federal unions are almost invariably mere historic stepping-stones from separate indepen- dent existence to national unity.' The line of argument that a federal state was but a way-station on a direct route to a unitary one was to surface often during the next fifty years.

The most punishing criticism of imperial federation was provided by Edward Freeman in the April 1885 issue of *Macmillan's Magazine*.[19] Freeman reminded his readers that the phrase 'imperial federation' was a contradiction in terms. The simple truth was that what was 'Imperial' could not be 'Federal' and what was 'Federal' could not be 'Imperial'. On looking at the British empire, Freeman found all the elements of a federation wanting: 'There is no voluntary union of independent states, keeping some powers to themselves and granting other powers to a central authority of their own creation. There is instead a number of dependent bodies, to which a central authority older than themselves has been graciously pleased to grant certain powers. This state of things is not federation, but . . . subjec- tion.' Moreover, if one looked at the American federal model the difference would be even more apparent. The American citizens of American states elected those responsible for foreign affairs, and the states in their legisla- tures chose the senators who either approved or disapproved of federal policy. As far as Freeman was concerned this proved that the difference between the position of an American state and that of a British colony was 'nothing short of the difference between federation and . . . subjection'. What was proposed for the empire, argued Freeman, was not only to bring in a new thing, federation, but in circumstances entirely novel: 'The proposal that a ruling state . . . should come down from its position of empire, and enter into terms of equal confederation with its subject communities, is a very remarkable proposal, and one which has perhaps never before been made in the history of the world.'

Was, asked Freeman, such a transition possible? He did not think so. 'No ruling state', he pointed out, 'has ever admitted its subject states into a federal relation.' To establish a real federation, 'certain states must agree to give up certain independent defined powers, foreign relations preeminently among them, to a central authority. The states which consent to this agree- ment, remaining independent states for certain purposes, cease to be inde- pendent states for certain other purposes.' Freeman thought it unrealistic to suggest that the United Kingdom be asked to give up its enormous power and become no more powerful in law than any other part of the proposed federation. Moreover, under such a massive change at the imperial level, would the United Kingdom remain one? Would it not be more in keeping with the federal principle for England, Scotland, Ireland and even Wales to have separate legislatures, each acting for its own local purposes, but leaving imperial concerns to a parliament of the empire? Freeman clearly thought this would be unacceptable. He also asked to whom was the federation to extend? To all the subjects of the Queen? 'Or only to such of them as are European by dwelling place or descent'? What, for example, of the people of India? These were embarrassing questions and imperial unionists must have squirmed on reading them. His final comments were especially telling: 'Perhaps,' he said, 'not one man in a thousand who has chattered about "Imperial Federation", has ever stopped to think what "federation" means'. Only confusion could result from using words 'without thinking of their meaning'.

The merits and disadvantages of the federal idea continued to be weighed throughout the eighties and nineties. It was clear that some of the writers had read Freeman's critique and were attempting to meet his reservations. But rarely did one find a fully-fledged and convincing rebuttal. More often the writers resorted to passion, sentiment and patriotic exhortation. No doubt such affirmations of faith in imperial unity stirred many a heart but it was rare to find specific schemes that could be analysed. Usually, the suggestions reflected a lack of understanding of 'true federalism' and more a penchant for ingenious constitutional tinkering.[20]

Even when the curious pressed for details about federal schemes they were usually met with suspicion or hostility as if asking a question suggested opposition. As Henry Thring pointed out in 1886,

> If you ask what is meant by Imperial Federation, that, you are answered is a matter of detail, and the inquiry itself indicates a 'parochial mind' in the inquirer hostile to Federation. If you venture to press a further question, 'But, apart from detail, what is the principle of Federation?' you are referred to the Constitution of the United States. There will be found both principles and details capable of being adapted to a system of Imperial Federation.[21]

On looking at that constitution himself, Thring came to different conclusions than the imperial unionists. Following Freeman, he concluded that to call a federation 'imperial' was a contradiction in terms: 'In so far as an institution is Imperial it cannot be Federal, and in so far as it is Federal it cannot be Imperial.' While the promoters of imperial union deserved recognition for their efforts to highlight the importance of the empire, Thring believed, 'There is danger in enunciating principles in which all men concur under guise of something new and unusual. There is danger in adding to such enunciations loose hints of schemes which are incapable of realization.'

F.P. de Labilliere appeared to take Thring's urging to heart. In a major address at the Royal Colonial Institute, the long-time proponent of imperial federation argued that the time had come for a more practical approach to the unity of the empire: 'the sentiment of unity must evolve the practical principle of Imperial Federation'.[22] Unfortunately, while he displayed a knowledge of existing federations and was sensitive to such key principles as equitable representation to ensure appropriate taxing authority at the centre and a division between general and local powers, de Labilliere also backed away from specifics and resorted in the end to an appeal to the heart and to the race, an all too common indulgence:

> Many great Empires have existed in the past. Their ruins may be seen thickly scattered over the old continents of Europe, Asia, and Africa. They were all raised by the sword and perished by the sword. Great Powers exist at the present day, but, with two exceptions, their very existence depends upon military strength. Not so with the United States and the Empire of Great Britain. Both rest upon the solid basis of the peaceful victories of our British race. Imperial Federation will consolidate, organize, crown, the greatest colonizing achievement the world has ever seen or can ever see. It will be the noblest union of free men, of self-governing communities, who, by their own free will, will find themselves in one indissoluble, world-wide nationality, under one flag, under one sceptre, in order that they may enjoy the greatest blessings of security, power and peace.

Such rhetoric appealed to those such as Sir Frederick Young who viewed the issue as a 'great national question' deserving of 'a sort of roving Royal Commission' analogous to Durham's that would visit the self-governing colonies and take evidence from leading colonial figures about their ideas on the subject. Presumably, by such a sounding a detailed scheme would emerge.[23] These comments reflected both the ardour and sincerity of the true believers and their woeful naiveté. As future 'roving commissions', such as those of Sir Frederick Pollock and the Round Table movement, were to discover twenty or more years later there would be much suspicion and hostility in the colonies once one moved beyond the predisposed members of the educated elite.[24]

During these years British readers were often assisted in their efforts both to understand federal government and to devise viable schemes by the willingness of colonial politicians, transplanted British theorists and American commentators to review the workings of both the United States constitution and the British North America Act and to provide fresh perspectives. Henry Parkes of New South Wales, Julius Vogel and Robert Stout of New Zealand, John X. Merriman of Cape Colony, C.R. Lowell of the United States and Goldwin Smith from Canada provided a variety of information, insights, cautionary comments and food-for-thought. In the late eighties there were numerous articles on the United States and Swiss federations and on the federal idea in general. They were primarily expository in nature and did not engage theoretical issues, but an avid reader of the journals of the day would have been left reasonably well informed if not a little overwhelmed by both the alternatives involved and the inherent complexity of federal government.[25]

Despite this widespread discussion of the federal idea it failed to secure a firm foothold in the thinking of most observers. Many, such as C.B. Roylance-Kent, clearly made a considerable effort to become familiar with the essence of existing federal systems but in the end concluded that it was not a form of government that could be readily adapted either to the empire or to the United Kingdom. Roylance-Kent recognized that 'Federal Union' would mean union without unity for 'the essence of a Federal Union is a divided sovereignty'. He viewed this as 'a palpable source of weakness' since a 'divided sovereignty always lacks strength'. Moreover, with divided sovereignty there is 'a tendency . . . to split up into coordinate and independent authorities, and therefore an uncertainty as to the ultimate sovereign body'. Whereas in the United Kingdom it was known that the ultimate sovereignty lay in the imperial parliament and that the law of parliament was the law of the land, in the United States it was not so easy to point out where the ultimate sovereignty really was. Roylance-Kent argued that written constitutions, i.e. federal constitutions, 'are intensely rigid and conservative. Where there is no written constitution, as in the case of the British Empire, it is far otherwise; all is elasticity.' Roylance-Kent's response was not unique, and given the pervasive influence of the arguments of such widely respected 'experts' as Freeman and Dicey his views were even predictable. The fundamental problem remained the presumed diminution of power that the central government would suffer in a federal restructuring of either the United Kingdom or the empire.[26]

After the late eighties the discussion of imperial federation and of federation *per se* gradually petered out, a reflection perhaps of the divided counsels within the Imperial Federation League. That body succumbed to the inevitable in 1893 and splintered into a number of discordant entities. The federal idea was also enveloped at the time by the controversy surrounding home rule for Ireland and the gathering interest in home rule all around. In so far as the federal idea was explored or toyed with in the 1890s it was primarily as a solution to domestic as opposed to imperial problems.[27]

The primary concern of those who in the late nineteenth century contemplated a closer political arrangement between the mother country and the self-governing colonies was to find a constitutional means of ensuring not only the continued union of the empire but also the involvement of the colonies in decisions of concern to them. Unfortunately, their ideas for achieving this were often confused. For example, the proposals for the inclusion of colonial MPs in the Westminster parliament were never very satisfactory. The proponents of the idea seem never to have addressed the constitutional and philosophic implications of having 'colonials' voting on purely local United Kingdom issues and being swamped by domestic MPs on matters of imperial concern. Similarly, the various boards of advice and the congresses and the conferences that were proposed would have had no executive authority to act on behalf of the colonies and would, in any event, have been completely undemocratic and thus unrepresentative in nature. None of these various proposals truly came to grips with the need to protect diversity while ensuring unity. As the self-governing colonies gained in autonomy, it became ever more apparent that some other constitutional form would have to be devised to accommodate the increasingly quasi-federal nature of the imperial relationship. It was only natural that a federal solution should be raised even though it had suffered from much criticism in mid-century as a result of the seeming breakdown of the American experiment. Those individuals who had some nodding acquaintance with the arguments and reasoning of *The Federalist* assumed that inherent in the federal idea was the resolution of the tension between the imperial metropolis and the colonial periphery.[28] It should be made clear, however, that while a federal solution was widely discussed in certain circles it was very much a specialists' preoccupation. It received no extensive public airing and no deep-rooted commitment. In fact, the proponents of the various supra-parliamentary schemes – the only ones that qualified as truly federal – seldom explored the constitutional and philosophic nuances inherent in such extensive changes. One is struck by how intellectually thin and superficial much of the discussion was. It was rare to find a challenging analysis and then more often than not it emanated from the camp of the disbelievers and usually from the pen of Edward Freeman.

Most observers thought any form of closer imperial union a hopeless cause and found a federal solution particularly wanting. The enormous distances separating the constituent parts of the empire, the unwillingness of the white settlement colonies to give up to a central federal legislature and executive any of their recently hard won self-governing powers, the seemingly insuperable problems associated with the raising of revenues, and the preponderant position that the United Kingdom would have in any federal legislature based on population were considered overwhelming problems, virtually impossible of resolution. To this list were added other issues: first, a marked colonial concern that involvement in such a union would lead to increased responsibilities and thus the possibility of being drawn into imperial wars; second, a resistance in the United Kingdom to the changing of its own status – after all, a federation would diminish the unique role of the mother country at least insofar as the white settlement colonies were concerned; third, a deeply-rooted British opposition to the loss of a constitutional flexibility that a federal arrangement would presumably create – most political theorists and commentators at that time tended to believe a federal, and therefore a written, constitution would be more rigid than the British constitution which was unwritten and based extensively on custom and precedent; fourth, it was generally held that it would be virtually impossible to enforce the federal will; fifth, there was a fear that a federal union which expected compliance on the part of the constituent units would lead to a break-up of the empire rather than to a stronger union; sixth, the failure of most proponents of a federal structure to face the problem of India and the place that it, and eventually other dependencies, would have in such a union; and seventh, the fear that a federal structure was nothing but a subtle conservative way of halting the progress of democracy, and thus of socialism at home and abroad.[29]

When the various arguments for imperial union, and especially for a federal structure, were examined closely it was found that many served the interests of the British rather than the colonies. Perhaps this was not surprising but it did raise a question about the conservative or liberating nature of federalism in the imperial setting. The champions of the federal idea often argued that as long as the self-governing colonies had no say in the determination of foreign and defence policies nor the right to declare war on their own behalf that they had not attained truly national status. It was therefore essential that the self-governing colonies be involved in such vital decision-making. A federal empire would allow that and thus would be a more democratic setting, enhancing colonial nationhood while strengthening and protecting the overall empire. Other writers were not persuaded by this argument. From their perspective the incorporation of the senior colonies into a federal arrangement in which Britain continued to predominate because of population and economic power would mean a further constriction of colonial potential, a centralization of power and a concentration of control that was counter to democratic advance and certainly a restraint on greater colonial nationhood. To these observers federation of the empire was an essentially conservative means of preserving not only imperial strength and potential but British control.

The same criticism was tellingly made about imperial defence. A federal government, it was suggested, would bring greater efficiency, conformity and centralization to both imperial and colonial defence. While this might certainly lead to greater protection and to a more integrated response to external threats it would inhibit local initiative and curb local input. It could be viewed, in other words, as an inhibitory rather than an expansive positive development. A similar conclusion was reached on looking at the commercial implications of federation. Promoters of federation argued that colonies standing alone were vulnerable to outside economic pressures but within a federation would be able to develop and mature their own industrial and commercial policies. To a degree this might well be so but the tightening of the bonds of empire that federation would inevitably bring would also mean that the colonies would be more closely bound to the economic policies of the mother country. Since many colonies disagreed with those policies federation had minimal appeal. It seemed a retrograde step given their achievements in the commercial realm since the mid-nineteenth century. The greater trading opportunities that federation might open up were not sufficiently persuasive to offset such scepticism. Also, when looked at from the vantage points of finance and investment it seemed clear that the British would benefit most from a federal union. It would mean a distribution of costs on a proportionate basis, an obligation to contribute and thus a consequent decrease in the burden to the British taxpayer. Also, Britain, a powerful financial juggernaut, would gain the most by an arrangement which consolidated investment opportunities. The impact of Britain on colonial development would be immense, and while there would be obvious pluses for the colonies there would also be a loss of discretionary control on the colonial side. In sum, all the presumably positive reasons for federation primarily aided the British. In the long run, and the not so long run, the colonies would be the losers, a part of a greater whole, but with individual discretion and growth curbed or tailored.

Finally, all the arguments in favour of a federal empire tended to assume the existence of an imperial sentiment that could easily be evoked in order to draw the colonies closer to the mother country. Appeals to sentiment were pervasive and shameless and were clearly designed to favour British as opposed to 'colonial' interests. Federation, it was argued, would unify and strengthen the 'race' and unite the 'British Nation'. It was no accident that the subtitle of George Parkin's 1892 book *Imperial Federation* was 'The Problem of National Unity' or that F.P. de Labilliere's 1894 volume on imperial federation was entitled *Federal Britain*.[30] These volumes assumed that all Britons living abroad were part of the British 'race' or 'nation' and that federation would unite those dispersed peoples into a greater, stronger, more efficient polity. Little consideration was given, even by George Parkin, a Canadian, to burgeoning colonial self-consciousness. He, like so many of his peers, tended to be mesmerized by the epic nature of the imperial adventure and convinced that the British, really the English, had a responsibility, a mission, to carry the fruits of British civilization to the rest of the world. A federal structure would ensure the success of such a quest within the empire and would enhance its prospects of success in the wider world.[31]

Some of these arguments undoubtedly appealed to the leaders of the Liberal and Conservative parties, and clearly prime ministers William Gladstone and Lord Salisbury were not immune to the sentiments that lay behind them, but two particular factors told against the federal idea. First, it was viewed by most Britons who thought about such matters to be an alien form of government, not at all attuned to British constitutional practice. The British were fond of thinking of their method of government as essentially more flexible and adaptive to circumstance than a federal one. Moreover, since the unitary system at home provided more obvious control over the regions than would a federal structure few politicians had given the federal idea any serious thought, if thought at all. Those who did recognized that existing federations, and there were no more than four or five by the 1890s, were either small compact entities or larger but contiguous groupings. The British empire was neither. It was widely scattered, highly diverse in peoples and climate, containing colonies and dependencies in various stages of political and economic change. Moreover, the relationship of the United Kingdom to the various colonies was in constant flux. The nature of the relationship between the mother country and both the self-governing colonies and the larger dependencies such as India and the West Indies was steadily shifting. How such changes would be accommodated by a closer union and particularly by a federal arrangement, was unclear. What did seem obvious, however, was that the presumed rigidity of a federal constitution, and here we witness the influence of Dicey's arguments, would be inappropriate and ultimately unworkable. Rather than unifying the empire, a federal arrangement might well sharpen tensions and lead to a more rapid disintegration. Best to let matters unfold without undue pressure. Perhaps Durham had been right. More informal arrangements based on cooperation and mutual interests might be more appropriate.

The second factor was simply the resounding lack of interest in colonial and imperial affairs generally and in constitutional relationships in particular among the general public. The more dramatic moments on the imperial frontier such as the Indian Mutiny, the defeat at Majuba Hill, the invasion of Egypt and the fate of Gordon at Khartoum could always be worked up by the press to attract widespread attention, but that faded quickly as the lurid details petered out. Interest in imperial matters in the United Kingdom as well as in the colonies was minimal. Moreover, the abstractions and technicalities of constitutional discourse appealed to only a few and even many of them were confused. Without a groundswell of support for the federal idea, or for any closer union proposals, no politicians and certainly no political party would waste time on its promotion. No political exigency equalled no political action.

The idea did not receive the support of any mainstream political party in either the United Kingdom or in any of the self-governing colonies. It was never publicly endorsed by any major political figure in Great Britain and only received occasional, flirtatious support, usually for parochial political reasons, from senior colonial politicians. Nevertheless, the debate surrounding 'federation' of the empire was an important if minor stream in British and imperial constitutional thought and is an integral part of the British engagement with the federal idea.

4 'Federation' of the United Kingdom

By the late nineteenth century there had been two developments on the British domestic front that were causing concern to parliamentarians and constitutional pundits. The first was the congestion of parliamentary business and the second was the gathering strength of the Irish demand for larger self-governing powers. These two issues became inexorably intertwined and the relief of one was often seen as a means of resolving the other. The parliament at Westminster was responsible for all manner of imperial, national and local business ranging from sensitive issues of foreign and imperial policy down to the complexities and ambiguities of local government. By the 1870s the parliamentary calendar was bulging at the seams and both participants and observers were complaining of a burdensome workload and the resulting inefficiency. The latter was compounded by the persistent and well-organized obstructionist tactics of the Irish Nationalist MPs as they made every effort to force the government to address Irish concerns, particularly their desire for some form of home rule. Over the next forty years, the federal idea was repeatedly offered as a solution to the twin problems of parliamentary congestion and Irish self-government.

From the 1870s to 1921 the Anglo-Irish relationship was rarely far from the top of the political agenda and, on occasion, it was decidedly the most important matter of the day. Since 1801 the Irish had chafed with varying degrees of discomfort in a union with England, Scotland and Wales. Neither a repeal movement – and thus a return to the pre-1800 relationship – nor hastily conceived revolutionary tactics had met with much support. It was only with the gradual emergence in the 1870s of a tightly organized Irish parliamentary party under the leadership first of Isaac Butt and then of Charles Stewart Parnell that Irish demands for some form of self-government had received any ready hearing from either Liberal or Conservative politicians. With Gladstone's decision in 1886 to introduce an Irish home rule bill debate over the relationship reached a fever-pitch, and it was in that context that the federal idea was first broached in a major way as a solution to British domestic constitutional problems.

Isaac Butt had, of course, promoted 'federalism' in the 1870s and had outlined in a preliminary way what he referred to as a 'federal' structure for the United Kingdom in which England (he did not mention Wales), Scotland and Ireland would each have separate 'national' legislatures and representation in a central 'imperial' legislature that would control such common concerns as imperial defence and foreign policy. Butt's ideas had not, however, been well developed and had not met with much response at the time. They had coincided with the surge of interest in imperial 'federation' and it was probably no coincidence that Butt, an avowed Unionist, saw federation as a means of maintaining both the union of the United Kingdom and the empire while granting Ireland some degree of self-government. Through the years this approach was to prove attractive to many Unionists who feared that without a formal tie such as afforded by some variant of 'federation' the United Kingdom and hence the empire would disintegrate. Butt was clearly familiar with the constitution of the United States and with various European federal experiments and he had recently studied the British North America Act. Nevertheless, his suggested solution for Anglo-Irish difficulties was not fully fleshed out and he had left a number of key issues unresolved, especially 'the question of the retention or non-retention of the Irish representatives in a British as opposed to an "Imperial" parliament'.[1]

Federal ideas attracted passing attention from both English and Irish writers in the early eighties but they were sharply criticized by the likes of Dicey and by that transplanted Englishman, and inveterate foe of federalism, Goldwin Smith. Few politicians had either the interest or the courage to promote federal ideas and the proposals and schemes that surfaced were strictly devolutionary in nature. Joseph Chamberlain did skirt with a division of legislative function in his 'central board' scheme in his desire to provide an opportunity for the Irish to achieve the fullest possible self-government in the management of their 'national' affairs. This preparedness to recognize the merits of the Irish demand did not stretch to a willingness to suggest a separate parliament for Ireland and he broke with Gladstone and the Liberals over that question. Chamberlain feared that a separate parliament for Ireland would lead to the disintegration of the United Kingdom. It was imperative to preserve the Union and to relieve the Westminster parliament of its excessive burden so that it could properly attend to both national and imperial affairs. It was clear to him that only a division and a sub-division of labour would resolve the problem. This led Chamberlain to suggest a scheme of boards at the county level (County Boards) and councils for each of the four countries of England, Scotland, Wales and Ireland (National Councils). The powers were to be delegated and the Westminster parliament would remain supreme, so the scheme was not a federal one. However, Chamberlain had openly recognized Ireland's need for a 'national' authority and he had extended the proposal to include England, Scotland and Wales. This was not federalism but it was not unlike numerous home-rule-all-round proposals that surfaced in the late eighties and throughout the nineties.

As the rumblings over constitutional change continued, and with the revelation in December 1885 that Gladstone had been converted to home rule, Chamberlain changed his mind yet again and this time did suggest that perhaps the only way to give Ireland what it deserved while preserving the Union was to adopt the American constitution. He proposed distinct legislatures for England, Scotland and Wales and possibly separate ones for Ulster and the rest of Ireland based in Belfast and Dublin respectively. A separate legislature at Westminster for foreign and colonial affairs and a supreme court fleshed out his now patently federal plan. For Chamberlain, this or a similar scheme was the only one compatible with imperial unity. He made it clear that this was not his first preference but if it would preserve the Union then so be it. As he put it, 'I am not going to swallow separation with my eyes shut.'[2]

Chamberlain never elaborated on his ideas of the mid-eighties and in years to come never pushed beyond the boundary of vague assertions in discussing the need for domestic and imperial union. But in his musings of those frantic months in 1884 and 1885, Chamberlain had intuitively recognized that only a 'federal' scheme would meet 'national' aspirations in the United Kingdom and preserve union. What Chamberlain meant by 'federalism' is unclear but it did seem he was ready to accept a division of sovereignty which is the mark of a true federation. Nevertheless, he left many problems, such as the nature of representation in the Westminster parliament and the vexed question of finance, unexplored.

Nor were they fully explored by Gladstone. In drafting his home rule bill, the Liberal leader had considerable difficulty over these two matters. His unwillingness to tamper with parliamentary sovereignty in order to preserve the Union drove him away from a federal solution, which, as Chamberlain had realized, would be the only logical way to resolve the problem, and towards a hybrid colonial-federal plan that had inherent and pervasive weaknesses.[3] In attempting to provide a degree of self-government to a portion of the United Kingdom while retaining the unity of that kingdom, Gladstone ran up against the interrelated problems of representation and taxation. Wishing to effect a clear division between local and imperial jurisdictions, he decided to exclude Irish representatives from the imperial parliament. This might have been acceptable to the Irish if he had transferred customs and excise to the Irish parliament, as he had initially wanted to do, but since such a transfer would have been abhorrent to business and commercial interests in England and potentially disastrous for the Union, Gladstone left those crucial taxing powers with the Westminster parliament. This led naturally to the century-old cry, 'no taxation without representation', a cry made louder and more penetrating by Gladstone's insistence that Ireland pay for its share of defence and that its consequent contribution to the imperial exchequer should be a first charge on its revenues.

Gladstone's problems in drafting a coherent home rule bill lay in his refusal to consider federalism. Not only was the federal idea little understood but those who had knowledge of it were convinced that it was essentially a weak and divisive system of government. That this was not necessarily so was hard to prove in light of the recent Civil War in the United States and the current problems over constitutional jurisdiction between provincial and federal authorities in Canada. Gladstone had attempted to reconcile unity with diversity by marrying features of both colonial and federal schemes. Under the existing British colonial system as it applied to the self-governing colonies, each colony was granted responsible government and control over local affairs. The imperial government relinquished all power to determine taxing policies. The colonies, in their turn, were not represented in the imperial parliament and were under no obligation to contribute to the costs of imperial defence. In this way, the colonies were not treated unfairly in the key areas of finance and representation. Gladstone had recognized that Irish representatives should not be in a position to interfere in English, Scottish and Welsh affairs, so he had, logically, *excluded* them from Westminster. Similarly, he had recognized that the Irish would still be a part of the United Kingdom and therefore should still contribute to its defence, so he had, logically, *included* them in that process. But logic led to illogic – taxation without representation. Gladstone's 1886 colonial/federal hybrid was a failure, as were those modelled on it of 1893 and 1912. The only logical way the issue could have been resolved was by adopting a truly federal solution which, modelled on Chamberlain's scheme, would have established not only separate legislatures for Ulster, the rest of Ireland, Scotland and Wales but would also have come to grips with the need to divide an oversized and all-too-powerful England. There was no support for such an idea other than on the margins of political discussion.

Federalism was simply unacceptable to a political community so deeply wedded to the concept of parliamentary sovereignty. It was natural that the English should view the division of sovereignty with some trepidation; it could mean a weakening of English dominance within the British Isles. More might have been expected from the Welsh and the Scots for whom the fragmentation of English power should have been attractive. But such was not the case. There was no more interest in the federal idea in Wales and Scotland – or Ireland for that matter – than in England. The furthest the Scots and Welsh would go was home rule all round, a strictly devolutionary device. National consciousness, such as it was, did not demand 'national' legislatures with clear sovereignty; all that was required were enhanced but delegated administrative and legislative powers within the comforting embrace of a unitary system of government. The Irish Nationalists, of course, to the degree that they considered the matter at all, approached it differently. To them, federation was simply a devious means of denying them greater autonomy on the colonial model. It might work as a means of resolving internal Irish tensions but it was not acceptable as a means of satisfying self-governing aspirations.

Despite the fact that federalism as a system of government had received more of an airing in the 1870s and 1880s than ever before in British history it was still not well understood by either the general public or the majority of politicians and publicists, and those who understood it did not believe it was applicable to either the United Kingdom or the empire. The root objection was to the division of sovereignty entailed in a true federal state. To those nurtured on the sanctity of parliamentary sovereignty the concept of separate but coordinate sovereignties was mystifying; even frightening. The potential weakness and loss of domestic and imperial control implied in such a division was an alarming prospect and thus a major deterrent. The debates and discussions of the next twenty years did little to shift these deeply embedded attitudes.

In the eighties and nineties, the primary concerns were the congestion of parliament and the Irish demand, backed to an increasing degree by the Scots and the Welsh, for greater self-government. Intertwined with these twin problems was a further need to ensure the continued unity of the empire by involving the self-governing colonies in the imperial decision-making process. The Scots, in particular, seemed increasingly alert to the fact that their country was becoming more and more a province of England. However, their translation of that understanding into political action was modest. They tended to argue that the maintenance of their nationality would not only be just to Scotland but would strengthen the empire of which Scotland was an integral part. They may, on occasion, have used the terms 'federal' and 'federal home rule' to describe their aim but their intent was clearly never more than conventional devolution. Sometimes they simply wished their nationality to be recognized by raising the minister responsible for Scottish affairs to cabinet rank and by increasing the number of Scottish MPs in the House of Commons.[4] Interestingly, the heightened self-consciousness was reflected in various references to Andrew Fletcher of Saltoun, rescued from almost two centuries of obscurity and hailed as the champion not only of Scottish nationalism but of a 'federal' solution to the Anglo-Scottish relationship. All these were but episodic comments and by no means involved a sustained analysis of nationalism nor of its relationship to federal governments. If anything, the Welsh were even more reticent on these issues and the comments that did surface tended to be somewhat defensive, asserting that 'so far as it is possible for a nation to exist without political institutions of its own, the Welsh are as distinctively a nation as a people numerically so small and occupying so small a portion of the earth's surface can be'.[5]

Not surprisingly, some of those interested in imperial federation believed it would be possible to accommodate both the domestic demand for self-government and the colonial demand for greater involvement in the decisions made about imperial defence and foreign policy. One commentator, G.B. Lancaster Woodburne, argued that 'In seeking the proper method of Imperial Federation, we must be prepared to accept some novelties – some constitutional changes – but, at the same time, we must endeavour, while adopting a thorough and successful measure, to maintain the Constitution of the mother country as much as possible in its present form.'[6] In his estimation, this could only be done by the establishment of an imperial assembly. The existing House of Lords and House of Commons would continue to legislate for England while the Irish and Scottish parliaments could be restored to do the same for their respective countries. An Imperial House would then contain representatives of England, Scotland, Ireland and the major colonies. By such an arrangement, Ireland would obtain home rule but would still be 'bound to us by sharing, in the Imperial Assembly, the responsibility of maintaining the interests of the Empire'. Unless some such scheme were soon implemented Woodburne believed neither the Anglo-Irish relationship nor the integrity of the empire could be protected.

As with so many such assertions, it was based on a flimsy grasp of the difficulties involved and was clearly fuelled by an almost apocalyptic paranoia. To Woodburne, and to those Englishmen who thought like him, imperial federation was

> an urgent necessity. We must choose either to go on dreaming of an Empire till that Empire has lost half its branches, or to act at once, and so make our paper Empire a reality. We must choose either to lose our colonies and have a separated and hostile Ireland ever menacing our peace, the gathering-ground of England's enemies, and a constant source of irritation and danger until such separation is effected, a probable deadlock in our Legislature owing to chronic Irish opposition to every Ministry, and the majority of the English members constantly out-voted by a combination of the English minority with the Scotch and Irish representatives; or, on the other hand, to have a number of happy states united in one great Empire, becoming daily more harmonious in their social and commercial relations, and proud and peerless in their power.

The quest for dominance and the patent fantasizing embedded in such effusions did little to advance any serious analysis or to win converts to the federal ideal. This was, in fact, nothing more than the adoption of federalism as a cloak for a cruder intent.

Not everyone agreed with Dicey that parliamentary sovereignty would be impaired by the adoption of a federal structure for the United Kingdom and the empire, but rather than demonstrating that sovereignty within imperial, national and regional jurisdictions would be sacrosanct, as any true federalist could have, those analysts who examined the interconnection of home rule and imperial union tended to emphasize that a system which simply conferred local self-government did not diminish the supremacy of the British parliament nor, therefore, work irreparable injury on the empire. Lord Thring, for example, in offering a strong defence of Gladstonian home rule highlighted the difficulties involved in marrying a *centralizing* of imperial power through imperial federation and the *dispersal* of local power through domestic federalism.[7] Such analyses did little to advance the federal cause.

Federal ideas, in the devolutionary form of home rule all round, continued to be pressed and discussed in the 1890s but in an increasingly tenuous fashion. Interest flared in the months leading up to the introduction of Gladstone's second home rule bill, but its rejection by the Lords and the return to office of the Conservatives in 1895 marked a down-turn in interest. The Scots and Welsh attempted to keep the issue alive in the Commons with a series of motions, but they were seldom fully debated and were given short shrift when they were. Few senior politicians took any of this very seriously and when someone of the stature of A.J. Balfour chose to intervene he was devastating in his criticism of self-government for the four 'nations' of the British Isles. The idea of setting up new elective bodies with considerable powers was not only premature but, in his estimation, 'absurd'. Throughout the decade the discussion of 'federalism' in all its forms was kept alive by a dedicated minority of concerned politicians, theorists and committed empire-watchers.[8]

This relative lack of interest in federalism, or in any form of home rule or home rule all round, persisted until 1910 primarily because the Conservatives remained in office until late 1905 and when succeeded by the Liberals the latter's majority was such that home rule was not a pressing issue. The Irish parliamentary party therefore had no leverage with either of the major parties and the Scots and Welsh nationalist organizations faltered in the general disinterest. In the main, imperial federation also suffered from the death of the Imperial Federation League in 1893 and the subsequent fracturing of its membership. To the degree that political integration of the self-governing empire was explored it was the embryonic colonial and imperial conference system that attracted attention and intellectual energy.

While the years 1900 to 1909 were thus relatively fallow, they should not be overlooked. Ideas continued to surface and percolate on the sidelines of imperial and domestic political life that kept discussion alive even if relatively unobtrusive. One particularly persistent advocate of constitutional change was J.A. Murray Macdonald, a Scottish Liberal who had sat in the House of Commons for Tower Hamlets in the 1890s. Macdonald did not believe that distance was any longer an impediment to imperial union but he felt strongly that the conduct of both domestic and imperial affairs was impaired by 'the fact that the Parliament that is at present responsible for the conduct of imperial interests is the same Parliament that is responsible for the conduct of the domestic interests of a part only of the Empire'. Since the range of its responsibilities in the two spheres was not coterminous any form of federal government would have to involve a delimitation of those spheres. Macdonald realized how reluctant people would be to tamper with a constitution under which the United Kingdom 'had grown great' and which was 'the model of political freedom for all the world'. Nothing but an 'over-ruling necessity, associated with its very growth and the continuance of its greatness, ought to justify or encourage us in making any alteration in its form'. Macdonald was convinced by 1900 that such a necessity existed. He believed the great self-governing colonies had earned the right to participate in sharing and determining 'the vast responsibilities involved in British rule and policy'. The choice was between a willingness to open up decision-making and the ultimate loss of those colonies. This was little more than the old hoary cry 'federate or disintegrate', but there was undoubted truth in his assertion that such vigorous, dynamic colonies could not continue to accept a position of dependence for much longer. But the need to increase the status of the colonies was not the only reason Macdonald offered for change. He pointed out what many before him had done: that the business of government had grown more extensive and complex and that the parliamentary timetable was congested with matters of essentially local or regional interest. This preoccupation with domestic issues distracted attention away from foreign and imperial policy. In his estimation, decentralization of institutions was necessary to ensure 'an ordered growth in the complexity of our social and political interests'. Therefore, change to the constitution, to reflect altered circumstances in both domestic and imperial spheres, was justifiable. He called for the delegation of local and domestic functions of the present parliament of the United Kingdom 'to the several countries it represents' and the subsequent involvement of the colonies in the imperial parliament for the control of larger empire-wide concerns. The initial stage would be 'Home Rule all round'; the final stage would be imperial federation. The key would be the separation of domestic from imperial interests.[9]

Macdonald's ideas were neither new nor original but they captured both the prevailing mood among imperial reformers and also reflected the nature of current thinking on the issue of domestic and imperial reform. Not surprisingly, there were no details. There rarely were. Before they could be tackled a willingness to consider change had to be nurtured. The problem for Macdonald and others who reasoned as he did and who supported him was the failure to recognize that to change effectively the conduct of both domestic and imperial business it would be necessary to establish a 'mezzanine tier' of government that would be responsible for the concerns and interests common to the whole nation-state and not peculiar to one portion or another of it. Such a 'tier' would be comparable to governments centered in Washington, Ottawa and Canberra and not to those located in provincial or state capitals. Lord Brassey, a friend and supporter of Macdonald, at least saw the weakness in Macdonald's scheme and advocated the eventual creation of a three-tier system involving imperial federation, the existing Westminster parliament responsible for country-wide issues, and local legislatures. Macdonald's plan fell well short of true federalism and while Brassey hinted at it his ideas were essentially devolutionary. What the two men had succeeded in doing, however, was logically connecting the need for an interlinked domestic and imperial awareness in any approach to constitutional reform within the United Kingdom and in the empire. This issue was to remain central to all discussions on the matter through to the 1920s.[10]

Macdonald was not unaware of the difficulties inherent in his proposal, but he did not believe they lay in demarcating the distribution of legislative and administrative powers between the imperial and local parliaments but rather in the division of taxing powers. In this he was, of course, absolutely correct. Gladstone had fumbled badly in grappling with the issue of taxation and Prime Minister Asquith's later efforts were to be no more effective. While isolating a matter of such primary concern, Macdonald seemed not much vexed by it, probably because he was not promoting true federation, only devolution, and under that scheme ultimate authority would always remain with the Westminster parliament. Delegated or devolved powers could always be withdrawn. He was quite clear about all this. In a letter to *The Times* in September 1904 he noted that the United States was a 'true federation':

> But though for convenience we loosely use the words 'federal' and 'federation' in relation to suggested changes in the machinery of our Constitution, no one has ever suggested that we should in these changes follow the lines of a true federal system. The very reverse is the case. The Imperial authority, under any scheme of devolution, would be the delegating authority, and would remain, after the delegation had taken effect, as absolutely and as completely supreme as it had been before. And it would exercise its supremacy in two ways . . . first . . . it would retain the right of refusing assent to measures passed by the Colonial Legislatures . . . second . . . the Imperial Parliament can never by any act of its own deprive itself of concurrent legislative power on any matter within the legislative jurisdiction of the National Legislatures; and from the very nature of the case no Act of a National Legislature could be filed in any Court against an act of the Imperial Parliament . . . the Imperial authority . . . would be absolutely unfettered in its power of determining whether any action of a National Legislature interfered with Imperial interests, and of dealing with that action either by legislation or by administration, or by both, as freely and as fully as Imperial interests required.[11]

Nothing could be clearer. The imperial federationists and so-called 'federalists' of the early twentieth century were obviously fully conversant with 'true federation' but did not find it applicable to either the empire or the United Kingdom. Dicey's arguments about parliamentary supremacy and the indivisibility of sovereignty were pervasive. The problem for advocates such as Macdonald was that stopping short of 'true federalism' rendered their otherwise perceptive analysis ineffectual. Ireland was not prepared to accept simply delegated powers regardless of what the Scots or the Welsh were prepared to settle for, while the self-governing colonies would certainly not give up any of their hard-won powers and return to the paternalist fold.

Their interest was in gaining more authority, not in relinquishing some or all of what they had. And as for the United Kingdom it was hard to imagine that it would be prepared to become but one component part, even if a very powerful part, of an imperial parliament. If one already had virtually unlimited powers why share or give them up unless there was no alternative? Beleaguered though it increasingly was in the early 1900s the United Kingdom was still one of the most powerful nations on earth and supreme within its own imperial realm. Under these circumstances, 'true federation' was but a pipe-dream and Macdonald knew as much.[12]

Federalism did not receive another sustained airing until 1910–14 when the complex problem of Irish home rule surfaced once more as a primary political issue and forced a reexamination of the British constitution. Those who advocated a 'federal solution' during those years or who wrote and reflected upon it invariably had a devolutionary solution in mind and not a 'true federal' one. Nevertheless, the variety of articles, editorials, pamphlets, books and memoranda that were published or distributed privately revealed a firmer grasp of federal principles and practices than the earlier musings of the late nineteenth century. Again, however, much of the musing and urgent pleading took place not in the decision-making centres of power but on the margins of political life. There was, admittedly, a brief serious examination of the federal option by the Liberal government, and two of its members, Winston Churchill and David Lloyd George, variously gave it their support, but in the main the discussants and protagonists were relatively minor figures. Their comments and insights were nevertheless often shrewd and perceptive and provided a necessary context and an analytic edge to the discussion. Not surprisingly, perhaps, given the tempestuous nature of the problem and the more general discordant political, social and economic pressures of the time, there was no considered reflection such as had been offered earlier by the likes of Edward Freeman and certainly nothing even proximate to the reflections of Baron Acton or the considered assertions of John Stuart Mill. It was true that Dicey was heard from but he unabashedly entered the lists as a protagonist on behalf of the Union and his febrile urgency and hectoring tone were not conducive to dispassionate appraisal. In the main, those who did write and comment on the principles involved tended to think a truly federal solution inapplicable to the twin United Kingdom problems of Irish home rule and parliamentary congestion.

This was so even for the Round Table movement which was actively engaged in discussing and promoting the federal idea after 1910. If the members' correspondence, memoranda and publications are examined one quickly realizes that, as yet, even they had not fully explored the implications of federalism and often were advocating a devolutionary solution rather than a federal one. They were clear, however, that 'federation' of the United Kingdom or, rather, home rule all round was not a necessary preliminary stage in the achievement of the 'federation' of the empire. Their concern with the issue was especially manifest in 1912 and again in 1913–14 when members endeavoured, sometimes successfully and sometimes not, to persuade the Unionist and Liberal leaders to take up the 'federal' cause.[13]

Insofar as there was an intellectual engagement with or, at least, an exposition of federal principles, it occurred in the article literature, usually as a by-product of commenting either on the constitutional crisis of 1910 or on Asquith's home rule bill of 1912 as it worked its inexorable way through the Commons. J.A. Murray Macdonald remained a persistent voice throughout these years. In July 1911 he reminded the readers of the *Nineteenth Century* that the congestion of business in parliament could not be suffered for much longer. In his estimation, only 'Federal Home Rule' would resolve the problem. In responding to the often heard criticism that such a scheme would weaken the British state and lead to disintegration, he argued that such a statement was no more than an opinion and should not be given undue weight. Nevertheless, he pointed out that the British North America Act of 1867 had effected two goals; first, it had brought several colonies together in a federal union; and, second, it had dissolved the Union between Canada East and Canada West, giving each independent legislative powers within the wider union. He suggested that the success of the British North America Act 'might at least encourage us to contemplate a modification of the terms of Union between the countries of the United Kingdom without the fear that it would weaken the cohesion of the parts or the strength of the whole'. He went on to argue that 'Federal Home Rule' was not inconsistent with the terms of the existing Union between England, Scotland and Ireland. Each of those countries had its own law and its own administrative system. Each, he argued, might be given independent powers for dealing with domestic interests without seriously departing from existing practice. This revealed that Macdonald really did not have a truly federal solution in mind despite his seeming understanding of the division of sovereignty enshrined in the British North America Act.[14]

Macdonald's Anglo-Irish colleague, Lord Dunraven, was also convinced that there was a need to recreate the British constitution. With the passage of the Parliament Act in August 1911 the constitution had, in his view, lost its ancient balance. The constitution should be rethought and reframed on 'federal' lines but for Dunraven 'federal' meant devolutionary. He was clear that the power of statutory parliaments was 'a delegated power'. For him, stability of the central authority was 'a condition essential to stability of the subordinate authorities; order cannot owe allegiance to chaos'.[15] As usual, his primary concerns were the relief of congestion and the containment of Ireland within a modified Union. In a follow-up article in November 1911, Dunraven asserted that it was 'only by proceeding on federal lines that the errors in the Gladstonian schemes of devolution can be avoided'. 'Federal Home Rule' would preserve the dignity of the Crown, would settle the second chamber questions, would reduce the representation of Ireland to its 'proper limits' and would remove the Irish grievance of English control and the English grievance of Irish control. It would clear the way towards imperial unity, and would bring about a better understanding between all portions of the English-speaking world. This extraordinary and all-encompassing panacea could not, however, be too closely modelled on the constitution of the United States. Its framers' purpose had been centralization whereas 'Decentralization is ours. They sought to create a central authority strong enough to secure homogeneity in all great national affairs without unduly encroaching upon the local authority of existing independent States. We desire to delegate to localities authority sufficient to enable them to manage their own affairs without unduly encroaching upon the power of an existing central authority.' This was not a 'federal solution'; this was patently devolution. Dunraven clearly understood true federalism but he did not wish to diminish either parliamentary sovereignty or the power and authority of a centralized state, for despite various legal and administrative forms ultimate power in the British state flowed from and to the centre.[16]

In November 1911, J.A.R. Marriott, Oxford historian and author of the recently published *English Political Institutions*, reviewed the various efforts of the 'federal home rulers' to reconcile and combine the 'little nationalisms' of the 'Celtic fringe' with the 'larger Nationalists' anxious to realize 'Pan-Britannic unity' and concluded that their well-intentioned endeavours rested upon a basis of 'intellectual confusion'. Marriott thought the idea of 'federal home rule' a 'superficially attractive' one that had not been properly or closely scrutinized. In his view, four questions needed to be answered: first, 'What precisely are we to understand by Federal Home Rule?'; second, 'Is the federal principle to be confined to Ireland or to be applied to other portions of the United Kingdom?'; third, 'If so, how is the lesser federalism of the United Kingdom to be reconciled with the larger federalism of the British Empire – the avowed goal of Federal Home Rulers?'; and fourth, 'What are to be the ultimate units of the Britannic Federation? Is the European unit to consist of Great Britain and Ireland? Or are England, Scotland, Ireland and Wales to be regarded as separate units, and to come into the Federal Empire on the same footing as the Dominion of Canada, United South Africa, the Australian Commonwealth, New Zealand and Newfoundland?' Marriott could nowhere find satisfactory answers to these questions. Any attempt to provide answers simply revealed 'a mass of political absurdities and Constitutional contradictions'. He believed the reason for this was simple: the 'federal home rulers' were 'on the wrong tack'. They were, he argued,

> misusing a term consecrated to a wholly different – indeed, a precisely opposite – process. Federalism implies, on the part of the related communities, not the acquisition but the surrender of rights; each unit of the federal whole is called upon to sacrifice some portion of its hitherto independent sovereignty. Federalism, therefore, is the bringing together, not the parting asunder, of related communities. It is, in a word, a centripetal, not a centrifugal, movement.

This was pure Freeman, and Marriott referred favourably to that analyst's view of the origins of federal states. Freeman's and Marriott's *ex cathedra* statements could have been countered but they were not, and Marriott was correct in pointing out the paucity of any hard-headed analysis by the 'federalists'. Their proposals and ideas went forth largely unexamined.[17]

The introduction of the third home rule bill on 11 April 1912 provided further opportunities over the next two years for both the affirmation and the dissection of the federal idea. The Liberals had considered introducing a bill based on the principle of home rule all round but in the end had decided to concentrate on meeting the Irish demand for greater self-government. Thus, despite Asquith's reference to the bill being the first step on the path to a major revision of the constitutional relationships within the United Kingdom, it had no 'true federal' features and, if anything, was anti-federal in nature. The bill fell clearly into the Gladstonian mould and was, in fact, closely modelled on the 1893 bill as it had emerged from committee.[18]

J.H. Morgan, the constitutional expert, was particularly emphatic in his criticisms. What struck him most forcibly was the sheer pragmatism of the exercise. The bill lacked any strong theoretical underpinnings. It was 'a singular triumph of empiricism. It defies the frontal attacks of the theorist, for the simple reason that there is nothing theoretical about it. It is not "Federalism", it is not Dualism, still less is it to be compared with a colonial constitution of the usual type.' The failure to honour theory and to ignore the insights that could be derived from examining the workings of the United States constitution had led Asquith and his colleagues to construct yet another colonial/federal hybrid that further complicated rather than simplified the task to be confronted. However, as Morgan was obliged to admit, even if the bill had been truly federal it probably would not have worked in the British context since the 'English people' were accustomed to meeting each political difficulty as it arose 'instead of roving the world of political speculation for far-fetched analogies and model Constitutions'.[19]

Morgan had, of course, put his finger on the British aversion to theory. It was rare to find either academic or popular writers in the United Kingdom plumbing the depths of philosophic reflection, particularly about concrete matters like government and constitutions. The British, particularly the English, liked to view themselves as problem-solvers and, in their estimation, problems were best resolved by adroit juggling of the practical options that had been worked out via discussion and compromise. Solutions based on theoretical premises had little appeal for them and especially so in such an emotionally laden context as the revision of the Anglo-Irish relationship.

But Morgan had also touched on another key aspect of constitution-making, or constitution-revising, as it played out in the United Kingdom. This was the pervasive and dominant influence of the *English* point of view. Unless the English could be persuaded of the merits of altering the United Kingdom constitution no significant change would occur either to the links between England, Ireland, Scotland and Wales or to the unity of England.

The latter point was underlined later in the year when in a speech at Dundee on 12 September 1912, Winston Churchill suggested that a workable federal system could only be established in the United Kingdom if England were divided into as many as ten or twelve self-governing areas.[20]

The anonymous constitutional columnist for *The Spectator* rightly pointed out that Churchill's scheme was not 'true federalism' but he scoffed at the notion that anything more than devolution was required to rid the United Kingdom of the current over-centralized administrative system and the inconvenient legislative methods. After all, he argued, 'true federalism . . . always means, and always must mean, the binding together of previously disconnected units. The modern federalists, who talk of introducing federal government by breaking up the United Kingdom, appear to have lost all historic sense. Every federal government in the world represents an amalgamation of governments previously separate.' Even more revealing than this public affirmation of Edward Freeman's thesis was the writer's assertion that Churchill's suggestion that England be broken up into a number of parliamentary jurisdictions lacked dignity: 'Most of us Englishmen, though we do not often talk about it, are proud not of Great Britain only, or of the United Kingdom only, or only of the British Empire, but proud also of England, and the idea of breaking up our country into seven or eight provinces, with separate parliaments and separate governments of their own, is utterly repugnant to our national pride.'[21] Here the writer had, of course, put his finger on a particularly weak spot in the federalist brief. England undivided would dominate any federation, but England divided was neither desired by nor acceptable to English nationalists.

One of the more experienced participants in the discussions and formulations of these years was Herbert Samuel, the Postmaster-General. Samuel had been an active member of the Pollock Committee which from 1903–7 had subjected both the imperial and the United Kingdom constitutions to a close analysis. More recently, Samuel, at the cabinet's request, had undertaken an examination of the financial relationship between Ireland and Great Britain. Thus he was one of the few individuals who had some detailed awareness of the complexities involved in readjusting the constitutional relationships within the United Kingdom. In a useful article in the *Nineteenth Century* in October 1912, Samuel frankly considered the question 'whether the United Kingdom and the British Empire have anything to learn from the Federal idea?'[22] Samuel admitted it was not easy to define federalism but he ventured that 'a Federal State is one in which there is a central authority that represents the whole, and acts on behalf of the whole, in external affairs and in internal affairs as are held to be of common interest; and in which there are also provincial authorities with powers of legislation and administration within the sphere allotted to them by the Constitution'. He challenged the prevailing doctrine that 'To federalize . . . is good when it means the surrender of powers by a number of separate States to a new central authority, but bad when it means the devolution of powers by a single central authority to a number of new local authorities.' He noted that it was 'urged *a priori* that for a loosely organized community of States like the British Empire to tend towards Federalism would be a measure of progress; but for the United Kingdom to do so would be retrogression'. How much proof was there, he asked, for this generalization?

Samuel recognized that the various movements for constitutional change over the centuries had, in the main, been centripetal but to elevate that disposition to a natural law would, he believed, be wrong and the consequences harmful. There could be no general rule that centralization was progressive and decentralization retrogressive. If such an assertion were held to be true then one should find federations developing over time into unitary states. But there was no such trend. 'Federalism', he argued, 'is not a ladder by which communities can climb to a higher level of political organization, and which they may kick down when they have reached it. Properly organized, in suitable conditions, it is a stable and a lasting system.' This was a shrewd comment and a salutary reminder to later analysts of federal systems.

British statesmen, continued Samuel, had to consider both the needs of the empire and of the United Kingdom. A balance had to be struck between central control and local liberty. It was currently claimed by many that 'centralization is weighted too heavily in the United Kingdom, too lightly in the Empire'. On analysing both constitutions, Samuel argued that the United Kingdom's was a hybrid of unitary and federal forms but that the empire's was clearly neither unitary nor federal nor even a hybrid. He doubted that a federal system would easily work for the empire but he suggested that 'elements of Federalism' would need to be turned to in both the imperial and domestic settings.

As the months passed and the passage of the home rule bill drew inexorably closer, greater attention was paid to the fate of Ulster. The Unionists were adamant that at least six counties should be excluded from the bill and the Liberals shilly-shallied and dawdled in the Asquithian way. As a consequence, the federal idea was much discussed as a possible solution to the dilemma and discrete pressure and hard bargaining ensued. It was during these years that a number of leading Unionists such as Austen Chamberlain, Lord Selborne and Walter Long paid increasing attention to federalism as the one possible means of resolving the Irish problem while preserving the United Kingdom. Spurred on by the advice and support of J.L. Garvin of the *Observer* and F.S. Oliver of the Round Table movement, Selborne and Chamberlain dallied more than most near the federal flame but even Long, one of the staunchest defenders of the Union, recognized by early 1914 that devolution in a federal form should be on the agenda of a new Unionist government. Predictably, Murray Macdonald, Lord Charnwood and Lord Dunraven, all veteran campaigners, poured considerable energy and passion into a 'last plea for federation'. Each believed, in Dunraven's words, that 'federalism offers, the best, perhaps the only, means of reconciling differences' and of holding both the United Kingdom and the empire together.[23] Unfortunately for the federalists such an argument had little impact. There was a widespread fear, particularly in Unionist ranks, that any move towards a 'federal' solution of United Kingdom constitutional difficulties would weaken the state and lead to disintegration rather than to a firmer Union.

This reaction to the federal idea was ironic because it is crystal clear that all the leading federalists were not in fact advocating true federalism. Their schemes, without exception, were devolutionary and not federal in nature. Even for those prepared to engage in constitutional change the supremacy of the Westminster parliament was sacrosanct. Lord Charnwood, for example, who did make an effort to define the distribution of functions made necessary by a 'federal' scheme for the United Kingdom, was clear that he envisaged no diminution in the 'unabated legal supremacy' of the 'Imperial Parliament'.[24] The Round Table group, more than most, does seem to have had a truly federal concept in mind, but since the members rarely indulged in protracted conceptualizing and offered no particular scheme during these years it is hard to be fully sure. At least one of the group's leading members, Philip Kerr, had doubts about both the Round Table movement's goal and the intent of various other 'federal' missionaries. Kerr thought the Round Table, and others, really had devolution in mind and that 'federation' therefore was a misnomer. Moreover, he was clear in his mind that in any Round Table scheme the imperial parliament would always retain its supremacy and that there would be no need for a supreme court to interpret the constitution. He was only prepared to accept 'federalism' as a better 'fighting word' than either devolution or home rule all round which most Unionists abhorred. The problem, of course, was that the term 'federalism' was equally unattractive, and across a wider spectrum. To believe that it might have merit as a 'fighting word' suggested that Kerr was somewhat out of touch with contemporary Unionist, Irish Nationalist and Liberal opinion. Moreover, most people still clearly did not have any proper understanding of 'true' federalism, so to promote the term confused more than it enlightened.[25]

The outbreak of war in Europe in 1914 brought an abrupt end to the intense discussion of Irish home rule and to the promotion of the federal idea as a solution both to that complex issue and to the more general problem of the congestion of parliament. It was only in the aftermath of the Easter Rising of 1916 and the abortive Lloyd George attempt to find common ground between the Irish Nationalists and the Ulster Unionists that federalism was again resurrected as a possible constitutional panacea. Lord Selborne, F.S. Oliver and L.S. Amery, supported by members of the Round Table movement, promoted the federal idea from late 1916 through to mid-1918. They held numerous meetings with politicians and civil servants, conducted a wide-ranging correspondence and published various articles and pamphlets. Their efforts intensified in the spring of 1918 when the Irish Convention staggered to a conclusion and Lloyd George appointed an Irish committee with Walter Long, a recent convert to federalism, as chair to draft an Irish home rule bill compatible with the adoption of a federal structure for the United Kingdom.

The discussions in the spring and summer of 1918, intense as they were, underlined yet again that most advocates of the federal solution had devolution and not 'true federalism' in mind. Selborne, Oliver, Amery and Austen Chamberlain, a recent and surprisingly staunch supporter of a federal United Kingdom, all emphasized that in a new federal state the Westminster parliament's supremacy would be unaffected. Even Walter Long, now more persuaded than most to accept separate legislatures for Scotland, Wales, England and possibly both Ulster and Southern Ireland and to divide powers between national and provincial jurisdictions, could not bring himself to take the final step and accept the division of sovereignty that 'true federalism' demanded. Perhaps his caution resulted, in part, from the difficulties that he and his colleagues had in determining the distribution of taxing powers. Long clearly favoured the retention of all significant authority at the national level. That, of course, would have resulted in a pseudo or, at best, an anaemic federal state. Simply by exercising its fiscal powers the central government would have circumscribed the freedom of decision and action of the various states or provinces of a new United Kingdom. Despite the widespread use of the term federal and the impassioned advocacy of its supporters, what they had in mind was clearly closer to the decentralized unitary system of South Africa than to the truly federal structures of the United States, Canada and Australia.[26]

Harold Cox, the editor of the *Edinburgh Review*, writing in July 1918, perceptively commented that most of the British politicians demanding federalism did so 'primarily because they think it would settle the Irish problem, not because they have seriously considered the merits of federalism from the point of view of England, or even of Scotland or Wales'. He thought that in 'their mouths federalism is little more than a phrase employed for the purpose of avoiding the hard facts of the real Irish problem' which, to him, was 'essentially a question of nationality'. He also quite rightly pointed out that many of those same politicians were concerned about congestion of government business and favoured the adoption of federalism on the assumption that 'it would relieve the pressure of work upon our present single parliament'. Like so many observers, the writer did not think federalism would work in the United Kingdom. It would not appease Irish nationalist desires and, in fact, would mean a loss of liberty for not only Ireland but also Scotland and Wales. To him federalism would mean the multiplication of parliaments which was both an expensive proposition and a potentially tyrannous development.[27]

In those hectic months in 1918 only one individual took the time to lay out the essential features of a 'true federal' state. J.A.R. Marriott had commented frequently and with insight at the height of the pre-war crisis and he now took the opportunity to offer his reflections.[28] He noted that 'federalism' had long been in the air and that it had 'come to be advocated as the most hopeful solvent of the acidities which for centuries past have poisoned the relations between Great Britain and the three southern provinces of Ireland'. Despite this general awareness, he believed the real meaning and implications of federalism were still 'imperfectly apprehended'. Marriott quoted Freeman, Dicey and Sidgwick in an attempt to get at the root of not only what federalism was but how federal states were created. He noted that Freeman and Dicey had argued that federalism was an integrative and not a disintegrative force while Sidgwick had claimed the reverse could as easily be true. There appeared to Marriott to be three primary conditions necessary for a successful federal union: first, 'there must be a group of communities, so far united by blood, or creed, or language, by local contiguity or political tradition as to desire union; but not so closely connected by all or any of these ties as to be satisfied with nothing short of unity'; second, 'none of the States should be individually so powerful as to be able single-handed to resist foreign encroachment, and maintain their own independence'; and, third, 'there should be no marked inequality among the several contracting States'. Federalism, Marriott emphasized, was 'essentially a compromise' and he quoted John Stuart Mill's favourable comments on the subject.

His wide-ranging reading, observation and reflection led Marriott to conclude that the distinctive characteristics of 'true federalism' were 'first, dualism of law; second, reduplication of political organs: legislative, executive, and judicial; third, precise definition of powers in written and preferably rigid constitutions; fourth, separation of powers; fifth, a supreme court of justice competent to act as interpreter of the constitutions and as arbiter between possibly conflicting laws; and sixth a bicameral legislature including a federal second chamber'. Marriott did point out that federalism could take a variety of forms but that one factor was invariable in federal constitutions: 'As opposed to the concentration of powers in a unitary State, federalism necessarily involves a division of powers.' This, of course, was the crux of the matter and it is surprising how few writers and 'federal' advocates recognized it, or, if recognizing it, accepted it. The majority were prepared to define as 'federal' what was really devolutionary.

The debate surrounding a federal solution to the twin problems of Irish self-government and parliamentary congestion had fizzled by the late summer of 1918. Lloyd George had been unwilling to disturb the political balance over such a contentious issue, especially in light of the prevailing indifference of the majority of English people to any tampering with the existing constitution. The end of the war also diverted attention and energy to other issues and it was not until mid-1919 that an opportunity arose once more for serious contemplation of the federal idea and its application to United Kingdom difficulties. On this occasion the public debate and the behind-the-scenes lobbying by various interest groups was less in evidence. Some of the key participants in the earlier discussions had died, others were preoccupied by pressing imperial and international issues while some, such as F.S. Oliver, had grown weary of fighting a seemingly losing battle. The main debates in 1919–20 took place inside government offices and in the cabinet, and the principal advocate of the federal idea was Walter Long, the First Lord of the Admiralty, who had been transformed since 1916 from a zealous opponent of home rule into the most persistent advocate of the federal idea. But while Long's tactics had changed his principal goals – the preservation of the unity of the United Kingdom and of the empire – had not.

Long and his colleagues knew that the Government of Ireland Act of 1914 would come into effect six months after the ratification of the peace treaties. While that Act was widely recognized by Unionists, Liberals and Nationalists as unsatisfactory, no longer reflecting contemporary reality, it was not easily repealed. Therefore, in October 1919 the cabinet charged a committee headed by Long to draft a new bill compatible with the federation of the United Kingdom which would be more in tune with Nationalist aspirations and Ulster Unionist fears. By the time Long and his committee began their work it had been emphatically underlined in debates in the Lords (March 1919) and the Commons (June 1919) that any form of federation or devolution for the United Kingdom as a whole was not feasible. Long and his committee therefore concentrated their energies on devising a bill that would allow the island of Ireland to remain in the United Kingdom while ensuring that the interests of Ulster and of Southern Ireland would be dealt with separately.

Long quickly persuaded his colleagues and subsequently the cabinet to accept a bill that gave parliaments to both the north and the south of Ireland and established a Council of Ireland with membership drawn from the two Irish parliaments. It was the hope of Long and the cabinet that the Council would serve as a stepping stone to the eventual reunification of Ireland and the establishment of a single legislature for the whole of the island. Powers were divided between the Irish and the Westminster parliaments such as to ensure that the latter was clearly supreme. Long's solution was 'devolution in a federal form' and was not truly federal. Despite his conversion to a more adaptable constitutional device, Long's essential aims had been to preserve the unity of the United Kingdom and to prevent that fragmentation of the empire which he was convinced would automatically follow from any split at the imperial centre. The federal idea had been adopted and adapted to meet an immediate political need. It had not been accepted as either a desired or attainable constitutional alternative.[29]

The Government of Ireland Act of 1920 proved, predictably, to be unacceptable to Sinn Fein who refused to recognize the southern parliament. The British government quickly abandoned efforts to establish a legislature in the south and concentrated on setting one up in Belfast. That parliament met for the first time in June 1920 and lasted in its attenuated form until 1972. The Ulsterites had not wanted a separate parliament nor a miniature statelet but accepted both as a protection against southern encroachment. The constitution of Northern Ireland had not been drafted with it alone in mind. Federal features had been pervasive in the 1920 Act and the restricted financial and constitutional powers of the northern parliament reflected preoccupations of men like Long who had hoped that through applying the 'federal' form a resolution might be found to an agonizing problem. Their failure underscored the difficulties inherent in approaching the resolution of national aspirations within the United Kingdom in a piecemeal fashion and from anything less than a full and truly federal perspective. Politicians such as Long were not political theorists or, in the main, reflective and philosophic men. While they no doubt read the articles by experts such as Marriott or Morgan and thus probably had a surface acquaintance with the principal tenets of a federal state, they could not break from the caste of mind that believed in the sanctity of the sovereignty of the Westminster parliament. They were therefore incapable of educating the British, especially the English, public about the merits of a truly federal form of government. They were only prepared to take certain features from it and the result was always a hybrid constitutional form which would not only exacerbate but indeed create problems.

What is particularly revealing about the debate over the future of the United Kingdom was the lack of attention the issues of nation and region received. In fact, over the forty years that the constitutional problems surrounding the Anglo-Irish and to a lesser extent the Anglo-Scottish and Anglo-Welsh relationships simmered on the political burner, there was no sustained analysis of such issues as ethnicity, culture and nationality that were and remain central to all explorations of the federal alternative. The discussion in the United Kingdom was essentially one over territory and over legal and constitutional boundaries. It may have simply been assumed that a federation which would ensure separate parliaments with discrete constitutional jurisdictions was, in fact, recognizing the unique 'national' or 'cultural' or 'ethnic' features of Scotland, Wales, Ireland and England. If so, there is surprisingly little dissection of these aspects of United Kingdom life. The discussants seem to have approached this issue in much the same way their peers approached the problem of determining colonial jurisdictions: lines were drawn on a map and existing boundaries were accepted without much thought being given to cultural, ethnic, linguistic and economic issues. Clearly the political necessities of the time determined the actions and thinking of politicians but the book, pamphlet and article literature, which one would expect to be more reflective, was surprisingly devoid of speculation and/or suggestion on these matters. One is left with the impression that the promoters of federalism for the United Kingdom had but a mechanistic, utilitarian approach to the federal idea and little true appreciation of its possibilities or its resonance. All were desirous of preserving the Union and thus of confirming central authority. This explains why so few of the schemes were truly federal. Parliamentary sovereignty, it was assumed, and often argued, had to be preserved. The federal idea did not have a strong hold on the British consciousness and was resorted to only when devolution for Ireland was clearly not a viable option. Those who did advocate pure federalism either did not really understand it or understood it only in a limited fashion, and their writings lacked subtlety.

In other words, when the federal idea was taken up it was as a tactical solution to an acute problem, not because the federal system of government was seen as an ideal resolution of domestic concerns. That this was so can be seen from the reaction of the small Scottish and Welsh nationalist movements. The Welsh never advocated federalism *per se* and pressed devolutionary ideas cautiously and the Scots, while admittedly more aggressive in asserting their position, did not advocate a federation of the United Kingdom. They, too, would seemingly have been content with a devolutionary solution to the constitutional and administrative difficulties bedevilling the country. Needless to say, the English, as a group, were almost uniformly uninterested in federalism, and without strong pressure from the largest 'nation' within the United Kingdom there was never any hope that a United Kingdom federation would be established.

Nevertheless, the debate had raised key concerns about the relationship of the Celtic fringe to the centre of power in London and how that linkage could be both ameliorated and preserved. Observers and, eventually, politicians had been obliged to recognize that any fundamental changes to the British constitution raised questions about the nature of parliamentary representation, the division of powers, particularly those related to taxation, and the overwhelming and overweening size and strength of England. The debate, fuelled primarily by the perilously balanced Anglo-Irish relationship and secondarily by the mushrooming congestion of parliamentary business, had also necessitated a look at a system, federalism, that would seemingly provide, at one and the same time, greater freedom for the people of the United Kingdom and greater stability for the British state.[30] These were awkward questions to address and most politicians and the public at large were either not interested in them or distressed by where the answers might lead. The major political parties were quite happy to leave the issue on the back-burner and, in fact, once the Irish Free State was hived off in 1922, to ignore it altogether. That the questions had neither been properly addressed nor answered and that the problems of the British unitary state had not been resolved would be dramatically demonstrated fifty years later in the 1970s. At the end of the twentieth century federalism or 'devolution in a federal form' would once again surface as a persistent theme on the political agenda and in constitutional debate.

5 The Round Table movement, the empire and world order

As we have seen, the issue of imperial union was never far from the centre of the debate over the constitutional form of the United Kingdom. In fact, from the 1870s through to the 1920s, the changing nature of the relationship between the United Kingdom and the white settlement dominions occupied a good deal of the time of politicians and civil servants in London and led to a protracted discussion about the goal to which all should be headed and how rapidly it should be reached. Similarly, the relationships between London and India and the other major dependencies also began to shift and these changes were accelerated by World War I. The debates and the various policy options that resulted preoccupied the attention of various empire-watchers from the early years of the century to the 1930s. At the centre of much of the discussion and involved to a considerable degree in the formulation of policy at particular moments was the Round Table movement. The federal ideas that emerged or the degree to which federalism was discussed as a possible solution to the larger imperial question and to particular colonial problems as well as to the whole issue of world order was primarily a result of Round Table initiative or influence.

The Round Table movement had been established in late 1909 and early 1910 by former members of Milner's 'kindergarten' who had been instrumental in promoting the Union of South Africa. The 'kindergarten' was a closely knit group of some dozen young graduates of Oxford, mainly from New College, who had gradually assembled in South Africa after 1900 as part of the influx of administrators brought in to help consolidate Lord Milner's reconstruction programme. The young men had worked more closely with Milner than others and had taken to living together in bachelor quarters and spending much of their leisure time together. With Milner's departure in 1905, the 'kindergarten' had thrown their energy into a move to bring the four colonies of the Cape, Natal, the Orange River Colony and the Transvaal together in a wider union. One of their number, Lionel Curtis, had drafted much of the famous Selborne memorandum which had provided the catalyst for union and another, Philip Kerr, had been instrumental in both the Closer Union Societies and in editing *The State*, a periodical founded to promote closer union, while a third, Robert Brand, had

worked closely with General Jan Smuts in drafting the South African constitution. When they had initially become involved in closer union activities,
the 'kindergarten' had favoured a federal form of government for South
Africa, but as their investigations and reflections continued they gradually
realized that fundamental issues such as railways and the treatment of the
'native' population would be more readily resolved, or at least handled, if a
unitary rather than a federal government was created. They threw their energies into the promotion of unitary government and it was in that form that
the Union of South Africa was established in 1910.

While the 'kindergarten' had not been primarily responsible for the
success of the closer union campaign they had played a key role, and given
their abilities and their natural self confidence it was not altogether
surprising that even before they began to return to England in 1909 a
number of them, especially Curtis and Kerr, had begun to think of working
for the closer union of the empire. Milner was a prominent imperial unionist
and they had imbibed deeply at his ideological well. Moreover, it was
increasingly clear by the early 1900s that the United Kingdom was threatened on all sides by the gathering industrial, commercial, military and naval
might of Germany, Japan and the United States. If the United Kingdom
was to continue to play a leading role in world affairs it seemed imperative
to many observers that it strengthen its position both in Europe and internationally by forming closer ties, perhaps an imperial union, with the white
settlement colonies of Canada, Australia, New Zealand and South Africa. It
was also argued, and here the Round Table was to play a key role, that as
matters currently stood the dominions were totally subordinate in the areas
of defence and foreign policy. They had no say in the formulation of policy
and contributed little to the imperial war chest. The 'kindergarten' reasoned
that until the dominions were treated as equals in these crucial matters they
would never achieve full nationhood. By becoming an integral part of a
wider imperial union with the full right to help formulate defence and
foreign policy each dominion would finally become a true nation. Thus, in
'kindergarten' minds, were nationalism and imperialism intertwined. These
assessments and assumptions were at the root of the formation of the
Round Table movement and were to be the driving force of the movement
and particularly of its two leading lights, Curtis and Kerr, until the end of
the war.

At first glance, the Round Table movement would appear to be the
natural successor to the Imperial Federation League. That both organizations were essentially founded in order to promote a closer union of the
empire is, of course, true but the parallels and linkages really cease there.
Unlike the League, the movement had a small group of close friends at its
core who shared a common and coherent set of beliefs and goals. Even when
individuals disagreed with a particular policy or a line of argument they
remained faithful to the central principles. This cohesiveness underpinned
the movement's activities in its early years and is a key to its persistence and

to its successes. Only when the founders of the movement aged and tired or became distracted by other commitments did the movement falter and lose touch with the pulse of the British state and its empire.[1]

The Imperial Federation League was never able to agree on a definite scheme and, in fact, was grievously divided between those who pursued the idea of a *kriegsverein* or military alliance, others who wanted a *zollverein* or imperial free trade area, and the remainder who aspired to some form of political union. By contrast the Round Table movement never took up the issue of preference, much to the annoyance of Leo Amery, and apart from isolating defence and foreign policy as the key areas of decision-making necessitating a unified empire, the members did not advocate a union solely for defensive purposes. The Round Table movement believed the empire needed to be strengthened and that the only way to do so would be for the dominions and the United Kingdom to come together in an imperial parliament, a 'federation' of the empire. Many of their number, Curtis most of all, were convinced that the stark choice facing the dominions was closer union or separation, federation or independence.

From the beginning, the Round Table movement assumed that some form of organic union rather than cooperation should be the aim of their activities. While all cooperative devices and forms, such as the emerging colonial/imperial conference system and the committee of imperial defence, should be encouraged they were viewed as no more than preliminary steps towards a tighter, more coherent union. That this more formal union should be federal in form seemed clear to most members of the London group. The vast distances separating the various dominions from each other and from London also seemed to preclude a unitary system. Only a federal structure would meet imperial needs and overcome inherent obstacles. Moreover, the congestion of business in the Westminster parliament that tended to interfere with the proper conduct of imperial affairs was as frustrating for the founders of the Round Table as it was for the advocates of a 'federal' United Kingdom. Shortly after his return to England in 1905, Lord Milner complained to George Parkin, now the secretary of the Rhodes Trust, about the mess the system of government was in: 'Here is everything depending on this rotten assembly at Westminster and the whole future of the Empire may turn upon the whims of men who have been elected for their competence in dealing with Metropolitan Tramways or country pubs.'[2]

An early insight into Lionel Curtis's thinking came the next year when in a letter to an old friend, and future critic, Richard Jebb, he scorned cooperation as the solution to South Africa's problems. 'Cooperation stands for everything', he argued, 'which Washington and Hamilton fought and overcame when they erected one government over the thirteen States of America, and gave her a place amongst the nations which today is second to none.'[3] This remark was revealing in two ways. It indicated a knowledge of F.S. Oliver's *Alexander Hamilton* which had been published earlier in 1906, and it reflected Oliver's passionate identification with Hamilton's highly centralizing tendencies. The federal structure that Hamilton had expounded, that Oliver admired and that clearly attracted Curtis was one which centralized power. It was not, at least at this stage in Curtis's thinking, a means of harmonizing diversity and unity. It was patently a means of establishing union and centralizing power in order to ensure that Great Britain, through its empire, continued to have a leading role to play in international affairs. This was the mark of the 'British Race Patriot' that Milner himself so proudly claimed to be. Despite Curtis's later identification of the British imperial experience with the 'Commonwealth of God' and his espousal of the 'principle of the commonwealth', it is hard to escape the notion that at root Curtis wanted to ensure the continuing presence of the British and their 'civilization' on the world stage.

Nevertheless, Curtis was astute enough to realize that to effect union through the use of arbitrary power might not work and certainly would not last. Far better that the union be effected voluntarily. That meant education and propaganda and ear-bending, all of which Curtis was good at. As he put it to Robert Brand, 'If the British Empire is to last it must be constructed on the principle of an arch with each stone so placed that its own weight constitutes the strength of the arch. If it is to be bound together by steel ties it is only a matter of time till the ties must rust and break.'[4] By the time of his departure from South Africa, Curtis was commenting favourably on the insights of Durham and Elgin who had earlier recognized the importance of transferring powers to British North America that had eventually enabled Canada and Australia and the other dominions to move rapidly towards nationhood. Curtis accepted that only by the transfer of self-governing powers could a firm union be achieved.[5]

It is also clear from their early writings that the Round Table members were fully conversant with the essential difference between a unitary and a federal system of government. Writing in the first issue of *The State* in January 1909, Philip Kerr pointed out that the 'real distinction' lay in the way power, or sovereignty, was exercised:

> In an Unitary Constitution the Central Parliament is all powerful, and has the power to alter at any time by Act the distribution of powers between itself and the local authorities. In a Federation both the Central Parliament and the States are limited to the exercise of the powers vested in them by the Constitution, and an alteration in the decision of these powers can only be brought about by the adoption of the special measures required for altering the Constitution, which are provided in that instrument. The distinction between an Unitary and a Federal Constitution lies, not in the manner in which the powers are divided in actual practice, but whether sovereignty resides in the central Government alone, or is divided between it and the local Governments.[6]

Despite this awareness of the essence of the federal idea, or perhaps because of it, not all members and associates of the movement were initially convinced that it could be readily applied to the empire. Even as early as November 1909, Milner's close confidant Leo Amery expressed doubt about the prospects of a federal empire. 'I don't think', he admitted to Alfred Deakin, the former prime minister of Australia, 'we shall ever get, at any rate within our time, to direct election all over the Empire of a federal parliament with direct legislative or executive authority.'[7] This was to some degree a surprising admission to come from Amery who was an ardent champion of imperial union but, in fact, it reflected his awareness of the gathering self-consciousness, even nationalism, in the dominions and the suspicion with which close imperial ties were viewed. He also recognized that the United Kingdom would be most reluctant to share power and decision-making with states of lesser status and stature at a time of gathering tension and increased talk of war.

Philip Kerr quickly came to share this view, especially after his trip to Canada in late 1909 with Curtis and William Marris, a Round Table associate who had befriended the 'kindergarten' in South Africa while on secondment from the Indian Civil Service. While Kerr strongly favoured closer union of the empire he neither thought the empire was a religion to be worshipped, as did Curtis, nor that the pace could be forced. He realized that Canada and presumably Australia and New Zealand were prosperous self-governing colonies basking in their gathering strength. He did not think Canada would necessarily break its ties with the United Kingdom but 'for the life of me I can't see why it should want to get any closer. I don't see that we can offer her anything that the United States can't offer just as well, and there are certain obvious disadvantages in the surrender of autonomy which is entailed in the creation of an Empire organization. . . . If you forced Canada to choose now between Imperial Federation and independence I think she would take independence.'[8]

Writing to Brand from Ottawa in November 1909, Kerr reconfirmed these feelings and admitted his differences with Curtis:

At the present moment we disagree so profoundly about Imperialism and the work our association is to do, that it looks as if all our plans might fall to the ground. I needn't go into the thing in detail now but broadly speaking the situation is this. Lionel believes that the only hope for the Empire lies in 'organic unity'. That is to say the creation of a central sovereign authority directly elected by the people of the Empire which shall control policy and services such as army and navy, and raise taxation through its own officers. I think, now, that 'organic unity' of that kind is impossible, at any rate until science has revolutionized communication and transportation, and that to try to bring on a movement of that kind would be almost certain to break up the Empire. It would get a certain amount of support – just enough to enable it to do damage. If Lord M. and he intend to work for the federation of the Empire in the strict sense I should, unless Lord M. can modify my opinions, feel forced to sever my connection with the whole business, if not actively to oppose it. . . . Of course I am still a strong Imperialist. I am more convinced by my visit to Canada than I was before that the Empire is going to hang together and will become a strong vigorous and living entity. I am further convinced that there is an immense amount of work to be done in bringing that about. But I am also convinced that any attempt to fit the Empire into the constitutional ideas which have suited the United Kingdom and the self governing colonies in the past is simply courting destruction.[9]

Curtis and Kerr did, of course, resolve many of their differences and the Round Table movement owed much of its energy over the years to their combined efforts. Nevertheless, despite his willingness to identify with Round Table goals, they were more a reflection of Curtis's beliefs than Kerr's, and the latter never completely moved over into Curtis's camp as an out-and-out federationist. He strongly believed in a united empire but was usually ill-at-ease with the schemes generated by Curtis. For his part, Curtis was aware of colonial nationalism and the need to transfer self-governing powers and he readily embraced the idea that the responsibility for public affairs had to be assumed by all those capable of exercising it. This led him to argue not only that the principles of representative government, involving an informed citizenry, should underpin any larger 'federal' structure but that such a union was the only way the self-governing colonies/dominions would achieve full nationhood. While Kerr shared Curtis's commitment to liberty coupled with the rule of law, his sensitivity to the gathering forces of nationalism in the white dominions led him to accept more readily that a looser empire/commonwealth relationship might be more realistic.[10]

At its final major organizational meeting held at Ledbury in January 1910, the Round Table movement agreed that its ultimate aim would be an organic union possessing the following features: first, the control of union affairs should be entrusted to an imperial parliament; second, such a parliament should be directly representative of the people, but the acceptance of this principle should not be taken to exclude from its composition an element chosen by some method other than that of direct election. It was recognized that

the more important functions of the Imperial authority would be executive and not deliberative, but the necessity of providing for the public discussion of Imperial affairs in some representative assembly, the importance of avoiding the evils and even deadlock incidental to the discussion of Imperial affairs by the national legislatures, and the need of some representative assembly to which the executive should be answerable, seemed to require the reproduction of the institutions of Cabinet and Parliament in the final Union of the Empire. The difficulty of avoiding the discussion of Imperial affairs in national legislatures if the Imperial assembly were constituted by secondary election; and the advantages which would follow from the separation of Imperial and national interests in popular elections, pointed to a majority of the members of the popular section of the Imperial Parliament being directly elected.[11]

Since the need for union of the empire arose out of external affairs, it was agreed that the central organization of the empire should have sole authority in conducting foreign relations and in determining the nature, strength, distribution and organization of the defensive forces of the empire as well as power to raise the revenue it required.

These decisions were not surprising given the nature of earlier discussions and the general familiarity the members had with federal ideas. Curtis's future writings faithfully reflected these general early guidelines although they were more detailed. It is not entirely clear what the movement's views were on the issue of sovereignty. Should the imperial parliament have supreme authority in all areas or just in those specific ones outlined in January 1910? It is a reflection of the movement's unwillingness to engage in a lengthy discussion of both specifics and of abstract principles that nothing in the record of these founding meetings is particularly helpful. Later in the year, however, in the context of the discussions surrounding a possible federal structure for the United Kingdom, Curtis, writing from Sydney, advised Kerr that

> no one should attempt to frame proposals for federalizing the United Kingdom, until he had been through the painful process of determining such things as What legislative and Executive powers could be devolved on Provincial Legislatures? How to divide the public revenues between the federal and provincial governments? What your areas are to be, e.g., Can you separate Wales? . . . By far your most difficult question is that of the division of public sources of revenue.[12]

It is clear from these comments that Curtis had been giving careful consideration to some of the fundamental questions involved in the creation of a federation but his use of the word 'devolved' suggests that he may not have had true federalism in mind, at least for the United Kingdom.

Kerr had also been paying more attention than usual to these issues, given the constitutional crisis in the British Isles and the sudden interest in federalism being displayed by J.L. Garvin in the *Observer* and by the Round Table associates Oliver and Amery in the press. The Round Table movement had been forced to look closely at the interconnection between federation of the empire and federation of the United Kingdom. Kerr explored these at length in a letter to Curtis at the end of September 1910.[13] He began by defining his terms. He would use 'Imperial' to refer to 'matters relating to the whole Empire or to more than one self-governing portion of it'; 'National' to refer to 'the affairs of the United Kingdom or of any of one of the Dominions'; and 'Local' to refer to 'the affairs of sub-divisions of the national or dominion units, e.g., Ireland, or Ontario'. He did not believe it was necessary at that time to examine the exact line between imperial, national and local affairs.

When the movement had discussed the form constitutional union might take during their organizational meetings in January it had been generally agreed that the sooner a line of distinction could be drawn in the United Kingdom between imperial and domestic affairs, 'by entrusting the control of each to a different assembly', the better. Such a measure had been seen as perhaps a necessary step on the road to imperial unity. Now, however, Kerr was not so sure and he wanted to explore exactly what was involved in the idea of 'separation', and 'whether it is practicable to prepare the way for Imperial unity by dividing the control of Imperial and national affairs between two different bodies before the Dominions are ready to come in and make a true Imperial assembly'.

He thought it would be conceded that 'any true Imperial assembly should only handle affairs which are the common concern of all the self-governing portions of the Empire. It should not, in addition to exercising its imperial functions, deal with any of the purely national affairs of the UK or Canada.' The reasons were obvious: 'because a large proportion of the members of an imperial assembly would not be representative of the people affected, would not be elected on the issues on which they were called upon to decide, and would have no knowledge of them'. On looking at the powers that should be entrusted to an imperial assembly, Kerr thought 'it would be generally agreed that the lowest common denominator of organic unity and the highest common factor of probable consent among the self-governing dominions, including the UK, are not widely separated'. The imperial assembly, therefore, should have control of foreign affairs, peace and war, the navy, the striking forces of the army, the dependencies and also 'the right to fix the amount of revenue it required for these purposes'. It would perhaps also handle minor matters such as shipping, cables and commercial law.

Having decided on the probable division of powers between imperial and national jurisdictions, Kerr asked if it would be possible to persuade the United Kingdom to entrust the imperial functions to a different assembly to that which conducted its national affairs. It was clear to him that the answer was no. He pointed out that

> So long as Great Britain alone controls the Empire, national and imperial affairs are so intimately connected that the assembly and Cabinet which represents the country in the most important of domestic affairs will represent it in imperial affairs also. . . . No scheme of devolution for the UK alone would produce the line of division between Imperial and national affairs. . . . The truth is that this Empire is still a national concern of the UK and so long as it remains so, will be handled by its national assembly . . . the final and complete separation of Imperial and

national affairs within the UK must wait the day when the dominions are ready to take their part in creating a true Imperial assembly.

Kerr was at pains to underline that 'imperial unity is concerned with the division between Imperial and National affairs, Federalism for the United Kingdom with the division between national and local affairs'. It was well to bear in mind the real distinction, he said, 'because it is usually blurred in the minds of those who talk about the subject'. For Kerr, 'Federalism for the Empire, and Federalism for the United Kingdom are two entirely distinct ideas.'

Kerr went on to remind Curtis that there was 'no general rule to serve as a guide to dividing powers between the several partners of a Federation'. Some matters would not be in dispute but many more would 'excite the hottest controversy. In practice the line is one of expediency. It depends upon the internal and external circumstances of the time, the traditions of the people, the pledges and records of the parties which bring the changes about, the prevailing temper of the day'. Here Kerr touched on a number of sensitive issues that were inherent in the problem of creating a federation but were particularly endemic in a situation where a national government had dependencies and thus imperial powers. This was to be an especially difficult problem to resolve in the federation-making of the 1930s to 1960s.

After looking at the existing administrative differences between England, Scotland and Ireland, examining the 1886 and the 1893 home rule bills, and studying T.A. Spalding's book *Federation and Empire*, Kerr concluded

> that the principle upon which a federal constitution is based is that the sovereign powers of a people are entrusted to and exercised by separate bodies, instead of being concentrated in the hands of one assembly as in the UK today, and that to create a federal council for the Empire would really be to isolate but a small portion of the sovereign powers of any of the self-governing peoples within it. The Imperial assembly would wield very important powers, those relating to peace and war. But the power to decide the commercial, social, moral, and even the religious code, as well as the administrative policy of the country – in some ways the more important of the attributes of a sovereign people – could still rest with the national assemblies.

In sum, Kerr argued that

> The Federation of the UK clearly is no necessary stage which must be passed before Imperial Unity can be achieved. The surrender of the Imperial functions can be made to an Imperial assembly just as easily by a unitary Parliament of the UK as by a federal Parliament. . . . In other words Imperial Unity has no essential connection with the movement for Federation for the UK, for it can be achieved without it, but it is intimately related to it, especially if the only satisfactory solution of the Irish

difficulty proves to be the complete separation of the national affairs of Great Britain and Ireland.

This letter touched on a number of crucial issues that most advocates of federalism in the United Kingdom chose either to ignore or of which they were unaware. That Kerr obliged his Round Table colleagues to address these fundamental concerns was positive but it resulted in a decision to concentrate their energies on examining the imperial problem and finding ways to achieve closer union. As a consequence, there appears to have been no further full-scale analysis of the federal idea which is regrettable since the group clearly had the background, the knowledge and the ability to offer a unique contribution. That it did not and that it continued to pursue a pragmatic path was more in keeping with the British/English predilection for the avoidance of the abstract and the theoretical. The result was a tendency to fall back on generalities and assertions and high-blown phrases rather than further rigorous analysis.

By 1910 the London members of the movement were content to leave the actual formulation of a particular scheme to Lionel Curtis and it was his plan which became the lightning rod for debate both inside and outside the movement. Philip Kerr appears not to have given much further close thought to the intricacies of federalism and once he became private secretary to Lloyd George in 1916 his attention and energies were concentrated elsewhere. Curtis first outlined his ideas in the major statement – the so called 'Green Memorandum' – which he had drafted in 1910 and taken with him on his recruiting tour to New Zealand, Australia and Canada. In that document he had gone over once again the need for the dominions to play a full and equal part in the determination of imperial defence and foreign policy if they were ever to achieve full nationhood, and the need to relieve the imperial parliament at Westminster from dealing with both national and imperial issues. In his estimation, the dominions should either federate with the United Kingdom in a larger and more formal imperial union or they should go their separate ways and develop their nationhood in that fashion. This stark alternative of union or disruption was not one fully shared by all his colleagues in the movement and certainly was not likely to appeal to a wider public. This did not seem to concern Curtis and he quickly moved on to outline his federal structure for the empire.

It was to have a lower house directly elected by the citizenry of the empire. Representation of each dominion would be proportionate to its population. The upper house would have equal representation from each state. A tribunal to serve as an arbitration panel when the dividing line between imperial and national responsibilities became blurred would be established. The primary responsibilities of the imperial assembly would be imperial defence and foreign policy and the issue of peace and war. It would have nothing to do with the internal affairs of the United Kingdom and nor, presumably, with those of the other dominions. Thus Curtis appears to have accepted the concept of divided sovereignty but he never specifically addresses the issue and the intent must be inferred. Curtis did appear to recognize, however, that such a union would only be possible if the United Kingdom was prepared to assume the same status as the other dominions. He obviously recognized that it would be difficult for the United Kingdom to relinquish any of the sovereign powers it currently had, but he seems not to have accepted that the dominions might be equally reluctant to part with recently hard-won powers. Nowhere do we have philosophic reflections from Curtis on these issues nor on federalism generally. He seems just to have accepted the brute logic that federalism would clearly make the empire more efficient. Unfortunately, brute logic was not enough.[14]

Curtis did argue in *The Project of a Commonwealth*, published in 1915, that by the early eighteenth century 'sovereignty had passed once and for all from the Crown to Parliament, or rather to the voters who elect it – the citizens, that is to say, recognized by law as qualified to choose representatives for the purpose of administering and changing the law. It is they, not the King, Cabinet, or Parliament, who are the mainspring of government in the United Kingdom.'[15] This was clearly an acceptance of the principle of popular sovereignty which had been at the root of the American colonists' argument with the British government in the late eighteenth century; however, Curtis dated the adoption of the concept earlier than most writers would now accept. Curtis also referred to the Scots' attempt to promote 'Federal Union' as misleading. It was important, he argued, 'not to be misled by terms. The plan proposed was in no sense a federal union, but merely a *zollverein* or customs convention, which left untouched the vital question of who was to control defence and foreign affairs. It was but one of many attempts to settle by contract between two states what in fact could only be settled by the creation of a single state claiming the unlimited obedience of the citizens in both.'[16] Curtis believed difficulties such as had arisen over Anglo-Scottish union would recur 'every time the necessity arises for extending the principle of the commonwealth'.[17] Curtis noted Fletcher of Saltoun's proposal to divide Europe into ten provinces and each province into ten or twelve sovereign republics. Agreement between the sovereign republics was to be secured in each province by a common prince, but Fletcher had not explained how the prince would achieve it. He was not, said Curtis, 'the last to argue that one titular crown will suffice to maintain the unity of dominions whose separate sovereignty has been recognized as absolute and complete'.[18]

In commenting on the negotiations that led to the Union of 1707, Curtis shrewdly observed,

> To none of the Commissioners . . . does it seem to have occurred that the continued existence in Edinburgh and London of provincial executives and legislatures, entrusted respectively with interests which were strictly Scottish and strictly English, was not incompatible with the policy

of merging Scots and Englishmen in a common state. The possibility of distinguishing local from general interests had not as yet been realized. The truth is that statesmen of that era had far less experience to draw upon than those who have followed the establishment of the American Republic. To the ministers of Queen Anne the only alternative to absolute separation was to centralize all government, local as well as imperial, at Westminster. The American method of preserving existing state governments as local organizations of the wider state into which they were merged had yet to be placed on the political market by its discoverers.[19]

In 1916 Curtis published *The Problem of the Commonwealth*.[20] Designed for a popular audience, it contained an analysis of the imperial problem and an outline of a federal structure for the empire. Curtis reviewed the growth of self-government in the British Isles and pointed out that the dominions were not yet self-governing because they had no control over defence and foreign policy. Until they had that control they would not achieve full nationhood. In Curtis's estimation, that control would only be attained by the creation of a federal imperial structure. The dominions would then be represented in an imperial parliament on the basis of population and would thus have a direct involvement in all areas of policy formation. But if they were to be participants in the formulation of policy they would have to contribute to the costs of mounting such policies. The imperial parliament would therefore have to have the power to both raise and collect taxes in each member state for imperial purposes. The amount of such a tax would be determined, and regularly reviewed, by a permanent judicial commission of assessors. In the event of a dominion defaulting, the imperial parliament would have the power to collect taxes from each individual citizen in that dominion.

This was a highly controversial proposal both inside and outside the movement and explains why Curtis was obliged to publish the volume under his own name. The movement was aware of the sensitivity in the dominions to any suggestions of taxation from the imperial centre and recognized that, if anything, the trend in Anglo-dominion relations was toward a looser, cooperative format rather than the tighter, more centralized arrangement that Curtis's federal plan clearly envisaged. But it was not only the taxing power of the imperial parliament that alarmed analysts of Curtis's federal scheme. They were equally concerned by Curtis's argument that since foreign policy and the supervision of the colonial dependencies were inseparable, the dominions would also have to assume a responsibility for the dependencies. Many empire-watchers, including some of his Round Table colleagues, were even more outraged by Curtis's failure to provide for the representation of India in his proposed imperial parliament.

These were highly complicated issues and Curtis's efforts to deal with them revealed what little thought had thus far been given to how India and other colonial dependencies would be accommodated within a federal structure. Would India be included on a par with the dominions? Would only one member of the new federal empire – the United Kingdom – be responsible for all the dependencies? Or would that role be shared? And what provisions would be made for 'raising' India and the other dependencies to full membership in the federal club? There were no easy answers to such fundamental questions and those Britons who were persuaded that the federal idea was the solution to British and colonial problems continued to wrestle with them into the 1940s.

India had first been given serious, sustained attention by the Round Table movement in 1912 when, at the urging of Kerr, questions about the pace at which India should proceed to self-government and the degree to which India should be involved with the dominions in decisions affecting defence and foreign policy and peace and war had been deliberately addressed. While most members of the London group, particularly Curtis and Kerr, now accepted that 'the principle of the commonwealth' – the extension of self-government to all those capable of exercising it – should be the sustaining ideal of the British empire, the problem was that India was not yet self-governing. Therefore, the involvement of India in a federal structure would be difficult, especially since the dominions would be hostile. Moreover, as one of the movement's advisors, Edmund Molony, an Indian Civil Service officer in Benares, pointed out to Curtis in June 1912, there were real difficulties associated with the creation of an imperial parliament that would be responsible for the dependencies as well as the key issues of defence and foreign policy. Such a parliament would have no control over the domestic affairs of the United Kingdom or the dominions but it would have authority over the domestic affairs of the dependencies, of which India was one. This would not be acceptable to political India.

In isolating this problem, Molony was raising an issue that was to be at the heart of the decolonizing process. There was clearly a serious anomaly because MPs would be elected on the grounds that they were sound on the subjects of defence and foreign policy but 'not on the ground of any special aptitude for domestic affairs in general or for sympathy with or knowledge of the coloured races'. Molony added that 'if the Imperial Parliament is considered unfit to manage the domestic affairs of the United Kingdom or Dominions there does not seem to be any reason to suppose it fitted to manage the domestic affairs of the Dependencies'.[21]

These were perceptive and telling comments and by the time war broke out in 1914 the movement had not been able to settle on a rational solution. Rather than divert their energies, the London group decided to concentrate on resolving the tensions in Anglo-dominion relations before tackling the formidably complex problem of India's status and stature within the empire/commonwealth. For the time being, the movement simply resolved to do all it could, first, to advance Indians towards self-government within the sub-continent and, second, to hasten the pace at which India moved towards self-government on a par with the dominions in the empire as a

whole. The simple explanation for Curtis's omission of India from the imperial parliament outlined in *The Problem of the Commonwealth* was that
neither he nor his Round Table colleagues had as yet tackled that issue.

Curtis went to India in 1916 with the intention of initiating the long-
delayed analysis of the Anglo-Indian relationship. By then, however, the
Round Table movement was being rapidly overtaken by events and its aspirations of the pre-war era were no longer relevant. World War I precipitated
a marked change in the Anglo-dominion relationship and by 1917 it was
obvious that federation of the empire was an impossible goal. The dominions were now clearly launched on the road to full self-government in the
key areas of defence and foreign policy, a status which was to be defined in
the 1920s and confirmed by the 1931 Statute of Westminster. The empire
was evolving away from a centralized 'federal' arrangement towards a looser
more cooperative grouping.

The impact of the war on India was, if anything, even more dramatic.
The imperial war conference of 1917 recognized the right of India, along
with the dominions, to a voice in the determination of foreign policy, while
in August of that year Edwin Montagu, the Secretary of State for India,
indicated that the goal of British rule in India was the grant of responsible
government. Indian nationalists immediately interpreted this to mean that
India would be given a constitution on the dominion model. Montagu and
the viceroy, Lord Chelmsford, held numerous meetings in India early in 1918
in order to gain a sense of constitutional possibilities. Their findings and
recommendations were submitted to the British government in 1918 and
markedly influenced the India Act of 1919.

The Act was designed to move India further along the path to self-
government. This was to be achieved through a system in the provinces
known as 'dyarchy'. Simply put, dyarchy was a means by which certain
powers such as law and order, finance, land revenue, control of the press and
famine relief were 'reserved' to the provincial governor and his executive
council while other matters such as education, agriculture, local government
and public health were 'transferred' to the control of Indian ministers
responsible to an Indian electorate. The Act also admitted elected Indians to
the new central legislature, enlarged the provincial legislatures and extended
the franchise.

Dyarchy had first been discussed in 1915 by the Round Table movement
and Curtis had become one of its principal champions. It was a scheme
which appealed to the movement because it allowed for a gradual transfor-
mation of the Indian domestic political scene while enabling the dominions
to become adjusted to India's presence at the imperial conferences. It also
fitted in well with the Round Table's lingering concerns about the level of
'civilization' that had been achieved in India. Dyarchy seemed to ensure a
means by which certain required modes of conduct would be instilled at the
same time that 'the principle of the commonwealth' was being realized.
Although after 1919 Round Table members were less directly or immediately

involved in Anglo-Indian affairs, when they did become caught up in the surge of events it was always in an effort to extend self-government within India and to create a stable nation-state that could take its place alongside the dominions in the commonwealth of nations. It was in that context that the federal idea was once again explored.[22]

Under the provisions of the India Act of 1919 it was necessary to review the workings of the new constitutional system after ten years. It had not proven popular with Indian nationalists and for a time the Congress Party had refused to participate. Once the Hindu-dominated Congress did reenter the formal political arena and began to operate as if it spoke for all of political India, concerns about the future of minority ethnic and religious groupings surfaced and led some observers to speculate about a federal solution to the problems of the sub-continent. Sensing the need to advance the appraisal of the 1919 constitutional reforms, the British in 1927 appointed Sir John Simon to preside over a commission to visit India and provide a first-hand report. Unfortunately, the Conservative government did not appoint an Indian member to the commission which infuriated the Congress leadership who refused to cooperate with the Simon commission and called for India to be given dominion status.

These developments prompted Philip Kerr to suggest to Sir John Simon that a resolution of some of the most immediate problems might lie with the federal idea. Kerr recommended the abolition of dyarchy in the provinces, its gradual introduction at the centre and a division of powers between the centre and the provinces in a federal structure. In keeping with his deep commitment to 'the principle of the commonwealth', Kerr argued that the Indian people would only learn to govern themselves by exercising self-governing powers. This would best be done initially in the provinces which would then become the buttresses of a federal system for British India.[23]

The Simon commission followed Kerr's advice and in June 1930 recommended the introduction of responsible government in the provinces, although not at the centre, and the eventual adoption of a federal structure. The proposed retention of British control at the centre and the failure to address the issue of independence drew the anger and repudiation of the Indian nationalists and the British reacted by calling a Round Table Conference in London to reassess India's constitutional future. The conference initially sat from November 1930 to January 1931 and Philip Kerr, who had recently become Lord Lothian, was one of four Liberal delegates. He now had a golden opportunity to push his ideas and he was given an unexpected boost when the Indian princes made it clear that they supported the principle of federation. In the end, the conference recommended and the prime minister, Ramsay MacDonald, accepted that the basis of a new constitution would be a federation for the whole of India. Dyarchy was now to be introduced at the centre, although defence and foreign affairs would remain the responsibility of the governor-general for a transitional period.

For the next four years, the constitutional future of India was a central concern and resulted in an intense debate between conservative gradualists, of whom Lothian was clearly one, and inveterate die-hards such as Winston Churchill who loudly and pugnaciously opposed any change in the Anglo-Indian relationship which would weaken the empire and thus the United Kingdom's international standing. Lothian played a significant role in the discussions, investigations and educational propagandizing that preceded and followed the granting of royal assent to the Government of India Act in August 1935. He was a delegate at the three sessions of the Round Table Conference stretching into late 1932. After the 1931 election and the formation of the National government he was appointed an under-secretary in the India Office, a position he held for a year. He also chaired the franchise committee, one of three specialist committees set up as a result of the Round Table Conference deliberations, which toured India in the spring of 1932 and whose recommendations markedly influenced the drafting of the new India Act. Lothian accepted these various duties, particularly the India Office position, only on the understanding that his primary interest was in 'the broad Round Table policy of placing real responsibility for government on Indian shoulders, both in the Provinces and in the Centre'.[24] For Lothian, federation was the key to a stable nation-state in the sub-continent and the realization of the 'principle of the commonwealth' was the only way by which federation would be achieved.

Once the federal idea had received the approval of the princes during the first session of the Round Table Conference in late 1930, a sub-committee on federal structures was established under the chairmanship of Lord Sankey and with Lothian as a member. It was the first time that the British government had participated in an extensive formal look at the federal idea. No such investigation had been set up to explore the applicability of the concept during the protracted discussion over the Anglo-Irish constitutional relationship nor during the heyday of talk about 'federation' of the empire. Not even Walter Long's constitutional committee of 1918, charged with the task of drafting a federal bill for the United Kingdom, had had the benefit of detailed analysis of federal variables.

The sub-committee was asked to examine the component elements of the proposed federation: the type of federal legislature and the number of chambers of which it should consist; the powers of the federal legislature; the number of members in the federal legislature and in each of its chambers and the proportion to be assigned to each of the federating units; the method by which representatives from British India and from the Indian states were to be drawn; and the constitution, character, powers and responsibilities of the federal executive. Sankey went over these responsibilities carefully and then referred his committee to the article on federation in the eleventh edition of the *Encyclopedia Britannica* which outlined the Swiss, the United States, the Canadian and the Australian systems. He made a point of emphasizing that each level of government in a federal system would be sovereign in its own jurisdiction and that citizens would owe allegiance to both levels.

There were constant references in sub-committee discussions to the British North America Act but it was soon clear that the problems facing the would-be federationists of India went far beyond those that had confronted the makers of the earlier federations of the United States, Canada and Australia. In India there were the Indian states – the so-called princely states – as well as British India. How were the British going to create a viable federation of these disparate elements on top of dealing with India's continued dependent nature within the empire/commonwealth? India had not yet achieved full self-government, let alone independence, and a federation to resolve internal sub-continent problems would still leave the central government stripped of many of the powers normally associated with the central government of an independent or self-governing state. There were to be parallel problems in Central Africa and the British West Indies after World War II, and there were no easy solutions. A federation *per se* did not necessarily resolve the tensions in the relationship between London and a colony or a group of colonies let alone resolve the problems between colonies. Any federation designed on the lines of those in the United States, Canada and Australia would have great difficulty functioning under these circumstances.

It is clear that the sub-committee members were well supplied with various memoranda dealing with India's economic and ethnic divisions but were given little on federal institutions. The only historical study on federations made available was by Arthur P. Newton, a much-respected historian of the British empire, entitled 'Federal and Unified Constitutions'. The committee did have access, however, to expert opinion in the university community and Lothian especially was able to take advantage of his contacts there. In December 1930, shortly after the federal idea had been broached as a solution to India's problems, Lothian received a perceptive memorandum entitled 'Federalism and Legalism' from Professor Herbert A. Smith, Professor of International Law at the University of London.[25]

Smith suggested that 'a federal solution of the Indian problem' had been thrust so suddenly into the foreground that the delegates to the Round Table Conference and the public had been taken by surprise. Both Montagu-Chelmsford and the Simon commission had only thought of it as a distant goal. They had fully realized the practical difficulties. Smith suggested that it 'does not seem to be generally realized that we have to choose between a federalism that rests upon understanding and a federalism that rests upon strict law'. Smith pointed out that to a large extent the British empire itself was 'federal in practice without being federal in law'. Legal federalism always involved the enactment of some form of words which purported to define the boundaries between local and central powers, but in the empire there was no legal limit upon imperial powers, and the powers of the dominion parliaments, insofar as their relation to Great Britain was concerned, were only defined in their constitutions by the vague words 'peace, order and good government'. If the empire had a formal federal constitution the British could, in law, overrule the dominions and dictate policy, but since the dominions were treated as equals this did not happen.

Smith argued that in a defined federal structure jurisdictions inevitably overlapped and therefore it was important to define the authority by which doubtful questions might be determined. In the United States, Canada and Australia it was the courts and the result was endless litigation. The difficulty in determining the precise limits of central and local powers became greater with the build up of case law. However, for Smith, complexity and litigation were not the worst of federal evils. He pointed out that 'the courts are compelled to assume responsibilities for which they are naturally unfitted. Issues which are in substance political are presented in legal form . . . the function of the judge becomes confused with that of the statesman'. Moreover, he argued, under 'a system of legal federalism experience shows that each party is perpetually trying to strain to the utmost its strict legal rights. Neither side will concede an inch of territory to the other.'

Smith suggested that the general effect of rigid constitutions was to reproduce in constitutional law one of the most serious defects of international law: they served to consecrate the right of obstruction by obstinate minorities. 'Real danger', therefore, 'lies in the fact that constitutional rigidity in a federal system may prevent the carrying out of necessary changes by peaceful and legal means. It screws down the safety value and thereby increases the risk of an explosion.'

Smith contended that India was formidably complex and diverse and not therefore easily adapted to a federal system. Also, existing federations were the result of long discussions and practice and the patient adjustment of conflicting interests. Smith reminded Lothian that probably 'only a very few have given any close personal study to the general question of federal government or its special application to Indian conditions'. He cautioned that a move towards strictly legal federalism for India would be a move in the wrong direction.

Smith's advice had strong Diceyan overtones but much of what he said was sound. Federation for a polity the size of the sub-continent with its vast diversity of ethnic, religious, caste and cultural groupings had never been tried before. Leaving aside the complicating factor of India's continued dependency within the empire/commonwealth, the internal complexities posed major problems for the federal theorists.

Smith's concerns were repeatedly echoed in the Commons and the Lords during the debates of the early thirties. Winston Churchill, who had earlier dallied with the federal idea as a solution to the 'Irish problem', spoke for many observers when he claimed a federation for India on the line of federations in the United States, Canada and Australia was impossible given the political, social, cultural, racial and religious conditions there. 'To apply the democratic institutions of Australia and Canada rigidly and pedantically to

India', he argued, 'would produce measureless tyranny and misery, ending in bloodshed and probably utter confusion.'[26]

While the sub-committee noted the arguments of Smith and Churchill, the members were not persuaded. Much of the discussion in the sub-committee was by and between the Indian delegates. Lothian, an acknowledged expert, intervened only occasionally in order to try and steer delegates onto the proper federal paths. By his suggestions he revealed what he thought should be done, but he did not push and the decisions taken were Indian. Lothian did, however, emphatically point out that the division of sovereignty was a fundamental principle of a federation and that it could not be transgressed. It was therefore essential, he said, to make a clear distinction between central and provincial powers for it would be impossible for a federal government to tell the province what to do in the areas of provincial jurisdiction.[27] Speaking in the Lords on 8 December 1931, Lothian argued that the only way that the problem of Hindu–Muslim relations could be solved and the only way the princes could be brought into an 'All India' solution was by dividing the powers of government between states and provinces on the one side and the federal authorities on the other, with each level respecting the other's jurisdiction. And, he continued, it was only by building into the structure of the constitution real guarantees for individual liberty and for minority rights that a constitution could be erected strong enough to be a security 'for internal order, for liberty and peace, as the British power is gradually withdrawn'.[28] In making this plea, Lothian knew he had the backing of the influential Nizam of Hyderabad who was convinced federation was the only way the rights and individuality of the princely states could be preserved vis-à-vis the provinces, each other and the centre.[29]

The sub-committee's findings and its recommendations had a major impact on the government's decision to accept the federal idea as a solution for India's problems. A considerable amount of the sub-committee's time and attention had been devoted to examining the financial relations between British India and the Indian states, and of both with the centre. Despite all the problems inherent in those relationships it is clear that federation was viewed as the way to resolve majority/minority problems as well as the problem of British India's relationship with the princely states, even though Professor Smith had advised otherwise.

As Sir Samuel Hoare, the minister responsible, pointed out to the House of Commons, the British had had to decide between a federation with a strong centre, such as Canada had originally had, and one with strong units as in the United States and especially in Australia. The British government had 'deliberately chosen' the second option. 'We have made that choice,' he explained,

for the very obvious reason that the great sub-continent of India . . . is much too big and much too diverse a unit to be managed by a highly centralized Federal Government. On that account, the basis of our proposals is that for the Federal Government there should be a definitely limited field of activity confined to the specified federal subjects, and the Federal Government should, of course, have sufficient revenue to meet its federal obligations, and that the provinces should be given the fullest field for autonomous development.[30]

The decision to create a federation with a weak central government and then to delay the full implementation of the federal structure until half the princely states had decided to join underlined the extraordinary difficulties involved in applying the federal idea to so complex a setting as India and gave the opponents of that idea ample opportunity for criticism. Viscount Wolmer, who, ironically, was the son of Lord Selborne, a committed feder-alist, summed up much of the concern when in December 1934, during the debate on the India bill, he referred to the 'insane experiment of Federation . . . this vast, complicated, unprecedented, extraordinary, Alice-in-Wonderland federation that is to come into being not now but at least five years hence in circumstances which may be totally different from what you can visualize at the present moment. Could anything as a matter of practical politics be sillier than that?'[31] Leo Amery, a passionate advocate of federa-tion for the United Kingdom only twenty years earlier, agreed with Wolmer. He argued,

> the Federation which is set up, if you make no change in the structure of the Centre, is a bad Federation because of the inherent weakness of the present system of government at the Centre. When you have, as you have at the Centre today, an irremovable executive face to face with an irre-sponsible legislature, the experience of the whole world, of every British Dominion and Colony, of our own past history, shows that you have created a system which involves endless friction.[32]

Amery also argued that if you set up the provinces with autonomy, dead-lock would result. Wolmer picked up on this point in April 1935, during the committee stage of the India bill. He argued,

> If you are going to have complete Provincial autonomy, then you will not get a federation that is a federation. It will simply be a collection of inde-pendent States, all of whom will be liable to pursue their independent and perhaps conflicting policies, with the result that one day you will get a breakdown. I think that the example of Australia shows us the dangers that apply to any Federation where the residual powers reside in the provinces rather than at the Centre.[33]

Wolmer did not think the Indian federation would stand the test of time. While others did not pursue Wolmer's philosophic point many speakers did address the contradictions in the bill, revealing as they did a knowledge of how a federal structure should work. Implicit in these comments was a firm understanding of federal principles but no one elaborated on those principles at any length.

In the debates in the House of Lords in the early thirties many of the same points were made. Viscount Brentford pointed out in December 1931 that in creating a federation in India the British would be dealing with one set of parties which were democratic and founded upon local parliaments and the other autocratic and not constituted the same way. 'Every other federation that I have known in the world', he said,

> has been formed from homogeneous States – States of the same race, with the same language, with the same thoughts, the same ideas, and the same legal administration. There has been a common basis on which they have built up a Federation. There is at present no common basis on which you can build up this Indian Federation. Then what are the safeguards? How is it possible that these safeguards, which are the negation of responsible government, can be dove-tailed in with the responsibility which the Indian politicians are asking for at our hands today?[34]

Lord Salisbury also had a sound criticism. He pointed out that the British were attempting to establish a constitution for a federation at the same time as working out the constitution of the units that would form the federation. That was unexampled in history and presented formidable difficulties, amounting almost to recklessness in those willing to undertake a federation without knowing the units that were going to federate. As far as he was concerned, the bill did not meet the profound communal difficulties in India. He pointed out that the princely states would be able to vote on matters affecting the provinces but not vice-versa.

Others such as Lord Lloyd continued to point to the endless litigation inherent in a federation. He was convinced that federation was no longer a good system: 'Times have changed since Federation was first the fashion. Today with the ever growing intricacy of the modern machinery of government, the undivided supremacy of one Legislature has become every day more imperative.'[35] Lord Phillimore wondered why the government insisted on federation. There had been no real reason given. He thought chaos could be resolved by other means. Federations did seem to work for the United States, Canada and Australia but they had been pioneering communities. 'Possibly,' he suggested, 'we ascribe to Federation something which is only due to the expansion of peoples in a semi-developed state. Possibly we have got it into our minds that because Federation coincided with the very rapid and very successful development of those countries, Federation is a kind of solution that you can apply in all circumstances, in all places and in all cases. It is beginning, in fact, to have the kind of virtue which is attached to a well-advertised quack medicine.' He doubted if federation would work in one of the oldest civilizations of the world. For him, federal constitutions were too rigid.[36]

When war broke out in 1939, the federal provisions of the Government of

India Act of 1935 had still not been implemented. The war ensured that the Act would never come into effect. The debate surrounding its genesis and ultimate passage through the British parliament had provided a fascinating insight into the perceptions of federalism that prevailed in the United Kingdom in the inter-war period. In many respects, the attitudes and assumptions differed little from those that had dominated discussions of 'federation' as a solution of imperial and Irish 'problems' at the turn of the century. The misgivings and prejudices of the prevailing authorities, Dicey and Freeman, were still very much in evidence. But it was also apparent that there was a much better grasp of federal principles among the participants than had usually been present in the earlier debates. The division of sovereignty was now generally accepted as the essence of the federal idea and was not automatically viewed as an impossible concept. What now bedevilled federal theorists and gave fuel to their critics was how to adapt the federal idea to a polity of such extraordinary internal diversity as India while remaining faithful to the shibboleths of responsible government. The task was compounded by the fact that India was not yet self-governing and that the United Kingdom government, let alone imperialist die-hards such as Churchill, was unwilling to relinquish power at the centre. Even if a credible federal solution had been found to the sub-continent's complexity, how would a federal state function fully at the centre if its powers were restricted by the continuing control of an imperial master?

Lothian did not have a ready answer to all these questions. All he could do was recommend a solution he was convinced had the only chance of long-term success. He advocated and defended the federal idea passionately in public and private in the 1930s. He was the Round Table movement's most consistent member in reminding all who would listen to him that the root of all constitutional advance in India must be adherence to the 'principle of the commonwealth' within a federal framework. There was a danger, of course, that Lothian had fallen victim to what Phillimore had described as a 'quack medicine': that federation was 'a kind of solution' that could be applied 'in all circumstances, in all places and in all cases'. Some commentators of the late 1930s thought that was exactly what had happened not only to Lothian but also to Lionel Curtis, since both men now saw in federalism a solution to the problems besetting the world.

Lothian had been concerned about the evils inherent in rampant national sovereignty since his days as editor of *The State* in South Africa and he had repeatedly returned to the question in the pages of the *Round Table* during World War I. Lothian and his Round Table colleagues had advocated the creation of an international system based on the rule of law in which the participants would work and deliberate together for the common good. Running through these arguments was the movement's commitment to the 'principle of the commonwealth'. Lothian and Curtis had done much to promote that ideal during the war and by 1920 they were convinced that the British commonwealth could serve as an exemplar of a new world order. At that time, both men believed a League of Nations would serve as a first step in the realization of international peace.

Curtis undertook to trace the manner and ways by which humanity had gradually learned to cooperate and form larger and larger stable polities. He was convinced that the essence of good citizenship lay in extending loyalty to others. For him, the mutual obligations of citizenship were found in purest form in the British parliamentary system enshrined in the commonwealth of nations. He elaborated these arguments and ideals in his three-volume *Civitas Dei*, published in the 1930s. While Lothian and Curtis had different daily preoccupations in the inter-war years, they always agreed about the primary importance of the 'principle of the commonwealth', and in his various articles and speeches Lothian continually referred to Curtis's publications to support his own contentions. Lothian's idealism was rooted in philosophic idealism as reflected in his Round Table activities, but since 1914 it had also been nourished and vitalized by his conversion to Christian Science. The nature and extent of his religious commitment pervaded his speeches and various publications in the 1920s and 1930s.

The state of the world in the inter-war years gave him much on which to ponder. The refusal of the United States to join the League of Nations was but the first indicator that national interests still prevailed over the common good. By the late thirties, the League was completely ineffectual and national sovereignty held sway wherever one looked. Since Lothian had always been critical of nationalism and national sovereignty it was not surprising in the aftermath of a war attributable to the perversions of sovereignty that he should argue that the world would always be at war or face the threat of war until national sovereignty was harnessed, preferably within a federal system. He spoke fervently, if repetitively, on this issue in 1922 and 1923 at Williamstown, Massachusetts, in the late 1920s in Germany and repeatedly throughout the 1930s, most notably during his Burge lecture in 1935. These speeches differed very little from each other. The same examples and the same phrases were often used. He pointed to the breakdown of the international system, particularly of the League of Nations, the hopelessness of relying on disarmament and cooperation to prevent war, and pointed to the eventual formation of a federation of mankind as the only solution. Increasingly, in these speeches Lothian referred to 'the principle of the commonwealth' as the guiding force. Only by the gradual but inexorable extension of self-government and of democracy within a federal framework could the world be assured of peace.[37]

Lothian's ideas were best summed up in an essay entitled 'The Ending of Armageddon' written early in the summer of 1939, shortly before he was appointed the British ambassador to Washington.[38] He pointed out that the primary cause of existing troubles was international anarchy, at the root of which was unbridled national sovereignty, and he contended that only by dealing with the basic cause would it be possible for the world to climb permanently out of its present distress. He believed that anarchy would not be ended by any system of cooperation between sovereign nations 'but only by the application of the principle of federal union . . . only by . . . pooling some part of national sovereignty in a common organism which represents, not the national units nor the governments, but the people of all the member nations as a whole'. Only by adopting a federal system would it be possible for each nation to set aside the idea that its own interests, rather than those of the world, should come first. Lothian reasoned that 'until there is an organism representative of all, which can limit armaments and economic nationalism and act for the benefit of all, every nation will remain bound to provide for its own security first, and that necessity compels it to put strategic and military considerations ahead of international justice and fair play'. For Lothian, 'national sovereignty is the root cause of the most crying evils of our time and of the steady march of humanity back to tragic disaster and barbarism. It is a denial of the brotherhood of man and of the principle that there ought to be one law or sovereignty, based on moral principle, uniting and governing the whole earth.'

In his view, the final remedy was 'a federal union of the peoples' so that while every nation was completely self-governing in its own internal affairs all the people would be united into a single 'commonwealth of men' for their common affairs which would comprise 'order and defence, the regulation of international trade and migration, citizenship, currency, and some forms of debt and taxation, inter-state communications, and the administration of the common assets and responsibilities of the federal union'. For Lothian this was the only way the pacifist ideal could be realized in practice; the only way in which the artificial dislocation of trade and employment by economic nationalism could be ended; the only way individual and national liberty could be made secure and war ended. All of this could not be achieved at once but a start could be made with nations sharing certain common values. Lothian suggested 'that the nucleus should consist of nations which accept the principle that government must be conducted with the consent of the governed, and who base their political life upon the freedom and responsibility of the individual. . . . Successful federalism must rest upon the acceptance of certain common principles, and free institutions seem to be the only basis for a federal community of nations.'

As for the particular form such a federation would take, Lothian admitted that was hard to foresee. He reminded his readers that while democracy had been developed in the Greek city states and the rule of law in the Roman empire, neither had survived without the principle of representation. That had developed in England, making possible the

> combination of the rule of law with the principle that government must be with the consent of the governed, which is the foundation of the Parliamentary system and made possible democracy on a national scale. The Americans confronted with the problem of uniting states which, in

separating from Great Britain, had already established their own sovereignty, discovered the federal principle whereby the powers and functions of government were divided between states and common-wealth. This discovery made possible the development of a system of federal union which combined complete state autonomy with democrati-cally controlled reign of law on a continental scale.

As Lothian saw it, the task now was to develop a 'world commonwealth patriotism' and to create the institutions which would give full play to both national differences while organically uniting all their inhabitants under 'a constitutional law which will end war, preserve liberty and make property secure'. After all, he argued, 'the essence of federal union is to unite the peoples under a government of laws and principle rather than of men'. The 'principle', of course, was 'the principle of the commonwealth' that Curtis and Kerr had long championed.

This was an eloquent plea for the abandonment of selfish sovereign nationalism, but Lothian's analysis was not unique. Many others were writing about sovereignty, analysing the causes of war and speaking on behalf of the peace movement.[39] What was different was Lothian's continued affirmation of 'the principle of the commonwealth', about which he had written extensively in the *Round Table* during the war, and his continued linking of that principle to federation. It was his bridge from a federation designed to consolidate British power and stabilize the interna-tional situation to an international federation of the democratic, mostly white, nations who would continue to assume trusteeship responsibilities in those colonies/territories/countries that had not yet 'matured' sufficiently to take on the responsibilities of democracy and self-government. When exam-ined closely, Lothian's international federation was suspiciously like a Western power bloc, but his ideas were suffused with 'principles' and reli-gious fervour and his shaky thinking was not closely analysed.

The power of Lothian's rhetoric was such that his ideas stimulated the British organization Federal Union, founded in 1938, and the Italian move-ment for European federation – an idea that Lothian, ironically, was not much attracted to – which flourished after 1945. The appeal was to those anxious to quell the fear and anxiety in and around them. A coming together of 'mankind' in a mutually cooperative super-state on federal lines was understandably and naturally attractive. Who could not be swayed by such an ideal? The problem, of course, as even Lothian realized, was that it was not even remotely possible in the short term. There was simply too much anger and bitterness, too much 'history', to overcome to make any such goal, even in a limited form, immediately realizable. Moreover, Lothian, and others who wrote as he did, Curtis among them, were never specific and were never anything but exhortative. Exhortation was, of course, important. Without ideals and goals and injections of emotional energy little of consequence would be accomplished. But neither Lothian nor Curtis ever analysed the federal idea nor explored its possible problems. They simply accepted the stark technical description of the federal state as created by the Americans in the 1780s as their goal. That is, an international federation where all member states would retain responsibility for their own affairs while pooling their sovereignty over defence, foreign affairs and relinquishing the necessary taxing powers in order to ensure that the federal, or central, government in the federation would have the means to fulfil its mandate. Beyond these broad postulates Kerr and Curtis did not venture.

In the inter-war years the federal idea was adopted as a possible resolution of India's complicated political, economic, cultural and religious problems. Lothian's contribution to those discussions was important, as was his and Curtis's continued promotion of a federal solution to the problems of world order. Their commitment to the federal idea resulted in a searching and constructive analysis and ensured that the British seriously considered it as a solution to pressing colonial and international problems while their sustained advocacy had a marked impact on a generation concerned with the stability of the world and the maintenance of peace.

6   Federal Union

Federal Union was an organization formed in the autumn of 1938 in the midst of European crisis by three young men, Derek Rawnsley, Charles Kimber and Patrick Ransome. Rawnsley and Kimber were the originators of an effort to prevent war by a reform of the League of Nations. They wanted to promote the creation of a European-wide organization with sufficient power to control the nation-states. In their estimation, national sovereignty had got out of hand and it would only be through some wider form of union that peace would be assured in the world. They called their embryonic organization Pax Union but when Patrick Ransome joined he persuaded them to change the name to Federal Union.

Rawnsley and Kimber had known virtually nothing of federalism, federal theory or federations until Ransome enlightened them. A former student of international law under Hersch Lauterpacht at Cambridge and a student of Harold Laski's at the London School of Economics, Ransome was well-versed in federalism and quickly persuaded Rawnsley and Kimber that they should adopt that political form as their major goal. Within a few weeks an initial pamphlet had been drafted, a statement of aims drawn up and an impressive band of backers and associates had been attracted to their ideal. A research department was established in late 1939 with the help of Sir William Beveridge, Master of University College, Oxford, and meetings were soon being held of various experts to discuss the economic, constitutional and colonial questions raised by a federal solution of the world's ills. This research department was reconstituted as the Federal Union Research Institute in March 1940 with Beveridge as director and Ransome as secretary. A series of federal tracts were prepared and eventually published.[1] Meanwhile, contributions were invited for a discussion of the principles of federalism and these appeared in early 1940 as *Federal Union: A Symposium*, edited by Melville Channing-Pearce.[2] Two annual reports of the research institute comprising the working memoranda and comments of the expert committees were circulated in August 1940 and August 1941.[3] Along with the *Federal Union News* and a number of individual contributions by its members this varied material represents the core of Federal Union thinking on the adaptation of the federal idea to the resolution of European and world problems as of the late 1930s and the early 1940s.

The organization had enormous popular success in the early months of the war and hundreds of local branches were formed with thousands of individual supporters. The appeal was primarily to the young and to those who had survived the horrors of the 'war to end all wars' convinced that the power of the nation-states must be curbed for the common good. As the war dragged into its third year, Federal Union lost many of its young supporters to the armed forces and most of its leadership to government service. From the summer of 1941 its efforts were minimal, but a residue of commitment survived the war and is still active in the Federal Trust and the Lothian Foundation of today.

Federal Union was born against a background of gathering tension and increasing aggression and the clear failure of the League of Nations to resolve the various crises confronting it. There was a general appreciation that the nation-state, certainly in its European form, was out of control and that the existing international apparatus designed to mute friction between states had proved ineffectual. Men like Lothian, Curtis, Bertrand Russell, H.G. Wells and Leonard Woolf had periodically called for a rethinking of the approach to the resolution of the world's problems. Lothian and others had claimed the primary cause of contemporary instability was national sovereignty. Something had to be done to control or curb or leash it. To Lothian and Curtis the obvious answer had been federation, preferably a transatlantic one involving the United States, but certainly one involving the democracies. It was not surprising, therefore, that when Rawnsley and Kimber initially sent out personal letters to some 500 individuals whom they had identified as interested or involved in international affairs that Lothian and Curtis should have been recipients, nor that they responded quickly.

Lothian and Curtis rapidly became two of the principal advisors and counsellors of the three young men whose concern and ideals appealed to them and reminded them of their younger selves in the earlier heady days of the 'kindergarten' and of the Round Table movement. In fact, Curtis wanted to have a relationship to Rawnsley, Kimber and Ransome similar to the one that Milner had had to the 'kindergarten' when it was founding the movement. Lothian and Curtis were to be very helpful to Federal Union in its early days but there soon developed a strong difference of opinion between the older and younger men. Lothian did write an initial pamphlet for Federal Union but he wanted the group to adopt the title 'Federal Union Now' in support of the American, Clarence Streit, whose book *Union Now: A Proposal for a Federal Union of the Democracies of the North Atlantic* had first been published in March 1939 and had quickly sold in the tens of thousands on both sides of the Atlantic.[4] The three founders of Federal Union had resisted because they believed that the organization should aim at a European federation in the first instance rather than a transatlantic one.

Curtis finally broke with Federal Union in 1941 in order to take up the cause of world-wide federation.[5]

Despite this rupture there was a considerable link between the ideas of the elder statesmen of the Round Table and the young federalists of the late 1930s and early 1940s. Both agreed that war could only be prevented if national sovereignty were curbed within the framework of a wider union. Both preferred a federal solution because it was the one political/constitutional arrangement that enabled two levels of sovereignty to coexist within a single form – one at the supranational level and the other at the national level. They also shared a commonality of opinion on the nature of the state and the mutual obligations of the citizens within the state. For them the state existed for the citizens, not the citizens for the state. Lothian and Curtis adhered deeply, of course, to the 'principle of the commonwealth' and both, although for slightly different reasons, believed federation was a commonwealth in constitutional form. Lothian had also had a deep abhorrence of the excesses of national sovereignty since the early years of the century and his experiences during the war, as one of Lloyd George's secretaries, and at the Paris Peace Conference, and in the years since, had simply confirmed him in his earlier convictions. Where they differed, however, was in their approaches. Rawnsley, Kimber and Ransome wanted a European-based federation while Lothian forever hankered after a transatlantic one. He found Streit's scheme compelling while the others did not. For his part, Curtis thought Federal Union should undertake a public campaign to raise awareness about the merits of federalism rather than espouse particular proposals which the expert committees were prone to do.

What strikes the reader very soon after starting to sort through the literature and the ideas generated by Federal Union is that in a few short months more probing attention was given to the federal idea and its implications for economic and political arrangements than at any previous time in British history. Under the threat of war and during the early years of World War II minds were highly concentrated on the federal solution in a way not achieved even at the height of the Anglo-Irish imbroglio or of Anglo-dominion tension. It was clear that while the general public might have only a passing awareness of federalism there were individuals in British society who not only had such knowledge but who had already begun to think and write about the federal idea. The Federal Union organization offered them an opportunity to explore the concept with other like-minded or, at least, open-minded individuals in an intense hot-house atmosphere, productive of imaginative thinking and probing analysis. Most admitted that world federation, even European federation, or a federation of democracies, was not imminent but they were agreed that the world had reached an impasse in its constitutional arrangements. The nation-state had at one time been a bold and stabilizing development in an age of competing groups, regions and monarchies. Now it was acting as those earlier smaller units had done with little thought for the larger whole and with paranoid aggression in every sphere. It was clear to them that the world must move on to a wider-ranging form of international unity. Cooperation seemed to have failed. The confederate underpinnings of the League of Nations system had proved as vulnerable as those of the United States in the early 1780s. What was necessary was a systematic analysis of the economic and constitutional implications of federal union. And since many of the potential members of a new federal order were imperial powers with colonial possessions it would be essential to explore how those colonies would be managed and what arrangements would be made to ensure their full economic and constitutional development. All these questions, and others, were tackled by Federal Union during its first two years – the heyday of its existence.

The first major publication to receive the support of Federal Union, although not considered by it to be an official statement of its views, was *The Case for Federal Union*, published as a Penguin Special in the autumn of 1939 and written by W.B. Curry, the headmaster of Dartington Hall School in Devon.[6] It was a cogent, eloquent, passionate cry for 'a sanely organized world order' free of the continuous preparation for mutual slaughter where liberty and diversity could be combined with effective government. Curry argued that the solution was federal union, beginning with the democracies but ultimately extending over the whole world.[7] While he had thought about the problems associated with rampant national sovereignty for many years, he had not been moved to write until he had read Clarence Streit's *Union Now*. Impressed by Streit's proposals and convinced that 'if the leading democracies could be persuaded to federate . . . they could become the nucleus of a democratic world order', Curry hurried to add his voice to those in Federal Union who were arguing 'that peace is not a matter of good intentions, but that it can only result from effective ordering of the common affairs of mankind'.[8]

Curry pointed out that war always wreaked a devastating toll and since science had recently drawn nations closer together, making of them a community, it was doubly imperative to achieve lasting peace through federal world government. Curry argued that the root cause of war lay with the rivalries and aggressive postures of nation-states and the consequent fostering of unthinking nationalism. Clearly, the power of the nation-state to wage war virtually at will had to be eliminated or, at least, controlled. This would mean the curbing of sovereignty for, as Curry put it, 'Whatever may have been its utility in the past, the sovereign State has now become an unmitigated nuisance, wasting our lives and frustrating our hopes. While it continues to exist and make its preposterous claims, mankind has no hope of a peaceful or even a tolerable existence.'[9] Nevertheless, Curry realized that any new world order had to be based on democratic principles that protected both the interests of the individual and those of the nation-state.

As an indispensable minimum, Curry argued, the national states would have to relinquish certain powers; they would have to, first, hand over to a world government the independent control of foreign policy; second, there would have to be a pooling of all armed forces; third, the economic relations between states would have to be governed by the world community; fourth, international finance would have to be brought under world control; fifth, the problem of colonies would have to be handed over to the world government, as would, sixth, the control of international communications; seventh, there would have to be international control of currency; eighth, the international migration of peoples would have to be placed under the control of a world government; and, ninth, the world community would have to ensure the free movement of information and ideas in order to create an informed and alert world citizenry.

What form should such a world government take? Curry quickly rejected the confederal League of Nations as too much constrained by the powers of the nation-state and he soon dismissed a world super-state because it would involve almost complete surrender of autonomy by the nation-states. To Curry, the only reasonable solution was a federal arrangement which at one and the same time would allow the 'world' government to have sovereignty in key supranational areas while ensuring the sovereignty of the individual nations in internal national affairs. Neither level of government would have the right to interfere with the functions or powers of the other. Moreover, each level of government would be directly elected by, and thus directly responsible to, the voters in each nation-state. A 'world' government under the federal model would therefore govern directly, as would a 'national' government. Thus under a federal system each citizen would have dual citizenship of her/his own state and of the world-wide federal union.

Curry pointed out that

A federal system is the logical application to the whole world of liberal democratic government, already discovered by mankind to be the only way of combining liberty with order. By assuming control over those matters that concern mankind as a whole, the federal government gains all the advantages of a world super-state. By retaining separate national governments, having authority in those matters of mainly local concern, we retain local diversity and maximize liberty. By making the individual a citizen with democratic rights both in his national state and in the federal area as a whole, we develop loyalties to the federal union which make it unlikely that serious conflict between a single state and the federal government will arise.

By defining, in terms of a constitution, the areas of government respectively under the control of national and federal government, we retain constitutional safeguards for the Rights of Man. By setting up a federal government, which acts directly upon individuals, and not upon nations, we make law enforcement possible without resort to anything resembling warfare. Because law enforcement is possible, because justice is secured in advance, because under this system State aggression becomes unthinkable, total disarmament, save for local police forces, becomes not an idle dream but the simple common-sense of the system we have set up. The union of free men for the preservation of their liberties and the fostering of their common purposes is the basis of democracy. Federal Union is the doctrine that enables us to apply throughout the world the only system of government which has hitherto proved either tolerable or durable.[10]

Curry recognized that world government was some way off and that considerable educational efforts would need to be made in order to effect so radical a shift from traditional ways of conducting international affairs. Nevertheless, he believed a start could be made, if not with the fifteen states suggested by Streit, then by another small grouping of European and/or transatlantic countries. The first step to that end might, he thought, be a convention analogous to that convened in Philadelphia in 1787.

Curry's book was a timely *cri de coeur* and it sold rapidly to thousands of people fearful of war and desperately anxious for any solution of the world's ills that would lead to permanent peace. Curry was clearly fully familiar with the essence of federalism and the crucial division of sovereignty as the heart of the system. His suggestions were therefore in keeping with a 'true federation' as opposed to devolutionary or home rule schemes but he did not engage in a full-scale analysis of the application of a federal system to the world's affairs nor did he explore the ramifications of such a system in the economic, social and religious realms. He did address some of the questions often asked, such as why not socialism rather than federalism? What of the USSR? And what of India and China? But his answers did not open up in any systematic fashion an analysis of federalism.

The first tract written for Federal Union was 'Peace by Federation' by Sir William Beveridge.[11] Unlike Curry, Beveridge was firmly of the opinion that 'the federal principle is not now, if it ever will be, applicable to world government'. Instead, he recommended a federation of the western European countries of Britain, France, Germany, Denmark, Holland, Belgium, Norway, Sweden, Finland, Switzerland and Eire plus the four self-governing dominions of Canada, Australia, New Zealand and South Africa. In the main, the area was limited and therefore manageable and the countries to a large extent shared a common culture, comparable standards of life, close economic relations and all but one, Germany, were democratic. Beveridge argued that Germany would have to be included in order to ensure peace, while the dominions should be included because 'Britain could not go into a European federation turning her back upon the British Commonwealth'. Anyway, the experience of the dominions in working democratic and federal systems would be invaluable. Beveridge, like others in Federal Union, wondered about India but concluded it could not be brought in because it would distort the federation if representation was to be based on population. Perhaps it would be possible for India to have a special relationship with both Britain and the federation. It was obvious from this that

Beveridge and his colleagues had still not come fully to grips with the imponderables inherent in Britain remaining a colonial power nor with the difficulties posed by states of varying size and political temper.

Beveridge was clear, however, that his federation should follow the American example in the division of powers. Named powers should be given to the federal government and everything neither transferred to the federal level nor reserved to the people by constitutional guarantees should be left to the national governments. Beveridge suggested the key federal powers should be defence, foreign policy, dependencies, currency, trade and migration. The federal legislature should have two houses, one based on population and chosen directly by the citizens and one with equal or nearly equal representation of the separate states. A federal executive should be responsible to the federal legislature and there should be a federal judiciary.

Beveridge pointed out that while federalism was unfamiliar in Britain, its problems had been the subject of intense study and practical experiment for generations elsewhere. Problems had proved capable of solution, as they arose, in existing federations and so, he suggested, would they in a wider setting. The new departure now was federation across long-established national boundaries. He, for one, was convinced that it was the only possible means of securing peace and world order. Responding to widespread criticism that such a scheme was utopian, Beveridge claimed it was based on harsh realities but he did admit that it could be seen as utopian because it implied a vision of the world different from the one they now lived in. Perhaps, he defiantly argued, it needed to be utopian because 'the choice is between Utopia and Hell'.

Beveridge's dramatic and defiant claim was made in response to a telling critique by J. Middleton Murry, 'Pre-conditions of Federal Union', published in early 1940 in a book of essays addressed to the adherents and critics of Federal Union.[12] Murry acknowledged that the difficulties in the way of achieving some form of international federal union were not insuperable but they were far more formidable than many enthusiastic advocates appreciated. The most troubling as far as he was concerned was the economic difficulty. Murry was convinced that the creation of a large free trade area would create acute distress, unleashing socially disruptive forces that would compound the development of 'the fantastic and macabre nationalism' that international federation was designed to ameliorate and overcome. Unless Federal Union recognized the absolute necessity of suspending free trade within the federated area and establishing central control of industrial production and distribution, it was bound to fail. Without the resolution of economic difficulties, 'the most extravagant and bellicose forms of exclusive nationalism' would result. Until Federal Union realistically investigated the problem and proposed an appropriate solution, it would be little more than 'the latest refuge for escapist idealism' offering not much more than 'a utopian scheme'.[13]

Similar criticisms were levelled at Federal Union from inside the civil service. Federal Union had drawn the attention of the British Foreign Office as a result of its advocacy of European federation. In particular, its involvement with a possible Anglo-French union in the early months of 1940 had aroused general comment in the Office. The eventual failure of the British overture to France in June 1940 could not be laid at the door of Federal Union but the impressions formed at that time underlined the difficulties the proponents of the federal idea were to face.[14]

A memorandum on Federal Union was prepared in the Foreign Office in April 1940.[15] It was factually accurate but caustically dismissive, suggesting that much of Federal Union writing suffered from 'inebriated optimism' and vagueness while the organization was overhung with

> an opaque miasma of belief in the perfectibility of man. This humanitarian enthusiasm is most regrettable, and it is aggravated by a tendency . . . evident in most of the English authors (chiefly Sir William Beveridge) to invest with the rubber stamp of God the purely political theories which they expound. . . . Sir William ends his pamphlet with the words 'The Choice is between Utopia and Hell'. . . . Most of the writers on Federal Union claim to be inspired, but they are all in fact merely distended with their own conceits. It is this which makes their works, for the most part, so infinitely tedious to read. And their empty conceit has a practical consequence. For the verdict of history has not been kind in the long run and sometimes even in the short run to those who believe, like Oxford Groupers, that they are divinely guided. Unless Federal Union can purge itself of this element it will not easily catch the popular imagination, nor having done so will it be able for long to put its theories into practice. It would be a pity if the purge did not take place, because the theory in itself has many attractions.

Writers such as Beveridge and Curry were easy targets and left themselves open to such patronizing criticism, but the cynical dismissal of their 'humanitarian enthusiasm' was in itself revealing of the blinkered national perspectives that Federal Union had to overcome. As Orme Sargent, the permanent under-secretary in the Office, had earlier remarked, the 'idea of the Federation of Europe can make its appeal to public sentiment so long as it appears only as a vague Eldorado about the details of which we need not bother our heads at present'. Even he recognized, however, that the application of the federal idea to a concrete case such as Anglo-French union would demand more detail and 'a considerable amount of education'.[16] One of his colleagues agreed and made a further telling point:

> Thinking in this field seems to be dominated by a desire to work out complex logical frameworks which have, perhaps, the merit of looking ship-shape and being – abstractly – workable. In no instance does a proposed organization for mankind appear to be based on a careful observation of what the peoples in question really feel about each other,

or of what their range of sentiments consist of. A marriage will not last merely in virtue of an initial ceremony and a system of laws governing the relationship. A real desire to maintain this relationship and a sufficiently compatible background and set of sentiments is a sine qua non for success. Exactly the same comments apply with even greater force to any arrangement for Union between countries.[17]

The criticisms levelled at Federal Union by Middleton Murry and certain officials in the Foreign Office were generally sound and certainly isolated the fervour and idealism that were such a marked dimension of its activities. Nevertheless, such criticisms did not provide a fair insight into the work of Federal Union. As Patrick Ransome pointed out, unless the proposal for federation across national boundaries was 'accompanied by a thorough and careful investigation of the many technical considerations which its adoption would involve' it would 'become yet another dream of the idealists, unacceptable because ill-considered, and dangerous because of its avoidance of reality'.[18] Accordingly, a research department was established at Oxford in late 1939 with Beveridge as director and Ransome as secretary.[19] Three research committees were then set up to examine the economic, constitutional and colonial aspects of an international federation. These committees were active into the early months of 1941 and their deliberations resulted in key problems being explored systematically for the first time in the United Kingdom. When their discussions were ended by the press of other commitments a draft constitution had been prepared and various informative and educational essays had been published.

One of Federal Union's first tasks was to define for itself and to clarify for a wider public exactly what was meant by federation. To that end, Edward Mousley prepared an essay entitled 'The Meaning of Federalism'.[20] For Mousley, federalism was the intermediary arrangement between confederate and unitary systems; its basic condition was 'willingness and readiness to unite'. Mousley pointed out that although federations had a written constitution, a clearly divided sovereignty and a superior court, giving them a certain 'fixity in the face of any change', it should not be assumed that federal union was a static constitutional form. Its internal features could be adapted to particular circumstances and the division of powers could be varied from situation to situation. The purpose of all federations regardless of particular differences was 'wider order and wider peace'; peace which depended on law and democratic government. Mousley countered suggestions that federalism was designed 'to unite artificially things which are naturally divided and naturally disunited'. On the contrary, federalism was designed 'naturally to unite what only artificially was divided and what surely was most unnaturally disunited'. He cited the United States constitution as a good example of the latter.

In sum, Mousley contended that a federation should be both a recognition of and an adaptation to diversity and should not have as its primary aim unification and centralization. His essay was a refreshing change from the Diceyan-driven analyses that had dominated discussion of federation through the late nineteenth century and the early decades of the twentieth. When Mousley's essay was read in conjunction with two others prepared under the auspices of Federal Union's research department, Duncan Wilson's 'The History of Federalism' and Ivor Jennings's 'Federal Constitutions', with its detailed look at their dominant features, the uninformed reader would have had an excellent introduction to both the federal idea and to federal practice. Equally, the essays provided clear benchmarks and much food for thought for those actively engaged in attempting to devise a world-wide, or even a regional, federation.[21]

As valuable as these essays were, it was left to Kenneth Wheare, an Australian-born constitutional expert based at Christ Church, Oxford, to outline in late 1939 what federal government was, and was not.[22] Wheare's essay was the best short description of federalism yet published in the United Kingdom. Cogent, discerning and widely informed it lacked the moral fire of the writings of Lothian, Curry and Beveridge but it ensured that anyone who read it could be in no doubt as to what federalism was. Wheare acknowledged immediately that federal government was not something about which people in Great Britain and Northern Ireland either had direct personal experience or much knowledge. It was likely they did not understand it when confronted with it and probably had no idea why such a system of government had been invented. The people in Great Britain and Northern Ireland were used to a form of government

> one of the leading characteristics of which is that one single legislature, the King-in-Parliament at Westminster, has authority to make laws for the whole of the United Kingdom on all matters whatsoever; and these laws duly made prevail over rules made by any other body in the Kingdom and are accepted by the courts as valid law and supreme law. The result is that people in this country may doubt whether acts of parliament are good laws, but they cannot doubt that they are good law. In a federation, it is otherwise. There it is possible to doubt not only whether the acts of some legislature in the federation are good laws but also whether they are good law, and it is possible for a court to declare acts which are almost universally recognized as good laws to be bad law and no law at all. This intentional obstruction, in a federation, of the will of the elected representatives of the people as expressed in acts of the legislature, appears to us to be a strange device. Why do people adopt such a form of government and why do they continue to put up with it?

Wheare pointed out that the people of Northern Ireland had some experience of what a federation was like in that they were subject to the legislation of two legislatures, that of Westminster and that of Stormont. But he was quick to add that while such a division of functions between legislatures was a characteristic of federal government that was not sufficient to constitute federalism. What existed vis-à-vis Northern Ireland was not federalism, it was devolution. The parliament at Stormont was subordinate to the Westminster parliament which could override or abolish the Stormont parliament at any time. Stormont held its powers at the pleasure of the United Kingdom parliament and derived its powers from that same parliament.

If devolution was not federalism, then what, asked Wheare, was federalism? In essence, he explained, 'in a federal system the functions of government are divided in such a way that the relationship between the legislature which has authority over the whole territory and those legislatures which have authority over parts of the territory is not the relationship of superior to subordinates as is the relation of the Parliament at Westminster to the Parliament at Stormont, but is the relationship of coordinate partners in the governmental process'. The allocation of powers between federal and state governments, once made, could not be altered by either level of government acting alone nor could either level of government interfere with the exercise of the other's powers. In sum, 'Federal government means . . . a division of functions between co-ordinate authorities, authorities which are in no way subordinate one to another either in the extent or in the exercise of their allotted functions.'

In considering why a federal system might be adopted, Wheare suggested devolution would serve the citizens well if they were happy simply 'to regulate local affairs locally as a general rule' and to leave a national parliament with a potential supremacy over all matters, national and local, throughout the country. Such a system was obviously thought appropriate for South Africa and it was the system in use in Northern Ireland. But where regions or states or provinces desired, for whatever reason, to have an absolute, guaranteed, exclusive control of certain matters then devolution would not do and federalism was more appropriate. 'Therefore,' said Wheare,

> it is only when a group of territorial communities are prepared to cooperate with each other for the regulation of certain matters but for those matters only, and when they are determined at the same time to remain separate and supreme, each in its own territory, for the regulation of other matters, that federal government is appropriate. Federalism provides for this desire for cooperation in some things coupled with a determination to be separate in others.

Of the key essential features of a federal government the first would be a written constitution which would clearly define the division of functions and bind all state and federal governments throughout the federation. From such a constitution 'all state and federal authorities derive their powers and any actions they perform contrary to it are invalid. It must be the supreme law of the land.' Secondly,

> if the division of powers is to be guaranteed and if the constitution

embodying the division is to be binding upon federal and state governments alike, it follows that the power of amending that part of the constitution which embodies the division of powers must not be conferred either upon the federal government acting alone or upon the state governments acting alone. It is preferable, though not essential to federalism, that the power should be exercised by the federal and state authorities acting in cooperation.

Thirdly, in a federation it was necessary to have a body – preferably a court – other than the federal and state governments to adjudicate jurisdictional disputes between the two levels of government. Finally, 'if the governmental authorities in a federation are to be really coordinate with each other in actual practice as well as in law, it is essential that there should be available to each of them, under its own unfettered control, financial resources sufficient for the performance of the functions assigned to it under the constitution'. Each level of government must be able to do its job and carry out the functions assigned it. If state governments found their resources inadequate and had to call on the federal government for subsidies then they would no longer be coordinate but, in fact, subordinate to it. 'Financial subordination', asserted Wheare, 'makes an end of federalism in fact, no matter how carefully the legal forms may be preserved.'

Wheare admitted his tone was dogmatic. It had been his aim to put forward an uncompromising position with respect to 'the delimited and coordinate division of governmental functions'. Nevertheless, he recognized that federal government would have to adapt to circumstance in order to ensure good government. It had to be remembered, above all, that federalism was not an end in itself. It was simply 'a means to providing a system of government in circumstances where people are prepared to give up only certain limited powers and wish to retain other limited powers, both sets of powers to be exercised by coordinate authorities'.

Wheare concluded his pamphlet by acknowledging that it had usually been hard to establish a federal government: 'The forces of separation and individualism which make federalism necessary make any super-state government at all almost impossible.' And when a federal government had come into existence it continued to exist only with difficulty. The operation of a federal system required great skill and tact and depended upon patience and 'an enormous capacity for compromise among the statesmen who work it'. As a result, 'swift and decisive government is impossible. Deep dividing issues must be avoided. Changes can come about only at the pace of the slowest. Federal government is conservative government. Federal government is above all legalist. It is created and regulated by a legal document; it is safe-guarded by a court of law.' 'Compromise, conservatism, and legalism': these, said Wheare, 'are at once the virtues and vices of federal government. It is wise to recall them when one proposes to set up a new federal government in the world . . . to recall that federalism is a form of government which is not always appropriate or always easy to work. It is fair to recall at the same time that federal government is at least government; it is order, not anarchy, it is peace, not war.'

Wheare's was a crisp, pointed introduction to the federal idea but he had not pulled his punches in outlining what would be required of both the exponents of federalism and the states that might consider joining in a federal government. What was of particular interest was that Wheare, like Mousley, Wilson and Jennings, had decidedly distanced himself from the negative and ultra-critical stance adopted toward federation by Dicey and Freeman. While not backing away from the essentially conservative and legalistic nature of a 'true federation', Wheare had underlined the adaptive capacity of federal government. The degree to which it was adopted would depend on those involved at the two levels of government. If the polity that had resulted from federation was considered worth maintaining despite occasional, or even persistent, problems then cooperation would be its underlying feature, ensuring a healthy and viable state. Wheare's clear-headed analysis was to become a benchmark in the history of federal thought. It laid the basis for his classic *Federal Government* published in 1946 which, in turn, was to be the primary guide for all those in London and overseas who grappled with the application of federalism to colonial problems in the 1950s and 1960s.

Wheare, along with Beveridge, Jennings and Curtis, took an active part in the deliberations of Federal Union's constitutional committee.[23] In conjunction with A.L. Goodhart, Professor of Jurisprudence at Oxford, he prepared a draft constitution for consideration at two conferences in November 1939. In light of those discussions a full-scale draft of a constitution for a 'Federation of Western Europe' was submitted to the committee's scrutiny in March 1940 by Ivor Jennings and was published later that year.[24] As Jennings pointed out in his introduction to the published version, '"Federation" is not a magic formula. It is nothing more than the name of a complicated system of government which nobody would wish to see established anywhere if he could think of a better.' There were 'vast difficulties' to be confronted in any such attempt but he and his colleagues recognized the desirability of replacing international anarchy by international government and 'ultimately' of replacing sovereign states by world order. Although he and many of his associates did not believe that such a dramatic shift in attitudes was possible in the immediate future, it was essential to explore the practical problems and see what would be involved and necessary for a federal resolution of the world's problems.[25]

The committee agreed that its deliberations should proceed on the assumption that the federation would be composed of democracies located primarily in western Europe but that provision should be made for the subsequent admission of the dominions. Jennings's final draft not only reflected the advice of the constitutional committee but also of the committee of economists, all of whose meetings he had attended.[26] The economists had generally agreed that the federal level of government should be responsible for defence, foreign policy and control of the dependencies, but as 'a further safeguard against war and as a means of raising the standard of living among all peoples and of removing insecurity' the federal government should also control trade, currency and migration.[27] Opinion had not been unanimous on these latter issues but all had finally accepted that the federal level of government should have the power necessary to carry out whatever policies were thought desirable for the preservation, prosperity and efficient functioning of the union. Therefore, in drawing up the articles of the constitution, it would be necessary to enumerate only the federal powers; the powers of the states would be residual. In effect, this meant that the west European federation would follow the United States pattern rather than the Canadian, although in his draft Jennings did recommend the adoption of the system of responsible government in line with the British tradition.[28]

The constitutional committee had gone over the draft constitution prepared by Wheare and Goodhart in some detail, exploring such issues as the number of houses in the legislature, their composition, the powers of each house, how deadlocks would be resolved, the role of the president and of the supreme court and the division of powers between the federal and state levels. The committee was well aware of the difficulties involved in federating sovereign states and made every effort to ensure that the sensitive issue of sovereignty was realistically addressed. Nevertheless, the utopian underpinnings of the exercise were clear because there was no alternative, given the task at hand, but to assume that nation-states would be willing, first, to join in a federation, thereby sacrificing a considerable degree of sovereignty, and, second, to compromise and cooperate once they became members of a federal state. Jennings, who was later to become a much sought after constitutional advisor and draftsman in such complex settings as Malaysia, Ceylon and Pakistan, faithfully reflected these concerns and the recommendations of the committee in his draft constitution. It was the first effort since Lionel Curtis's in World War I to prepare such a document, certainly by a group of knowledgeable Britons. It envisaged a Europe vastly different from the one in existence and was based on the assumption of a shared vision of the future of mankind. That the assumption was false and the vision but a chimera should not lead to a quick dismissal of Federal Union's efforts. The problems the three research committees confronted and explored could not be ignored if some form of closer cooperation across national boundaries was to emerge from the chaos of war. Better they should be addressed than ignored, and in taking the initiative Federal Union did concentrate the attention of experts on a number of difficult and contentious issues.

One of the issues of particular concern was the future of the dominions and the colonial dependencies. For example, should the dominions become members? Should India? And what of those colonies which unlike India were still thought to be far from self-governing status? Should they continue to be administered by the colonial power even after that power became a constituent member of a European federation or should the colonies become the responsibility of the new federal level of government? Parallel to concerns over admission and administrative control ran questions related to the economic future of colonies. Should an open door policy be involved or should a system of local tariffs be permitted? And finally, what of the inhabitants of the colonies? Should they be consulted or not? And if so, how and to what degree? These were serious questions with no clear-cut answers and, not surprisingly, Federal Union found many different opinions within its ranks. The speculation and discussion generated by pondering these and other more technical issues brought into sharper focus the complexities of international federation at a time when empires had not fully waned and a sense of trusteeship still vied with a desire to preserve the economic benefits accruing from colonies, to say nothing of the prestige associated with colonial possessions.

William Beveridge had made it clear that he believed the dominions should be included in a federation because the United Kingdom should not turn its back on them. He carried that argument into the discussions of the constitutional research committee where it was accepted that the dominions needed special consideration. While they obviously could not be coerced to join the federation they also could not be deprived of the military protection so long afforded them by the British. The committee suggested the dominions be offered favourable terms such as the right of secession, a right which would not be available to the European members of the federation. An alternative would be to allow the dominions to join a customs union as a step towards unqualified membership of the federation. Either way there was a strong feeling that the dominions should be involved.[29] The discussion was a revealing one and underscored much of the difficulty that the United Kingdom would face in any effort to maintain ties with its Commonwealth while drawing closer to Europe. The deliberations within Federal Union in the early 1940s foreshadowed the divided counsels surrounding entry into the European Economic Community some twenty years later.

India posed somewhat different problems. It was not yet fully self-governing, although presumably well on the way to that status, and it had a massive population. Its inclusion as a separate member would pose particular difficulties for both constitutional draftsmen and the day-to-day functioning of the federation. In fact, as Professor G.W. Keeton, the director of the New Commonwealth Institute, pointed out, if the federation were based on adult suffrage and racial equality then the federation would be completely different from one confined solely to white, west European states. Not to include India, however, might lead to the formation of an Asiatic federation which would simply perpetuate power politics and the threat of war. Keeton was emphatic that 'democracy, the rights of man, and social justice' had to be the pillars of world peace. Nevertheless, he was forced to conclude that India could not reasonably be included in a European federation. Even in a world union India and states such as China would have to be represented not on a population basis but in accordance with some more limited form of representation applicable to countries with large populations.[30]

The discussions surrounding India underscored the extraordinary complexity inherent in creating a federation. Even when nation-states were willing to surrender some of their powers to a central authority, the resulting federation might be inoperable because of the demographic size of one of its components. This factor had surfaced repeatedly early in the century during the debate over the adoption of the federal idea as a solution to United Kingdom difficulties, and it had always been an obvious impediment to a federation of the empire where the United Kingdom had a population so much larger than even the combined populations of its white self-governing colonies. The British were to run into this problem repeatedly in the 1950s and 1960s as they strived to establish a number of colonial federations. The discussions also revealed the degree to which paternalist and racist assumptions, often disguised as trusteeship, prevailed even amongst the more enlightened of colonial experts. It was clear that most participants in Federal Union conferences still believed that India would still need to be administered and guided and protected for some time to come and that full participation as an independent entity lay some time in the future. There were close parallels in the deliberations of the 1940s with those of fifty years earlier surrounding the place of India in a federation of the empire. If anything, Federal Union's analysis confirmed the problems inherent in creating a federation involving states of disparate size, in various stages of constitutional development and differing in ethnic, cultural and religious composition. Such a multiplicity of seemingly conflicting variables would confront the British constantly only fifteen years later as they sought to create stable political and economic polities in their rush to decolonize.

Federal Union also gave special attention to the place of the colonial dependencies in a federation of western Europe. Unlike India, the dependencies were not considered potential members of the federation because it was universally assumed by the discussants that the colonies would be dependent for some considerable time to come. The problem was which government should administer them, the new federal authority or the nation-state to which they 'belonged'? Moreover, what principles should undergird administrative practice and inform general policy? Should they be those of trusteeship and self-determination as enshrined in the League of Nations Mandates Commission or should each colonial power determine its own approach? These problems were, of course, important but they were peculiar to the stage at which colonial relationships had developed since World War I, and any recommendations reached in the early 1940s could be little more than fleeting reactions to a rapidly changing process in which the colonies more than the imperial powers increasingly forced the pace or proved unamenable to persuasion or coercion from the metropole.

One expert, Georg Schwarzenberger, a lecturer in international law at the University of London and secretary of the new Commonwealth Institute, pointed out that federation was 'essentially a democratic concept'. In his estimation, federation would be unthinkable without self-government and representation of the individuals who composed it. Nevertheless, he had to admit that 'quite apart from all egotistical interests of colonial powers, there are colonial territories which have not yet reached the stage in which they could join a federation on a basis of equality'. In these cases, it was obvious that the principle of trusteeship would have to be applied to the colonies of the imperial powers. He believed it would be in the best interests of the colonies if the member states were entrusted as mandatories by the federal government with the administration of their former colonies and mandates. This would mean the coherent, organic development of policy; an opportunity for the sharing of experience and cooperation among colonial powers; and the effective supervision of the trust by a federal colonial commission.[31]

The colonial research committee which met in January and May 1940 agreed in the main with Schwarzenberger's analysis. Professor Norman Bentwich, Lionel Curtis, William Beveridge, Lord Lugard, Lucy Mair, Arthur Creech Jones, W.M. Macmillan and Sir Drummond Shields were among its members and rarely could a more informed group have been assembled.[32] They focused on Article XVI of Ivor Jennings's draft constitution which dealt specifically with the 'Dependencies', and after extensive discussion, fuelled in part by two memoranda from the reigning colonial expert, Lord Lugard, the committee advised the establishment of a federal colonial commission. Its responsibilities would be to ensure 'the well-being and development' of all the people of the dependencies. There were differences among committee members on some points but all appeared to accept the underlying assumption that the role of empire would not end with a federal Europe, and while some clearly favoured a steady progress from trusteeship to the grant of self-government others urged that general references to ultimate self-government should be avoided in any constitution.[33]

The discussions on colonial issues were to prove more pertinent in the short term than those on purely European matters. While the latter would come to dominate political and constitutional discourse in the late twentieth century, the problem of colonies and their future advanced to the top of the political agenda more rapidly and abruptly than most observers expected. For much of the fifties and sixties, the issues of independence and federalism were, if not twinned, certainly entwined in the minds of those involved politically and academically with the affairs of the British empire and Commonwealth.

By the time the research committees concluded their work in June 1941 the initial impetus that had launched Federal Union was waning. Increasingly, the bevy of experts who had either joined the organization or been drawn into its deliberations were siphoned into war-related activities while the general membership was distracted by the day-to-day demands of the war. Federal Union survived the war, albeit in an attenuated form, and a core of dedicated federal unionists, through the medium of the Federal Trust, an educational organization, ensured that the federal idea continued to be given a steady if not high-profile airing. The initiative of the three young men, Rawnsley, Kimber and Ransome, in founding Federal Union in the late thirties had resulted in the most intensive analysis and coherent discussion of the federal idea and its complexities since it had first been seriously broached in the nineteenth century as a solution both to the problems besetting the empire and those bedevilling the efficient and fair functioning of the United Kingdom. The stimulus given to such individuals as Kenneth Wheare and Ivor Jennings was considerable and their ideas and advice were to be frequently sought and followed after 1945 by those in London and in the colonies who saw in the federal concept a means of facilitating decolonization.

7 Federalism and decolonization

Federalism had not been considered seriously by the British government as a solution to the 'Irish problem' or to the congestion of business in the Westminster parliament. It had never attracted mainstream politicians concerned with the maintenance of imperial unity. It had not received close philosophic attention by those studying the constitution. Its adherents, as with the Federal Union movement, had been essentially unknown or lesser known public figures. Few politicians of rank and/or influence had supported the federal idea in the United Kingdom since the late eighteenth century. Despite the initial enthusiasm for a 'federal' resolution of the problems besetting the international order in the late 1930s and early 1940s, it had quickly petered out as national cause by 1941. Nevertheless, it was not entirely surprising that after 1945 the British sought a federal solution to some of their most pressing colonial problems.

If the federal idea had ever had much encouragement in British political life it had been in the imperial setting. What was unpalatable for the metropolis was often considered eminently sound, even essential, for the colonial periphery. A federal solution for the problems besetting the Canadas had been explored in the 1830s and 1840s and had finally been adopted in the 1860s in the form of the British North America Act. This legislation had united Nova Scotia, New Brunswick, Quebec (Canada East) and Ontario (Canada West) in the Dominion of Canada which soon stretched from sea to sea with the addition of Manitoba (1870), British Columbia (1871) and Prince Edward Island (1873). This was the first 'true federation' in the British empire and the British North America Act and Canada's ongoing political fortunes had received much attention from both British and colonial politicians, especially those concerned about Irish home rule and the unification of the colonies in Australia and in South Africa. The colonies in the southern continent had, in fact, united in 1901 as the Commonwealth of Australia in a federation modelled on that of the United States rather than the more centralized Canadian version. The four South African colonies had united in the Union of South Africa in 1910 but not before much attention had been given to a federal rather than the ultimately adopted unitary system.

The federal idea, of course, had pervaded discussions of the Anglo-Irish relationship from the 1870s to the partition of Ireland in 1921. Although not formally adopted either in Ireland or in the United Kingdom, the federal idea had determined the nature of the Government of Ireland Act of 1920 and thus much of the Anglo-Irish and the Northern Ireland–Southern Ireland relationship thereafter. The federal idea was formally broached in 1930 as a solution to the incredibly complex cultural, religious, ethnic and regional problems of India, and after much discussion was adopted as the basis of the Government of India Act of 1935. Thus when the British began to give serious attention during the 1940s to the future of their colonial empire a federal solution to innumerable intractable problems seemed sensible and, above all, acceptable to the home authorities.

The British were not alone in turning to the federal idea as a possible solution to complex colonial or regional issues. In 1946 Brazil reaffirmed a commitment to federalism and in the same year Yugoslavia adopted a constitution modelled on the USSR's federal variant, while in 1949 the West German federation was established. Both the Dutch in Indonesia and the French in Indochina attempted in the mid-1940s, unsuccessfully as it turned out, to establish federal states in colonial territories, and by the late 1940s the discussion of a west European federation was already well advanced, owing in no small measure to the stimulus provided by the publications of Federal Union.[1]

Despite these parallel developments the problems the British faced in their colonial empire were unique. Many of their colonial possessions were small, both in terms of size and population, and were not considered to be viable either economically or politically on the international stage. In addition, many had mixed populations where either several ethnic groups resided in rough parity of numbers or where one group was clearly dominant in a society containing one or more smaller groupings. The plurality of societies such as Trinidad, Nigeria, British Guiana, Malaya, Southern Rhodesia and those in East Africa and Aden and the South Arabian Protectorate suggested that a unitary system of government would be inappropriate for them. This was especially so when it was remembered that by the end of the war 'the central purpose' of British colonial policy was 'to guide the colonial territories to responsible self-government within the Commonwealth in conditions that ensure to the people concerned both a fair standard of living and freedom from oppression from any quarter'.[2]

That commitment had been reiterated in 1948 by Arthur Creech Jones, the Secretary of State for the Colonies in Attlee's Labour government. Creech Jones had been an active participant in the deliberations of Federal Union's colonial committee, so he was fully conversant both with the difficulties confronting small colonial territories and with the proposed federal solution. In a memorandum on 'smaller colonial territories' prepared for his colleagues on the cabinet's Commonwealth Affairs Committee, Creech Jones had taken pains to emphasize that 'full independence can be achieved only if a territory is economically viable and capable of defending its own interests'. Many territories in South-east Asia, the Caribbean and East and Central Africa would have to be united, probably in some form of federation, in order to achieve full self-government.[3] As Attlee himself affirmed in January 1949, the British government 'should not encourage the natural separation of small colonial communities by an exclusive preoccupation with the constitutional objective of self-government within the Commonwealth. Our aim should not be to create a large number of small political entities, technically independent but, in reality, isolated and feeble; but to develop new principles and methods of association and integration.'[4]

The British government's continuing search for new principles and methods often led it back to an old but proven method, federation. This was so under both Labour and Conservative administrations. For example, in January 1957 Harold Macmillan, the new Conservative prime minister, asked the colonial policy committee to estimate the probable course of constitutional development in the colonies in the years ahead, taking account of economic, political and strategic considerations. Ian Watt, the secretary of the committee, agreed to do so but emphasized:

> It is also desirable, indeed essential, to take account of the fact that the very basis of the United Kingdom's Colonial aims and Colonial policies rest upon an obligation to the peoples of these territories to advance their welfare and prosperity in every way. Certainly there are territories where our strategic and financial interests are more obvious than in others, but in none of them can we afford to neglect our obligations to their peoples; and these obligations in turn must continue to govern, as in the past, the nature and pace of the constitutional changes in them.[5]

Watt was not alone in holding these views. His colleague P.R. Odgers, in preparing the draft report of the committee, asserted, 'In many territories it is only British authority and administration which enables peoples of different racial or tribal loyalties to live in peace with one another.' In his estimation, the United Kingdom bore 'some responsibility for encouraging, directly or indirectly, the immigration and settlement of non-indigenous peoples. The present responsibility is to persuade the races to tolerance and cooperation; this is a slow process.'[6]

By October 1957, the Colonial Office staff were reflecting on a memorandum entitled 'The Smaller Territories' prepared by Sir Hilary Blood, a former governor of the Gambia, Barbados and Mauritius and a widely recognized constitutional expert.[7] Blood recommended federation as a means of meeting Britain's responsibilities and obligations and of resolving the problems confronting many small, plurally diverse territories. He argued that in order to assume the burden of national sovereignty a country must have a certain size and a certain population and an adequate income, either actual or potential. It also must be sufficiently advanced politically to have thrown up leaders rather than demagogues and to be able to staff most of its own civil service on both the administrative and technical sides. It should also have developed 'a national sense' and so have solved its mixed society problems, and its free development should not be hindered by strategic considerations requiring responsibility for external and internal security to remain either with the United Kingdom or with another sovereign power of the Commonwealth.

Blood admitted there were no set rules and that each case would have to be considered individually. Nevertheless, many colonies would not satisfy the requisite criteria and would never, in his estimation, achieve national sovereignty on their own. However, some colonies were either so situated or grouped that they could very well achieve full self-government and thus eventual independence as a federation. He referred specifically to the proposed federation in the British Caribbean as an immediate example of what he meant, and pointed to the earlier federations in Canada and Australia and to the more recent Central African Federation as further proof of both successful and potentially viable nation-states. In looking at British interests in the Far East, he suggested that a federation of Malaya, Singapore, Brunei, North Borneo and Sarawak would be feasible. Certainly, he thought 'it would be wise to make it plain now that these territories cannot hope for anything more than internal self-government unless they are prepared in due course to join in a Federation'. Blood concluded his memorandum by recommending that 'the possibilities of federation, either as a new creation, or as an addition to an existing federal set-up, should be kept in mind wherever possible'. He pointed out that federation was 'a tried, and has been a successful, solution in a sufficiently large number of instances to put it well in the forefront of any planning in connection with the non-viable territories'.

Blood's memorandum was written near the end of the United Kingdom's experiment with federation as a solution to the perplexities and complexities involved in decolonization. It fairly summarized the various concerns that had dominated discussion in official circles, and few would have argued with his analysis of the dilemmas confronting smaller territories. What was not as clear from a reading of Blood's memorandum was the range of motives underlying British responses. Undoubtedly many British politicians and civil servants truly believed that the British government had an obligation to observe the principles of trusteeship through to the end of the decolonizing process – whenever that might be. But the federal idea was not turned to simply as a means of ameliorating past actions. It was often viewed as a way of ensuring continued economic and strategic stability. The British were interested in the creation of larger, more integrated markets for themselves and not simply for the colonial populations. Similarly, the British were anxious in the post-war world to ensure a minimum of military flashpoints. The consolidation and cooperation of small states within the framework of a larger federal structure would hopefully achieve that. There was also during those Cold War years a pervasive fear of the 'left', and the federation of Malaysia was clearly encouraged by the British as a way of offsetting the influence of Peking in an independent Singapore and the possible creation of a government of the 'left' in that strategically and economically important island colony. Underlying many of these considerations was post-war Britain's lack of money. This added an urgency to the decolonization process and prompted the British to hasten independence, and by the federal route if need be, so that it could concentrate its resources on more central domestic and foreign concerns.

The mixed motives of the British government in pursuit of the federal idea in the colonial setting should not surprise the student of empire. What is of particular interest is how the British proposed to use and adapt the federal idea to the particular problems posed by small and/or ethnically diverse territories. Only in the 1930s and in India had the British begun to confront the difficulties inherent in applying the federal idea to a complex polity, and only in the early 1940s as a consequence of the outbreak of World War II had they begun to familiarize themselves in a more systematic fashion with the central postulates of the federal idea and to consider how that system of government might be useful to them. As a result of those deliberations, the British now had a small body of home-grown literature on federalism to which they could turn and a small group of experts, among whom the two leading lights were Kenneth Wheare and Ivor Jennings, on whom they could call.

The experience of attempting to devise a federal government for India should have given the post-war advocates more pause than it did. Lord Hailey was one individual who by the early 1940s had sufficient experience of both India and Africa, and of federal and constitutional schemes, to comment shrewdly on the application of federalism to the dependent empire. In 1941 he was encouraging. On looking at the possibility of a federation of East Africa, of the two Rhodesias and Nyasaland, of the West Indies and of the West African colonies, Hailey suggested,

> the chief interest behind the promotion of these schemes had been the hope of securing greater efficiency and a more coordinated policy in the administration of matters of local concern. There has been a general agreement that union would help to secure these results. It is also clear that it would enable the Home Government to make a beginning of that process of devolution of executive authority which in Colonial conditions is an essential prelude to the extension of legislative powers. The arguments that have so far stood in the way are based in some cases on geographical and in some on political factors.[8]

Hailey pointed out that hitherto such factors had been decisive, but if such colonies were ever to have a sufficient presence in the world it might only be through uniting and that would supply 'a new reason for federation, and one which should be given full weight in the final decision of schemes of this nature'. By 1956 Hailey had had a few second thoughts. He acknowledged that 'there has throughout been manifested that spirit of adaptation and adjustment, that sense of practical rather than theoretic logic which is so marked a characteristic of the British people', but he now recognized that the mixed racial composition of some colonies was a major problem. 'It is certainly one of which the solution cannot be found by applying the strict logic of our own representative institutions.' Nevertheless, on balance, he preferred to see the attempt made rather than the British lapse into complacency.[9]

Hailey had touched on some of the difficulties in the way of federations but there were additional problems peculiar to an imperial relationship. For example, there would be a difficulty where none of the colonies was self-governing nor where responsible government existed. Such a place was Aden and South Arabia. Another problem would arise where one of the units was self-governing and the others were not, such as in Central Africa. There would also be difficulty where one or more potential members had responsible government but others were still fully dependent, such as in Malaysia. Yet another difficulty would emerge where partial responsible government existed but not full self-government, such as in the West Indies. Under these varied circumstances it was assumed that federation would be a prelude to full self-government or independence. But what would be the role of the British government in such a transitional relationship and what affect would the necessary involvement of that government in the affairs of the new 'colonial' federation have on the nature and operation of the federal constitution?

Some of these questions arose in discussions about a possible federation of the British West Indies. Federation was not an unknown constitutional form in the West Indies. A quasi-federal structure had existed in the Leeward Islands in the seventeenth century, purportedly giving one of its eighteenth-century citizens, Alexander Hamilton, a fruitful historical example of its possible adaptation to the mainland colonies. In the nineteenth century federal experiments of a limited nature had been either tried or suggested for at least the Leewards, and Gideon Murray, the Master of Elibank, had promoted a federal solution for West Indian difficulties from at least 1912. During the 1920s discussion in the Colonial Office and in the islands themselves was virtually continuous about a closer constitutional relationship, with federation the most favoured option. These deliberations quickly revealed that inter-island differences and angularities would pose major problems to the constitution makers. While such differences suggested that a federal structure might be the most appropriate way to achieve unity while protecting diversity, they also provided serious impediments to the establishment of a stable federation. The British West Indies was but the first of many examples where local peculiarities were so deeply entrenched that smooth constitution-making, of any kind, was virtually impossible.[10]

Edward Wood (later Lord Halifax and Viceroy of India), the Parliamentary Under-Secretary of State for the Colonies, had toured the West Indies in the early twenties in order to get a sense of the possibilities of federation. He admitted to the Commons it was 'a very attractive proposition'. But there were also problems.

> There is no doubt about the advantages of it. The advantages are not to be measured by pounds, shillings, and pence. It will redound to the greater influence of the West Indies in Imperial Councils and affect for good the level of administration and conditions of service in almost every direction. As to that there is general consensus of opinion, but there is considerable danger in some quarters of ignoring what I may call the more real and active lions that lurk in the path. . . . I believe it to be axiomatic that it is not wise to attempt to force a scheme on a reluctant community and still less in face of active opposition. I am at present driven to admit that public opinion in these Colonies is far too centrifugal to make West Indian Federation immediately practicable, and I am disposed to think, having given such thought and judgment to it as I can, that the grant of representative institutions is likely to be the most effective instrument by way of education toward broader policy, for this very simple reason. The real arguments for West Indian Federation are arguments principally known to Governments who realize how they are hampered and clogged and circumscribed by the narrow horizon of their operations.[11]

Both W.A. Ormsby-Gore, the Under-Secretary of State for the Colonies, and Gideon Murray agreed with Wood that anything that would bring cooperation between the heterogeneous islands and the sixteen or seventeen legislatures would be good. 'Ununited, and as single units, the West Indies could not hope to make any impression upon the Empire, or upon the world,' asserted Murray. He believed it 'absolutely necessary' if they were to take their proper place in the empire, certainly so far as commerce was concerned, for them 'to come together in regard to their common affairs to the greatest degree possible'.[12] Ormsby-Gore had to admit, however, that it was 'perfectly clear that the tentative proposals made by [Edward Wood] met with considerable local difficulties', and any progress in the direction of federation would have to be 'a plant of slow growth'.[13] These early soundings and conclusions were to echo down the years. The practical and economic reasons for union were to be made repeatedly but the 'real and active lions' lurking in the path were never to be fully overcome and in the end were to devour the federation that did emerge.

Whenever a union was suggested, it usually encompassed Trinidad, the Windwards and the Leewards in the East Caribbean, but the Colonial Office knew full well by the early 1930s that even in that more limited sphere Trinidad was reluctant to assume control over other colonies and the local populations were not ready for the abolition of their legislatures and treasuries. As for any more elaborate federal scheme, it was generally accepted that British Guiana, Barbados, Bermuda, Jamaica and the Bahamas would take no part. Observers were convinced federation would eventually have to come but acknowledged there was little point in attempting to force the issue. Although a commission visited the East Caribbean from November 1932 to February 1933 and recommended a union of at least the Windwards and the Leewards, the Colonial Office chose not to proceed and in 1938 the Moyne Commission, while finding the federal idea attractive, decided the time was not ripe. The British were clearly well aware of the various problems in the West Indies but before 1939 they were unwilling to ignore local opinion and force the pace.[14]

By the end of the war circumstances had changed considerably, and when Oliver Stanley, the Conservative Secretary of State for the Colonies, asked the British West Indies in March 1945 to consider the possibility of federation the response was encouraging. While the islanders had recognized the problems inherent in insularity, the communication difficulties and the costs involved in surmounting them, as well as the differences in speech, ethnicity and economic development, in the end the consensus supported further discussion of the federal idea and pursuit of that goal. Most West Indians who reflected on the matter in 1945 wanted to achieve dominion status as quickly as possible so that they could take their place in the world at large. Many believed federation would allow them to achieve that goal more rapidly than if they waited for each colony to obtain self-government. Others preferred to acquire self-government and then federate, as had been the pattern in Canada and Australia.[15] The mid-to-late 1940s marked the highpoint of federal commitment in the West Indies. As the larger islands separately moved closer to full self-government in the 1950s the attachment to the federal idea waned, and by the time the agreement to federate was signed in February 1956 the future of the British West Indies federation was already problematic.

Despite the decline in enthusiasm over the decade, the colonial and treasury civil service in London worked diligently from 1947 to 1956 to ensure that the federal arrangement in the West Indies was properly grounded. It is clear from the files that the London officials were acutely conscious of the great disparity between the individual colonies in constitutional development, in natural wealth and in probable revenue. Nevertheless, they doubted that such small isolated units could achieve and maintain either economic self-sufficiency or self-government on their own. The officials therefore strived to find within the parameters of the federal formula a means by which unity could be achieved and diversity respected. Throughout the internal discussions and deliberations the staff, particularly in the Colonial Office, was constantly aware that the islanders and not London were dictating both the pace and the direction. If the islanders preferred a decentralized federation on the Australian model then so be it. For London to insist on the more centralized Canadian variant would simply feed the suspicions and fears in each island not only of London's supposedly hidden agenda but of their fate in a federal structure.

Concentrated consideration of the application of the federal idea to the British West Indies began in February 1947 when Arthur Creech Jones, the colonial secretary in the Labour government, sent out a memorandum to the islands entitled 'Closer Association of the British West Indian Colonies'.[16] It reflected both how much thought the British had been giving to constitutional arrangements in the West Indies and how firm their grasp now was of federal principles in the aftermath of the debates in the 1930s over Indian federation and the publication in 1946 of Kenneth Wheare's *Federal Government*. The memorandum first canvassed non-federal alternatives, but each was found lacking. A unitary system would mean the loss of existing island legislatures and that was clearly unacceptable; governor's councils would mean unrepresentative government; while a West Indian Council would have no executive authority. That left a federal system which was carefully explained:

> The federal principle can briefly be stated as the division of powers between distinct but coordinate governments, a single central government on the one hand, and a number of local governments, on the other. The legislature of each of these governments has its own sphere of legislative authority. The fundamental problem in drafting a federal constitution is thus the division of powers, and in existing federations the problem has been resolved in a number of ways. In the United States of America, for example, certain powers are specifically assigned to the Federal Government and all other powers inhere in the State Governments. In Australia, the same arrangement obtains except that some powers are assigned for concurrent exercise by both Commonwealth and State Governments, although in the event of an inconsistency the law of the Commonwealth has overriding force. In Canada, on the other hand, there is one list of powers specially assigned to the Provincial Governments, while any residual powers (that is, not only all existing powers not otherwise assigned but also any new powers which it may become necessary for Government to assume) inhere in the Dominion Government, although for the sake of clarity, certain of the Dominion Government's powers are also specifically listed. In India, under the Government of India Act of 1935, specification is carried still further, and Federal, provincial and concurrent powers are all separately listed, the disposal of residual powers being left to the discretion of the Governor-General. Thus the division of powers need not be such that each is exclusive either to the federal government or to the local governments; but if there is a concurrent legislative sphere, it clearly seems necessary specifically to provide that, in the event of inconsistency, the federal law shall prevail. It is also vitally important that it should be known whether any residual powers inhere in the federal government or in the local governments.

It is clear that the British were at pains to assure the islanders that their specific local concerns could still be protected in a federal union and that much could be gained by the transfer of powers to a federal centre. The Colonial Office and Treasury staff were aware of the problems associated with an inappropriate division of revenues from customs and income tax. They believed that if federal government was to work in the West Indies it would have to have a strong centre with a consequent sacrifice of powers by the individual colonies. The officials had no difficulty with the divisibility of sovereignty; it was more the distribution of powers that concerned them. An earlier version of Creech Jones's memorandum had been quite explicit on the matter, but the relevant passage had been removed from the final version for fear it would unduly antagonize. The Office had stated a preference for the Canadian rather the Australian federal model because 'the Canadian system is closer than the Australian to the unitary integration which, in West Indian conditions, seems likely to make for the maximum efficiency and economy in the conduct of internal government'. It was thought likely 'that any shift of emphasis in a federal state is likely to be away from the Australian and towards the Canadian model, so that the nearer to the Canadian model a West Indian federation could approach, the more could it claim to achieve not only constitutional advance within its own limits but political progress in the wider framework of world history'.[17]

The West Indian section of the Colonial Office staff and the legal draftsman J.C. McPetrie undertook intense preparations for the September 1947 conference at Montego Bay. In March a small working committee was established to prepare papers on such key issues as the structure and powers of a federal government, the functions of a federal government in developing the area, and the constitutional advances, such as the adoption of universal suffrage, that would accompany any federal plan.[18] McPetrie was asked to prepare the brief on the structure and powers of a West Indian federal government 'on the basis that, although the West Indies could have the Canadian system if they wanted it, it was unlikely that they would be prepared to go beyond the Australian model'. The brief should therefore take the form of 'an outline' of what the Canadian system would involve if applied to the West Indies followed by 'a fuller statement' of what the Australian system would involve. The staff agreed the main questions to be explored were, first, the division of powers between the local and central governments and, second, the structure of the central government.[19]

McPetrie's draft was reviewed by the working committee on 3 and 17 June and the final version was ready by early July. McPetrie's draft clearly reflected the difficulties inherent in unifying in federal form colonies of varying sizes and constitutional maturity. Although an expert draftsman, McPetrie had to accept the more general conclusion that under such circumstances a more decentralized federal system might have the best chance of success and that a continued British role would be necessary to ensure a fair and functional government. Even at this early stage in the constitutional preparations, the civil servants must have recognized that the prospects for a successful West Indies federation were tenuous. What is especially obvious from the 1947 Office deliberations was that the British government was unwilling to intercede and control the form of the federal structure. They were aware of the antipathy that would be generated by any such action. It would strike the West Indians as yet another example of metropolitan imperiousness. As far as one can judge from the minutes and memoranda in Office files, the civil service seem to have genuinely believed the liberal shibboleths they espoused. It was not, in their view, appropriate for the British government to tell the West Indians what to do. The islanders would have to decide. The inevitable tension between patronizing efficiency and liberal open-mindedness so succinctly identified as the 'dilemmas of trusteeship' was much in evidence throughout the constitutional process.

In his draft, McPetrie openly conceded that

> the most satisfactory method in the case of the West Indian Federation would be to follow the Australian model and draw up a *Federal Legislative List* of subjects which shall be within the legislative powers of the Federal Legislature leaving all subjects which are not included in the Federal List within the legislative powers of the Member Governments. The alternative would be to draw up a *Colonial Legislative List* of subjects which shall be within the (exclusive) legislative powers of each Member Government leaving all subjects which are not included in the Colonial Legislative List within the legislative powers of the Federal Government as is done in Canada. . . . It is thought that in the West Indies where there are various colonial governments at different stages of constitutional development it would be easier to draw up, and agree upon, a satisfactory Federal Legislative list than it would be to produce a uniform and workable Colonial Legislative List.

This was a revealing comment for it indicated that the proposed decentralized federation was directly linked to the nature of past colonial relationships.

There were other parallel anomalies. McPetrie recognized that the smaller colonies would be vulnerable to adverse federal legislation and wondered whether there should be a special provision in the constitution in the event the federal legislature passed a bill adversely affecting a colony or a group of colonies. He suggested the governor-general should have the power to reserve such a bill. Similarly, the composition of the executive council and the proposed single chamber legislature posed problems given the different franchises and constitutional status of the various colonies. McPetrie suggested that the executive council should be composed of six non-officials and three officials while the legislature should have twenty elected members and three officials, the chief secretary, the attorney-general and the financial secretary.[20] It was unlikely that such an attenuated structure would appeal to the West Indians but its devising underlined the contradictions inherent in the whole federal exercise in the islands.

The Montego Bay Conference endorsed the goal of federation and a

Standing Closer Association Committee was established to explore both the nature and implications of a federal system in the West Indies. It reported in 1950, its recommendations were discussed throughout the British Caribbean in the early fifties and a modified version was approved in 1953. Unfortunately, by that time some of the ominous signs at the Montego Bay meeting had become formidable realities. The West Indians had pushed the suggestions of the Colonial Office for a federation modelled on the Australian variant one step further by leaving the main tax-gathering powers with the individual colonies and leaving the federal centre with little more than a distributive function. This was quite unlike the Australian example where the primary taxing powers lay at the centre. Even more alarming for the long-term fortunes of the federation had been the acceptance at Montego Bay of the separate development of the islands toward full self-government regardless of what happened on the federal front. During the 1950s the larger islands pursued the goal of independence with avidity and in doing so became increasingly detached from common goals and more preoccupied with insular advantages. The British civil servants should not have been surprised at these developments and clearly many were not. Nevertheless, they did all they could to facilitate the marriage of convenience and to make sure it was fully nurtured.

Both the Colonial Office and the Treasury worked closely together in the years following the Montego Bay Conference to ensure that appropriate constitutional and financial advice was offered. It was not unusual for representatives of each government department to meet to discuss specific issues. That is not to say there were not problems between the two, primarily because the Treasury came at everything from a purely financial perspective and often ignored the political realities that the Colonial Office had to contend with. The Treasury took the view that political independence without economic independence was unrealistic, but as the Office well knew the primary moving force for a federation in the British West Indies was political and the financial arrangements simply had to be fitted into that framework. This left much of the initiative and the control of pace and direction in the often wilful hands of the larger islands of Trinidad and Jamaica and subject to the strong personalities of their leaders.

Moreover, as late as January 1952 the feeling in the Colonial Office was that there was still very little interest in federation in the British West Indies, or understanding of its implications, outside a limited circle of politicians and civil servants. In fact, opposition on various grounds was strong in many of the colonies. Therefore, the officials involved concluded, 'any approach to the institution of federal government must be gradual at best'. The expectation was that not much could be expected before 1956. A great deal of detailed work needed to be done, and, as Jamaica's interest seemingly grew, that of others waned.[21] On the eve of the April 1953 conference in London to discuss the Standing Closer Association Committee report, the Treasury thought the prospects for a successful federation 'very unpromising'.[22]

The officials in the Treasury and the Colonial Office gave very close attention in the 1950s to the details of the proposed federation, and the files reveal not only the extensive cooperation between them but also the attitudes and tactics that were consciously pursued. For example, in March 1953 the Treasury argued that

> it is clearly important that HMG should not allow themselves to be involved in bargaining. There is already a widespread belief in the West Indies that the United Kingdom has an undisclosed vested interest in federation, for the sake of which it would be prepared to pay handsomely if pressed. It is essential that this illusion should be dispelled . . . and that HMG should therefore maintain from the outset that the extent and form of future financial assistance to the federal area must be decided on the merits of the case (bearing in mind the importance which is attached both in the West Indies and by HMG to the Federation becoming a strong and self-sufficient economic unit).[23]

A further Treasury memorandum added, 'In theory, we [i.e. the Treasury] agree with the Colonial Office that some form of federation is the logical answer in the West Indies. But the Colonial Office are not prepared to try and force it on them against their will, nor to offer them disproportionate inducements to enter into it.'[24]

Despite the general problems besetting the realization of a healthy federation and the increasing pressure from individual islands for a quick advance to full self-government, the Colonial Office remained convinced virtually to the end of the process of detailed negotiation that

> the sheer force of circumstances of the modern world makes independence on a unit basis a mirage. Independence or self-government as a Federation is however a practical possibility. . . . We do not claim that Federation will immediately and automatically solve economic and fiscal problems of the region, or that it cannot fail. We do claim that it will put in the hands of men responsible to the region as a whole, powers and opportunities, particularly in respect to the place of the region in world trade, which do not exist at present. Federation as such will not solve our problems, but will provide the conditions in which they can be dealt with. . . . We may place on record our considered and emphatic view that Federation, and only Federation, affords a reasonable prospect of achieving economic stability and through it that political independence which is our constant object.

As of 1955, the Colonial Office staff believed 'the major problems remaining to be dealt with are primarily administrative and financial, arising from the distances between the units of the proposed Federation and their comparative poverty'.[25]

The British Caribbean Federation bill was debated in the House of Commons on 29 June 1956.[26] There was a minimum of debate and no probing questions. The bill had uniform support and passed second reading easily. There was no committee debate and none on third reading.[27] The federation was on the Australian pattern with residual powers resting in the unit governments. The powers and resources of the federal government were weak compared with those of other federal governments, particularly in the economic and financial fields. Its budget had virtually a fixed ceiling of some £2 million a year. Centrifugal tendencies were rife and the relations between Jamaica and the rest of the federation were poor. In 1959 the Secretary of State for the Colonies admitted that the United Kingdom could do little but continue to give sympathetic support to the federal government.[28] Not surprisingly, the Federation barely lasted four years. It was formally dissolved on 31 May 1962 and was quickly followed by the independence of Jamaica and Trinidad.

The British had been well aware of the weaknesses in any proposed federation of their colonies in the West Indies, but they had persisted because, first, they were convinced none of the islands, except perhaps Jamaica, could survive alone on the world's stage; second, they believed a federation would provide economic and strategic stability in the region; and, third, they hoped federation would hasten the decolonization process and free the United Kingdom government from a politically inconvenient and financially draining burden. Once again the federal idea had been resorted to as a means to an end, and a blind eye had been all too readily turned to the fact that the federation the British devised catered to the insularity of the islands rather than obliging them to view their affairs in wider perspective. On the other hand, the British had had little alternative. Any effort to force a more centralized version of federalism would clearly have failed, especially since the British also held out the carrot of island independence parallel with the federal option.

During the years they had been nurturing the federal idea in the West Indies, the British had also supported it as a solution to problems they faced in Central Africa, Aden and the South Arabian Protectorate, Malaysia and Nigeria.[29] These areas all posed slightly different problems given their size, constitutional standing, economic viability and strategic significance. None, however, offered quite the mix of problems associated with joining Southern Rhodesia, Northern Rhodesia and Nyasaland into a Central African Federation. There were parallels to the West Indian experience but also significant differences. In the first place, the colonies were contiguous and not separated by vast distances as in the West Indies; second, one of them, Southern Rhodesia, was self-governing and white settlers dominated the political arena; third, the Colonial Office believed it had a special responsibility to protect African interests and therefore felt obliged to ensure that the involvement of Northern Rhodesia and, particularly, of Nyasaland was conditional on that protection being honoured; and fourth, there was a decided lack of support for the federal idea in the African population. African leaders believed such a scheme would perpetuate the dominance of the white settlers and extend the authority of the Southern Rhodesian whites into both Northern Rhodesia and Nyasaland. The Central African Federation was achieved in the face of extensive African opposition and disintegrated for the same reason.

The Bledisloe Royal Commission, appointed in 1938 to examine the possibilities of cooperation in Central Africa, concluded in its 1939 report that any attempt to federate the three governments of Southern Rhodesia, Northern Rhodesia and Nyasaland which 'enjoyed such different measures of responsibility and were in such different stages of social and political development' was unlikely to succeed. In the commission's view, 'the wide disparity between the three territories constituted a fundamental objection to any scheme of federation'. The commission recommended as an immediate measure that 'an inter-Territorial council should be set up with the functions of, first, examining the existing Government services of the three Territories and bringing about the greatest possible measure of coordination in these three services; and, second, surveying the economic needs of the whole area, agriculture, industry and commerce, and framing plans for future development in the light of that survey'. The United Kingdom government accepted the recommendations of the commission and immediately after the war a Central African Council was established by the governments of the three territories with instructions to coordinate policy and action in all matters of common interest.[30]

By late 1948 the British were having second thoughts and Arthur Creech Jones admitted to Roy Welensky, the leader of the unofficials in Northern Rhodesia, that the Labour government had 'come to regard federation as the possible political destiny of the Central African Territories'.[31] The change of heart was prompted by a variety of factors and, certainly, the economic argument was a powerful one in many circles, particularly in Southern Rhodesia. Nevertheless, the primary concern appears to have been a combination of the political and the strategic. The victory of the Afrikaner Nationalists in the 1948 South African election prompted the fear of undue South African influence in Central African affairs and led the British to promote amalgamation of their three Central African possessions. A federal rather than a unitary system was favoured because it would allow the component units to control African affairs, thus meeting a major concern of the African populations in Northern Rhodesia and Nyasaland. Moreover, a loose federal structure would more readily permit the maintenance of a direct link between the Colonial Office and the two northern colonies. When Kenneth Wheare was asked his opinion in 1949, he was not fully convinced by these arguments, foreseeing 'difficulties in creating a federation out of territories at such different levels of constitutional development as Nyasaland at one end and Southern Rhodesia at the other'.[32]

By the spring of 1950 Southern Rhodesia was so dissatisfied with the Central African Council that it decided to withdraw from it in 1951. Sir Godfrey Huggins, the prime minister of Southern Rhodesia, made it clear to the Colonial Office staff that he thought federation an impracticable alternative. There was neither enough money nor suitable people to staff and run separate state legislatures plus a federal legislature. As for the Africans, he thought 'it would be difficult to arrange for African representation in a lower chamber . . . although there were some intelligent and civilized Africans, and a certain number of literate Africans, the great majority were still savages'. This and similar comments prompted Sir Andrew Cohen of the Office to remind Huggins that development in Central Africa 'should be not only for Europeans, and not only for Africans, but should seek to provide for both'.[33] The context was thus set for the deliberations of the next three years.

The first crucial conference was held in London in March 1951 and the British were determined to be well prepared. The Colonial Office was particularly

> anxious to have associated with the work of the conference a recognized authority on the constitutional questions which arise in working out a degree of partnership between two or more Governments. What we want is not so much an expert in the drafting of a federal constitution as an authority who could keep us from going off the rails and could advise us on the ways and means of providing machinery for a partnership of Governments.

Such experts were not easy to find but they immediately thought of Kenneth Wheare, the leading authority on federal government, who had already been a constitutional advisor to the National Convention of Newfoundland in 1946–7. Wheare was approached and offered seventy-five guineas to act as advisor. He agreed in February 1952 and was immediately sent a copy of the 1939 Bledisloe Report and arrangements were made for a preliminary meeting.[34] Wheare's role would be to 'advise on the theory and practice of constitution making, point out omissions or inconsistencies in any drafts, and if necessary, answer with obvious impartiality any points on which the Central African Governments might have suspicions of ulterior motives if the reply was given by a United Kingdom delegate'.[35]

It was also agreed that

> there should be circulated, for information, to the Governments concerned a factual note, which would give a brief outline of various organizations which involved some form of merger, or loss of sovereignty, explaining in each case: (a) the constitution of the organization; and (b) how the organization operates in practice. The summary might, for example, include particulars of the Council of Europe, the Schumann Plan, O.E.E.C., and the East African High Commission. The covering

note could refer to the difficulties which had been encountered in the working of the Central African Council.[36]

In mid-February 1951 the Central African department in the Colonial Office circulated a position paper.[37] It was surprisingly cautious in its estimation of the application of the federal idea to Central Africa, although shrewd in its appraisal of African and British opinion. The author argued that it would be desirable for the United Kingdom delegation to be clear when it went into the conference 'which of the various possibilities could be regarded as practicable both from the point of view of acceptability to parliament in this country and to public opinion here and in Central Africa. We might also be ready to bring forward concrete proposals when the right moment in the Conference arrives. We certainly do not want to do so at the beginning.' Of the four possible methods by which some form of closer association between the Central African territories might be attained, the first was by the complete amalgamation of either the three territories or the two Rhodesias. The United Kingdom delegation would have to oppose such a scheme as unacceptable to either parliament or to Africans in Northern Rhodesia and Nyasaland. The same was true for the second proposal, 'the excision of one part of N.R. and its absorption into Southern Rhodesia, leaving the rest of Northern Rhodesia as a Protectorate or two Protectorates with a High Commissioner'. This solution would condemn those territories to permanent economic dependence on Southern Rhodesia which would be unacceptable to the Africans. The third solution likely to be put forward was that of full federation on the Australian or United States pattern. The writer argued,

> it will clearly be bad tactics in the conference to reject this out of hand, but in our view it will in the end have to be rejected. The three territories concerned differ so much in their stage of constitutional development that they could not enter such a federal union as equal partners; nor is it considered that they are as yet sufficiently far advanced economically or have a large enough population to support the elaborate paraphernalia of government that such a federation would involve. Politically, there would, it is believed, be almost as strong objections among Africans in Northern Rhodesia and Nyasaland to federation, with the territorial governments reduced to provincial governments, as there would be to amalgamation.

The fourth solution was some form of 'functional confederation' based on the joint administration of certain common services. This was the only solution possibly acceptable to parliamentary and African opinion. In many respects this was a perceptive document, certainly insofar as it assessed the problems inherent in a federal solution.[38]

Despite Office reservations, the merits and demerits of a federal solution to Central African problems were quickly confronted in the meetings of March 1951.[39] It was generally agreed in the eleventh session that major economic, social, strategic and political advantages would result from a closer union in Central Africa. There was a vital and urgent need to establish a British bloc in Central Africa, capable of resisting dangerous influences from outside and of unifying certain services. One member of the conference, A.D. Evans, claimed experience had shown that the unitary state was the most successful form of government. In true Diceyan fashion, he argued, 'One of the great drawbacks of any federal system lay in the power possessed by the judicature to declare legislation invalid, which led to undue legalism and a confusion of the legislative and judicial branches of government.' Moreover, a federal system of government also 'tended to rigidity', while the difficulty of amending a federal constitution was 'notorious'. In general, the Southern Rhodesians disliked the idea of African policy being fragmented; they preferred a unitary approach to 'Native policy'. They asked, reasonably enough, how African affairs could be divorced from other matters since they affected everything. Andrew Cohen, the Assistant Under-Secretary of State in the Colonial Office, addressed this issue in the thirteenth meeting on 14 March. He pointed out that whatever new body was proposed there would be difficulty in securing the acceptance of the Westminster parliament to any surrender of the United Kingdom's special responsibility for Africans in the northern territories. The need, argued Cohen, was to keep the lines of communication open between the United Kingdom parliament and a Central African Federation over native policy, and the best solution seemed to be one devised by Kenneth Wheare and W.L. Dale, a legal advisor in the Colonial Office. It involved the creation of a Native Affairs Board with direct links to the federal government and the United Kingdom government. The chairman of the Board would be an *ex officio* member of the federal cabinet.

The British had now openly endorsed a federal solution, and when asked by the Southern Rhodesians during the fifteenth meeting to give reasons for the United Kingdom's opposition to a unitary system, Cohen made a good case. He said, 'It would be contrary to the whole trend of present British colonial policy to create a state which would be entirely run by Europeans and established in the face of the expressed opinion of all Africans in Northern Rhodesia and Nyasaland . . . the United Kingdom Government would not contemplate the handing over of authority to a Government which was not fully representative of all the main communities.' Cohen personally thought the choice lay between federation and confederation, but in the end the conference opted for federation as the solution most likely to meet acceptance by all three governments. In doing so it had been guided by the political difficulties in the way of the acceptance of a unified system by the United Kingdom and of a confederation by Southern Rhodesia.

In the summary report of the March 1951 meeting, 'a true federal solution' was recommended on the grounds that 'We believe that this would enable the territories to be knit together effectively for communications in those spheres where it would be most beneficial to all of them, while leaving unimpaired the authority of individual territories in spheres where this seemed most appropriate, and recognizing the responsibility of His Majesty's Government in the United Kingdom towards the African peoples.'[40] Federal powers were to be specified and in all others the relationship of each territory to the British government would remain the same, as would the authority and constitutional position of each territory. The residual powers remaining with the territories were those closest to the African, but since African interests would inevitably be impinged upon there would be African representation in the central parliament and an African Affairs Board would be vested with special powers. There would also be a minister for African interests.

The report was generally well received in the Colonial Office, although J.J.S. Garner still had some concerns about the application of a federal solution to Central Africa. He commented:

> the obvious dangers in any Federal State are: (a) wasteful duplication of effort and (b) conflict in authority between the Central and the State Governments. No federal system seems to work ideally and there has been a good deal of creaking in the working of the Constitutions of Australia and Canada. Indeed if the plans for Southern Rhodesia mature I think there will be a lot to be said for bringing in an expert from Canada who has had experience of the working particularly of tax and economic relations between the Federal and Provincial Governments. I see that it is proposed that both the Federal and Territorial Governments should have the right to levy direct taxation: it seems to me that a very close degree of harmony and understanding between the two will be necessary if this is to work without friction. It is also suggested that the Federal Government should be responsible for economic planning throughout the whole area though it will largely be the responsibility of the Territorial Governments to carry out this planning. I wonder whether this also may not be a cause of friction. One wants if possible to set up Governments with a reasonable division of functions though I suppose it may be questioned whether the area of British Central Africa is really sufficiently developed to support four separate Governments.[41]

G.H. Baxter, to whom Garner had written, recognized the merit of Garner's critique but saw no real choice. 'Admittedly,' he wrote, 'a federal system is always complex and requires in its working even more good will than is called for in working other types of constitutions.' Nevertheless, this would simply have to be faced given the more serious disadvantages of any alternative. James Griffiths, the Secretary of State, agreed. It was federation or nothing: 'To do nothing would be fatal, since the Union influence would undoubtedly spread.'[42]

One key figure who opposed federation was Hastings Banda of Nyasaland who wrote to James Griffiths, Secretary of State for the Colonies, pointing out that federation was seen in Northern Rhodesia and Nyasaland as a step towards dominion status which would give the Europeans, i.e. the Southern Rhodesian settlers, control over the Africans in the same way the South African government had control over Africans.[43] It is clear that a fear of the extension of South Africa's apartheid policy to the Rhodesias and Nyasaland led to the acceptance of federation by the British. In fact, Griffiths later stated emphatically that South Africa's apartheid policy needed to be withstood and that union in Central Africa was urgent.[44] Nevertheless, Banda was right to be suspicious. While the Southern Rhodesian representatives had not liked the federal idea, many Europeans in the two Rhodesias saw federation as a means of controlling the 'advance' of Africans which they saw as 'too rapid'.

In the preparation of the draft federal constitution the staff in the Colonial Office were constantly looking to the Australian, Canadian and United States examples, but in settling on a format they consciously used the West Indian model outlined in the Report of the British Caribbean Standing Closer Association Committee of 1948–9.[45] Kenneth Wheare did not take part in these in-house preparations although his influence was pervasive. His participation in the 1951 conference had been 'a great success' and 'members of all teams tended to look to him for guidance and as a touchstone of the wisdom or practicability of particular proposals'.[46] But it was also clear that Wheare and Colonial Office officials did not always see eye-to-eye. Wheare was anxious on such important issues as amendment of the constitution to ensure that the interests of the territories were protected, while the Office staff were acutely conscious of the political context. Southern Rhodesia, for example, objected to the territories having the power effectively to veto federal decisions. Similarly, the United Kingdom would not agree to a weakening of any of its powers then or later. These problems underlined the difficulties inherent in creating a federation in so explicit a 'colonial' relationship and between two discordant racial groups. The key was power. Some had it and wanted to keep it; others did not have it and aspired to it. Wheare frankly said he would give his opinion at the conference if asked but, 'He would, however, naturally look at the problems arising out of the Draft Federal Scheme through the eyes of the United Kingdom delegation.'[47]

In the scheme that emerged from the April–May 1952 meetings powers were divided between the federal and the territorial legislatures which in their exclusive spheres were 'in no way subordinate to one another'. It set out a number of subjects on which the federal legislature alone might make laws, and also set out a number of other subjects with which both federal and territorial legislatures might deal, provided that in case of inconsistency the federal law would prevail. It also allowed the federal legislature to delegate powers to legislate on federal matters to the territorial legislatures, and within certain defined spheres allowed them to delegate power to the federal legislature. All subjects not specifically allotted to the federal legislature remained the responsibility of the territories, and care had been taken to ensure that the territorial legislatures retained control of those matters which most closely concerned the daily life of the African population.[48]

These provisions formed the basic framework for the conference in January 1953 which drew up the final scheme. The federal apparatus was modelled to a degree on the Australian and Canadian examples, but it was a constitution devised to meet particular problems and was not, therefore, anywhere near a carbon copy of the dominion models. Wheare again attended as an advisor and he could not have been happy to see the African Affairs Board downgraded to a committee of the legislature. This clearly made African interests more vulnerable and seemed to bear out Banda's concerns. The fact that no Africans from Northern Rhodesia or Nyasaland attended the conference meant no sustained opposition had developed, but it also underlined the fragility of the scheme. The British, of course, remained convinced to the end that only federation could provide the economic and political power to benefit the whole area.

The Rhodesia and Nyasaland Act received royal approval on 1 August 1953. Despite the close attention given the federal idea by the civil service, it attracted no sustained attention in parliament. None of the colonial federal bills did. The British generally knew very little about federalism. They accepted that it had its uses for the solution of complex colonial problems but they saw little need to indulge in philosophic reflection about its use. Not altogether surprisingly, the Central African Federation lasted barely ten years, succumbing in the end to the determination of the Africans in Northern Rhodesia and Nyasaland to dissociate themselves from the white settlers of Southern Rhodesia.

By the time the Central African Federation dissolved at the end of 1963, the British had pursued the federal idea in three other areas. Perhaps the most bizarre attempt was that made in Aden and the Western and Eastern Protectorates; even more so because the Central African division of the Colonial Office was also responsible for the Arabian experiment. A federal union had first been proposed in 1928 but the Arab rulers had been too particularistic and the effort had come to nothing. The idea was raised again in 1944 but once more it was agreed a federal solution to the social, economic and political problems of the area was 'still a most distant goal'. In the view of one official on the spot, R.S. Champion, the 'idea of federation or cooperation is largely alien to Arab minds, which are steeped in traditions of individualism',[49] while the governor, Sir John Hathorn Hall, observed that 'Federation as a political system does not ordinarily commend itself to primitive peoples; the federal system, with its acceptance of the principle of sacrificing individual interests to the common good, demands a very high standard of political education on the part of those to whom it is applied.' In his opinion, 'the fiercely individualistic, selfish, undisciplined chiefs and tribes of the Western Protectorate were in no way ready for so sophisticated a political development'.[50]

In 1952 a new Governor of Aden, Sir Thomas Hickinbotham, decided another attempt should be made to initiate a federation of the Western Aden Protectorate. He pointed out that 'it has been an accepted principle of our policy in the Protectorate that eventually some form of federation would take place among the states'. He thought the British should move fairly quickly as the majority of the states could not separately achieve economic independence: 'I have felt that our aim should be to integrate the states with the object of pooling their resources and unifying the major services such as education, customs, communications and health, with a view to reducing expenditures on administration, and thereby effecting a reduction in the annual grant by H.M. Government, and at the same time expending the States limited resources to the best advantage.' Hickinbotham wanted to improve relations between Aden and the Protectorate; to help the people take a larger part in the 'management' of their own affairs; and to relieve the financial burden on the British government.[51]

The Colonial Office agreed with the general principles but thought it 'important not to rush things or to appear in any way to be imposing a ready-made scheme from on top'. Nevertheless, the Office did not believe either the colony or the Protectorate was a 'viable' unit without the other. More cooperation should be encouraged in order to lay the base for future change. While recognizing that federation could lead to political and economic stability in the region and therefore should be encouraged, federation 'should only proceed on condition it obtains the genuine approval in principle of the rulers involved'.[52] One member of the Office staff was particularly concerned. On 6 February 1953 John Marnham, an assistant secretary, minuted that he had been preoccupied with the Central African Federation but now had read Hickinbotham's dispatch 'which proposes to initiate yet another Federation – that of some of the hotchpotch of two penny-half penny States, Sheikhdoms and Sultanates in the Western Aden Protectorate'. He reminded his colleagues that they should only proceed on a line involving 'a greater measure of direct British executive action than hitherto . . . if, and only if, the Rulers concerned can be persuaded to want it. (We cannot I think contemplate at present forcing another federation on an unwilling populace).'[53] His colleagues agreed. They were well aware that the proposal was out of step with the current British policy of disengagement. The proposal involved assuming a good deal of executive responsibility in an area where, except in exceptional circumstances, the British had confined themselves to advisory functions. Therefore, only if the rulers agreed could the British go ahead.

The Treasury also had its doubts. On 29 July 1953 J.W. Kennedy agreed that federation might be a logical step, but he did not find much evidence that it would produce the benefits expected. He was left with the impression 'that even if agreement on federation is achieved the parties concerned would be very uneasy bed-fellows. The eternal triangle basis, with one state being sought after to further the aims of either of the other two states, would not seem to make for the best relationships.' Colonel Russell

Edmunds agreed: 'Federation, as we know qua Central Africa and West Indies, is not without its disharmonious side. Whether this stems from aversion to change or from other roots, it is the balance of all considerations which should guide a decision.'[54]

As it happened, the rulers decided in January 1954 that they were not ready for union. While accepting federation in principle as a solution to their region's difficulties, little specific accommodation could be found between the nineteen statelets – ranging in size from 1,000 to 125,000 people – to translate principle into action. The proposal was raised again, however, in 1958 and this time by the rulers themselves who now realized that if the Protectorate with under one million people was to develop economically and politically unity must be achieved. Not only had their security been increasingly menaced by Yemeni aggression and subversion since 1953 but the rulers also thought union would assist them in containing the anti-Western influence of Arab nationalism in their various states. The British cabinet's Colonial Policy Committee thought it desirable to support this 'progressive' move by the rulers. 'It was recognized that this would involve some reversal of our previous thinking, in that the creation of a more powerful political unit in this area was likely to lead to greater independence of British control, and our experience of federations has not been entirely satisfactory.' Nevertheless, there were political advantages 'if a new Arab State which was friendly to the West was created in this strategically important area'.[55] There was, of course, considerable concern at this time about Yemeni hostility and Egyptian and Saudi disapproval of any federation.[56]

The Office went over the 1958 proposed federal constitution very carefully but never discussed federal principles *per se*. As for motivation, the British were quite calculating: 'Unless their vague but growing sense of nationalism is satisfied in a way which would allow coexistence with British influence they must be expected to come into direct conflict with it and, eventually, to look to a future in the United Arab States.' If this was to be avoided the rulers must be offered an acceptable alternative. There was only one: 'that of the Western and, preferably, the Eastern Aden Protectorate, evolving into an independent Arab State which would ideally and might eventually include Aden itself. This could only come about if the treaty states entered a federation which could acquire the political stability to manage its own affairs.'

The Office therefore believed the government should support the states wanting to federate. Finance, however, was seen as a problem since there were no separate federal taxing powers. There would simply be contributions from the states. The British were prepared to accept this in order not to alienate the rulers. As in the West Indies, the British were prepared to launch a weak federal structure in order to try and achieve their strategic and economic aims. They also realized they had little alternative in either instance. As C.A. Kirkman of the Colonial Office revealingly put it, 'the Federation is too weak financially and in powers of legislation vis-à-vis the states to be really effective but I believe that we must accept this at first until the Rulers see that their long term interests lie in making the Federation effective. The pressure for this may be applied through development money.' Here was British policy in a nutshell: create a federation to preserve strategic interests and then pressure the states via development money to ensure the federation did what the British wanted.[57]

The Federation of the Arab Emirates of the South was inaugurated on 11 February 1959. There were six members in all. The Colonial Office was not particularly happy with the outcome. As Kirkman put it, 'there is still a great deal of nonsense in the constitution but we have to accept it for the present'. The Office admitted that the federation was not ideal and that the constitution was 'essentially a Ruler's document'. The federation actually lasted longer than many expected and, in fact, Aden joined before it finally fell apart in 1967.[58]

An area which presented many of the same problems as the British Caribbean and Central Africa was Malaysia. The British had created the Federation of Malaya in 1948 by order-in-council after agreement had been reached between the Crown and the nine Malay Rulers both jointly and individually. The settlements of Malacca and Penang had also been included but Singapore had been left out of the arrangement. The 1948 Federation was highly centralized and the states had limited legislative powers. The high commissioner had extensive administrative and legislative authority and the Federal Legislative Council had both *ex officio* and official as well as unofficial members. It was not a 'true federation' and it was far from independent.

During the early fifties there was much discussion of a wider federation which would include not only Singapore but the three territories of Sarawak, North Borneo and Brunei. The British favoured wider union despite the inherent problems. Once again, as in the West Indies, the three territories had little in common either with each other or with Malaya. Separated by considerable distances there had been little inter-territorial trade, while ethnic differences only compounded the problems. Moreover, the Malays were fearful of the power Singapore would exercise in a closer union and Singapore was afraid of getting involved in the troubles of the Federation. Despite all these warning signs the British had decided by June 1953 that it would 'try to guide unofficial opinion in Malaya directly towards a real political federation'.[59]

After a good deal of dramatic negotiation it was agreed in February 1956 that Malaya would receive full self-government and independence within the Commonwealth as of 31 August 1957. One of the principal members of the commission appointed to draw up a new federal constitution was Sir Ivor Jennings who had been an active participant in the discussions of the colonial committee of Federal Union and who was now a widely respected constitutional expert. Jennings utilized his experience of the federations of Australia, Canada, India and the United States in drawing up memoranda on such sensitive issues as the allocation of financial powers and representation of the various states in an upper house. The strategy of adopting a 'federal monarchy' with a rotating head of state underlined the pragmatic nature of the new federation as well as its unique form.[60]

Thus far Malaya had resisted any effort to form a wider federal union with Singapore and the three territories, but in May 1961 the Malayan prime minister, Tunku Abdul Rahman, fearful of a possible 'leftist' government in Singapore, spoke favourably of a larger association. The British were very interested because it would get them out of 'an increasingly menacing situation' in Singapore and was likely to reinforce rather than undermine the security of South-east Asia in general 'and our own interests in particular'. The fear in Britain was that if this venture failed the government of Lee Kuan Yew in Singapore might fall and a government of the left take over. The British might then be obliged to suspend the constitution and assume direct administration of the island. The value of the Singapore bases would then be 'highly problematical'. The British also feared the influence of Peking on an independent Singapore. As for Lee Kuan Yew, he recognized there was a greater opportunity for independence by entering a union with Malaya than by remaining aloof.[61] In keeping with Tunku Abdul Rahman's wishes, the British conveniently satisfied themselves 'that the complications of jettisoning the existing constitution of the Federation of Malaya and drawing up an entirely new Federal Constitution are such as to make this proposal impracticable'. They examined the constitution of the Federation of Malaya and 'concluded that it could be taken as a basis for the purpose of the creation of Malaysia'.[62] Thus the constitution of the new state was based on the existing Malayan constitution and no new in-depth federal theorizing took place within the Colonial Office. As a consequence, the Malaysian Federation that was born on 16 September 1962 did not adequately resolve the potential for ethnic tension and it was not surprising that in less than two years Singapore left the new union, becoming a republic and an independent member of the Commonwealth on 7 August 1965.

In South-east Asia, as in the Caribbean, Central Africa and the West Arabian protectorate, the British had decidedly pushed federation as a means to resolve regional problems and to hasten the decolonization process. Complexities such as ethnic differences, poor communications, the lack of a 'national sense' and diverse political ambitions had been hidden beneath the cover of a neat, centralized federal carapace.

British efforts in Nigeria conformed to this pattern although, as in the West Indies, the dynamic lay at the periphery rather than in London. The Nigerians had very clear ideas about acceptable and unacceptable forms of government. The Colonial Office was obliged to recognize the determination of the primarily Muslim northern region to retain control over its own affairs. The leadership in the land-locked north realized the necessity of cooperating with the Yoruba and Ibo of the western and eastern regions but they drew back from entering a centralized system of government. For their part, the western and eastern regions, particularly the latter, did not wish to be slowed in their constitutional advance towards full self-government by being too closely tied to the more conservative and less developed north. It was clear to Andrew Cohen of the Colonial Office by the late forties, and to the British government by 1950, that federation was the only constitutional form that had any chance of success in Nigeria. The disparity in resources, ethnic composition, religious conviction, educational standards and constitutional status virtually dictated a federal system if the three regions, so artificially welded together early in the century, were to remain united. Once it had been agreed to keep them together the major issues were whether or not there should be more than three units and whether the federal structure should be patterned on the decentralized Australian example or on the more centralized Canadian version. The Colonial Office staff responsible for West Africa were highly sensitive to the rapidly changing political conditions in the area and constantly adapted their advice and ideas to shifting circumstances, but their one consistent belief was that too rapid a move towards the creation of a number of smaller units in Nigeria would lead to fragmentation and an unstable economy. They preferred to devise a flexible federal constitution which would allow the individual regions to move at their own pace towards regional self-government.

The 1954 federal constitution left residual powers with the regions but central government powers did include such matters as defence and external affairs (insofar as responsibility was delegated by the United Kingdom government). The discussions in the Office frequently referred to Kenneth Wheare's work on federalism and his insights often guided the staff, although he was not personally consulted on this occasion. The staff clearly recognized the need for a strong central government to keep Nigeria together but, at the same time, they had to bow to the exigencies of the Nigerian situation. As one official put it, 'Nigerian problems are largely *sui generis*'; while the study of other federal constitutions was generally recognized as useful there was obviously no exact replica of Nigerian circumstances to guide them.[63]

The Nigerian federation that was launched on 1 October 1960 was an unusual one in that the northern region was larger in both size and population than the west and the east together. The Nigerian federation therefore offended one of the principal tenets of classic federalism: that no single unit in a federation ought to be so large as to be in a position to hold the remaining component parts to ransom and so be able to impose its lone will on the general government. In the estimation of the British, local circumstances allowed no other solution if the whole area was to remain united. Once again, the British had adapted their federal response to the particular conditions but essentially they had been driven by the need to protect West African economic and political stability while disengaging as quickly as possible.[64]

The British involvement with the federal idea as a solution to colonial problems ended in the early sixties. It had been a continuous preoccupation since the late 1940s but had been arousing interest and increasingly sporadic attention since the 1920s in connection with British Caribbean and East African problems and, of course, had been stimulated and accelerated in the 1930s by the protracted analysis of federalism in its application to India. The British, whether on the spot or in the London enclaves of the Colonial Office, the India Office or the Treasury, clearly saw in the federal idea a constitutional form that would allow them to bridge the various ethnic, economic, religious, constitutional and communication gulfs that existed between and within many of their disparate colonial possessions. It had worked reasonably successfully in the United States, Canada and Australia. Admittedly, problems continued to beset those federal polities but at least through compromise and a coordination of powers they were still united and, in fact, thriving. There was every reason to hope that the passage of time would allow the constitutional cement to dry and the traditional suspicions and acrimony in the new federations to wither. Anyway, there was little other choice if the United Kingdom was to effect a reasonably rapid and ordered retreat from areas it had neither the power nor the will to hold on to any longer.

By the 1940s the British had a considerable body of writing on federalism to which they could turn and a number of internationally recognized experts upon whom they could call for advice. The grasp of the federal idea was firmer than it had ever been. For example, the Colonial Office files amply demonstrate that by the 1950s the civil servants were at ease with the federal idea both in theory and in detail. This was in stark contrast to the hit-and-miss and often blundering efforts earlier in the century. This shift in attitude in Whitehall and Westminster could easily have led an observer to conclude that the British might yet find the federal idea attractive in other forums than the colonial. This, of course, would have proved to be a mistake. The Colonial Office staff were not representative of either the British public or its politicians, so their ideas and actions had no broader currency. Moreover, it is clear that the staff were simply being professional in their advocacy and analysis of the federal construct. It was a means to an end – the preservation of harmonious relations in potentially divisive regions. As long as the British were playing with other people's sovereignty and not their own, the federal idea held little fear for them. Once their own sovereignty was affected, the reaction would be very different.

8 'The federal solution is not possible for us'[1]

In the latter half of the twentieth century the British grappled with two major constitutional concerns. The first involved the centuries-old question of what the relationship should be between the nations and regions of the United Kingdom. The second centered on the nature and extent of the United Kingdom's involvement with Europe. The latter discussion began in the late 1940s and continues to the present day, while the debate over domestic constitutional arrangements surfaced in an acute form in the sixties and seventies and still attracts ritual attention in the post-Thatcher nineties. In both instances, the federal solution has been suggested as a means, on the one hand, of creating unity while protecting diversity, and, on the other, of protecting unity while allowing diversity.

Despite the success of Federal Union in awakening an interest in federalism and in the possibility of a federal Europe in the stormy days from late 1938 into the early forties, the influence of the Union waned after 1941, and in the years following the war there was little sustained interest amongst the general public or in either the Labour or Conservative parties in the federal idea. This was not the case on the Continent.[2] In the mid-to-late 1940s the European federalists, many of them, ironically, inspired by the arguments of Federal Union members such as Lord Lothian, Lionel Robbins and R.W.G. Mackay, were much to the fore in the debate over a reconstituted Europe. To their mind only through a federal structure, or through constitutional and political arrangements that would eventually lead to a federal structure, could Europe and thus the world be spared the ravages of national sovereignty gone berserk. To them, acutely and often personally aware of the devastation resulting from competing nation-states, a stable Europe where law was respected and democracy ruled could only come from a cooperative pooling of sovereignty, a coordinating of varied interests, in a federal structure. To the British, behind their physical and symbolic moat, such thinking was unappealing. Ever the pragmatists, they preferred a more flexible and continuously adaptive process than either federalism or a federal state seemingly allowed.

The British did not ignore the federal idea entirely but when they did comment it was usually with scepticism. When Lionel Curtis initiated a debate in 1948 on Britain's future relations with Europe and the Commonwealth he came out, not surprisingly, in favour of 'organic union of the sovereign states of the Commonwealth'.[3] It was perhaps somewhat more surprising to find Curtis's old friend and associate from the early days of the Round Table movement, Edward Grigg, now Lord Altrincham, responding with a trenchant criticism of the federal case.[4] Altrincham pointed out that those who believed 'in federal union between Britain and western Europe or between the sovereign nations of the British Commonwealth' based their arguments primarily on history. The argument appeared 'formidable' given that the United States and subsequently Canada and Australia had adopted the federal form of government, but did it follow, asked Altrincham, that Britain should do the same in Europe and the Commonwealth? After all, 'all existing federations have joined together states or provinces or colonies with . . . primitive economics, no longer national traditions, for the most part no fundamentally different cultures, no great dissimilarity of institutions such as the difference between republics and monarchies, and few mixtures of language or none'. All the proposed members of a west European federation or of a federal Commonwealth were fully developed nation-states resolute in their determination 'not to merge their sovereignties in any wider union'. Altrincham concluded that arguments from history had little bearing on contemporary problems in either Europe or the Commonwealth:

> Ancient nations have at least as much to sacrifice as younger ones when they are urged to subordinate their individual sovereignties to that of a federal system in which majority interest and opinion must prevail. They bear no resemblance to the undeveloped provinces and simple primitive economies with which federal union has successfully dealt. The difference between the Protozoan and the Metazoan, between that is, the living animal of a single cell and that of many cells, is not more distinctive than the difference between primitive colonies on the eighteenth – or even nineteenth-century model and national systems of high development and great complexity like those of modern Britain or modern France. In the former case union involves no serious change in the economy, living standards, social system or internal character of any of the federated States; and colonies in an early stage of growth have no world status or responsibility to think about. In the latter case it may involve changes that completely transform a nation's internal economy and external power – make it indeed an entirely different kind of State, different in itself and different to all who may be connected with or dependent upon it.

Altrincham suggested that 'methods sufficient for the problems of America nearly two centuries ago are obsolete and inadequate in ours'.

Turning to a consideration of federal union as a solution to the problems facing the United Kingdom in the post-war world, Altrincham argued that its 'influence and standing in Europe' depended upon the cohesion of the

Commonwealth, and the United Kingdom could not hope to help stabilize western Europe if it entered a European union 'on any terms which seriously reduced her own strength and value by loosening her ties with the Commonwealth'. As Altrincham pointed out, the United Kingdom 'would no longer be a Great Power in isolation from the Commonwealth'. It followed therefore that if the United Kingdom became simply another state in a federal union it would 'forfeit elements of political and economic power which constitute her main value to both Europe and the Commonwealth. She would be a province of western Europe, and no longer an oceanic Power in her own right.' The proper path for the United Kingdom to follow was that of close cooperation with Europe, the Commonwealth and the United States 'unhampered by constitutional dogmas belonging to another age with a totally different and far less complex problem to solve'.[5]

Altrincham's arguments and assumptions were to become increasingly familiar in the following years as various analysts, pundits and commentators explored the interconnection of the United Kingdom, Europe and the federal idea. They were, in fact, already firmly rooted as of mid-century in both the official mind and that of the alert academic, and shifted little thereafter. For example, in May 1950, the same month that Robert Schuman put forward a plan for a coal and steel community, Max Beloff wrote an article for *The Times* entitled 'European Association: False Analogies from Federal Example of United States'.[6] He argued that both the American and the European proponents of a federal system for Europe were paying insufficient attention to the difficulties in the way. It was false to equate the conditions of the 1780s in North America with those in Europe in 1950. The thirteen states had language, cultural traditions and to a considerable extent race and religion in common. At least, said Beloff, 'the Protestant Anglo-Saxon element was universally predominant'. Even more important, 'since all of the states had been British colonies (some for a century and a half) they all had roughly the same political and legal institutions. . . . When the Founding Fathers assigned a function to the executive, the legislature or the judiciary, their decision had for them a perfectly definite and concrete significance.' Moreover, 'in the all important spheres of defence and foreign relations the separate units had always been ruled from a single centre'. Beloff also contended that the primary concern of the Americans had been political – to ensure that the states were not vulnerable to foreign intervention. For that reason there needed to be a centre strong enough in terms of powers and taxes to fulfil its responsibility of defending the interests of all the states. Beloff argued that the Europeans were not discussing the key point: 'what powers does a federation require in order to present a single front to the outside world, while allowing the units of which it is composed to retain the maximum of autonomy in their purely internal affairs?' Furthermore, there did not exist in western Europe any powerful groups, similar to those that had existed in the United States, 'passionately convinced that their interests would be served by federation, no political parties whose organizations are not bounded by national frontiers, and none in any country prepared to fight the cause of federalism in the Parliaments and on the hustings'.

Certainly, there were no such powerful organizations in the United Kingdom and neither the Labour nor Conservative governments paid the federal idea much heed. For its part the Foreign Office was patently hostile. This can be seen from a January 1951 memorandum prepared by the Research Department of the Foreign Office at the request of the Colonial Office. The memorandum, entitled 'Closer Union in Africa: The European Pattern', had been prepared in the context of the British government's intention to unite the two Rhodesias and Nyasaland in a Central African federation.[7] The writer was obviously familiar with federal government as practised in the United States, Canada, Australia and Switzerland, and he was at pains to make it clear that in working out its future relationship to Europe the British government was 'opposed to anything that smacks of federation'. He cited Beloff's recent article in *The Times* as evidence of the faulty reasoning behind the application of the federal idea to Europe, and he quoted from the speech made by Ernest Bevin, the Foreign Secretary, in the House of Commons on 4 May 1950. On that occasion Bevin had assured his colleagues that the Brussels Treaty of 1948 did 'not provide for union in the sense of some pooling of sovereignty or the creation of a European federated State'; it expressly safeguarded national sovereignty. The writer acknowledged that federalism had become a 'blessed word' in recent years and that it had a 'specious appeal to ideologues and reformers'. On a theoretical level, the advocates of federalism were right enough – the world's ills could probably only be solved by world federation – but in reality 'World Federal government . . . is clearly nonsense today; and life, anyway, is not a thing of logic'.

The opinions, assumptions and attitudes embedded in this memorandum and in the writings of such observers as Altrincham and Beloff remained at the base of the British response to the federal idea through much of the next five decades. Cooperation and intergovernmental arrangements were always possible but anything suggesting a more integrated European polity which might diminish, even in the slightest, British sovereignty was given, initially at least, no more than rhetorical attention. The British of all political hues were adjusting after 1945 to a harsh new world which they did not yet have in clear focus. The degree of their own fall from first-power status had not fully hit home nor had the nature of the rapidly accelerating changes in their relationship with various members of their colonial empire. Well into the 1960s the British gave short shrift to the rapid developments towards European integration and cooperation taking place on the Continent, and clung to the twin aspirations of a continuing strong bond with the United States and a world role through the medium of the Commonwealth. The problem was that the British leverage with the Americans was never what the British thought it either was or should be and it was badly affected by the split over Suez in 1956. Similarly, the rapid pace of decolonization meant that by the early 1960s the British no longer had the same relationship to their former colonies and thus could no longer stride the world stage with the same ready assurance.

During these years the British did join the United States-backed North Atlantic Treaty Organization but remained pointedly distant from the Jean Monnet- and Robert Schuman-inspired European Coal and Steel Community (ECSC) of April 1951 comprising six members, France, West Germany, Italy and the Benelux countries. Again in June 1955 the British only sent a senior civil servant to the Messina Conference on the assumption it would accomplish nothing. It, in fact, laid the basis for further European integration enshrined in the Rome treaties of March 1957 which established the European Economic Community (EEC) and the European Atomic Energy Community (EURATOM) with again the six nations of France, West Germany, Italy and the Benelux countries as members. The British responded by helping to found a much looser European Free Trade Area (EFTA) in July 1959 but the real impetus towards some form of European union lay with the Rome treaties and especially the EEC.

By the early sixties the United Kingdom had begun to disengage rapidly from its overseas empire and to reevaluate its options in the international community. It was patently obvious by then that the EEC had proved to be an enormous economic success and that the United Kingdom was falling badly behind in its readjustment to a different and vastly more vigorous economic climate. The Conservatives in 1961 and the Labour government in 1966 both attempted to climb aboard the new economic juggernaut but in each instance the application was vetoed by General de Gaulle who was suspicious, first, that the British were still too closely tied to the Americans and would attempt to deflect the EEC towards essentially American objectives, and, second, that the British would challenge French authority within the Community. By the time the British did join in 1973 the bloom had gone off the economic rose. The world was beset by an oil crisis that plunged the Western economies into various degrees of recession. That parlous economic condition still continued in the mid-nineties and left the United Kingdom with serious problems. By remaining aloof from Europe for twenty years the United Kingdom had done itself a disservice. Once it joined, the world-wide economic downturn ensured that no dramatic benefits were reaped. This disappointment in part explains the continuing widespread suspicion of Europe that pervades many strata of British society.

While uncertainty about Britain's international role was undoubtedly important in preventing or inhibiting the British from exploring the European possibility, there were other more deeply felt but less tangible reasons for holding aloof. The British had had a pugnacious relationship with Europe for centuries, and in the previous three hundred years either France or Germany had been formidable foes. The natural suspicion that would be aroused by such historical – and contemporary – memories and experiences was compounded by a sense of invincibility. The island nation had not been invaded successfully for centuries and only a few years earlier the dramatic rescue at Dunkirk and the victorious Battle of Britain had seemingly confirmed its invulnerability. The British were therefore understandably cautious about becoming too entangled in Europe. Experience had taught them that complications and dangers more often than not lay across the Channel. Moreover, the British were deeply wedded to their constitutional and political institutions. For them, as we have repeatedly seen, the idea of the sovereignty of parliament and by extension their national sovereignty was at the core of the nation's being. It was incomprehensible to most Britons, politicians or not, that even a modicum of that sovereignty would be surrendered. The lack of any sustained open discussion of constitutional alternatives had led to a fixation on the overriding merits of a unitary system where if powers were shared at all they were shared primarily at the most local of levels and rarely at either the regional or national levels. Those powers could, of course, always be revoked, and sometimes were, in the most dramatic fashion.

This preoccupation with parliamentary sovereignty and its indivisibility led the British to be suspicious of any step towards 'ever closer union' with the continent of Europe, and particularly leery of anything that appeared to be federal in nature or a move towards a future federation. To most Britons federation was anathema. Perhaps it was a tolerable system for colonial territories but not for the mother country. Federation meant the sharing; the division, of sovereignty. That would mean the diminution of British authority. Restrictions on the conduct of the nation's interests would ensue. Decisions made 'in a faraway place of which they knew nothing', or very little, would dictate the pace and nature of British political, social and economic life. The thought was appalling.

Kenneth Wheare, the constitutional expert and former member of Federal Union, summed up the prevailing British attitudes in a perceptive article entitled 'Federalism and the Making of Nations', published in 1955.[8] Wheare reminded his readers that nationalism was often too strong in existing states for them to be readily combined in a federal structure. He pointed out that 'People of differing nationality cannot form a federal union unless they are prepared to accept a government in which those who differ from them in nationality have some share.' Also, while some nationalities had their own way in their own state, they might well be in a minority in a federal union. Furthermore, a federal union usually implied that those who joined were 'expected to develop some common nationality in addition to their distinct nationalities'. When people of different nationalities were unwilling to accept those consequences, federal union would not work. Wheare believed those who were advocating a federal Europe would do well to realize that what they were proposing had never been successfully achieved before. He did not believe there was 'sufficient common sympathy between the peoples of the national states of Europe, even of Western

Europe, for us to say that they have, over and above their national feelings, a sense of common European nationalism'. He was quite certain 'that if Britain is included in one's notion of Western Europe, no such common European nationalism exists'. In Wheare's estimation, the British were not Europeans and therefore would not easily or readily join a federal European union. Given these pervasive attitudes, it was not surprising that the British were suspicious of any supranational entity in Europe and that they preferred intergovernmental arrangements.

British attitudes to European union in a federal form, or to any form of union that posed a threat to national sovereignty, were reflected in the debates in the House of Commons in 1967 and 1971–2 when members considered British entry into the EEC. On both occasions fear was expressed about the loss of United Kingdom sovereignty and the standing of the United Kingdom parliament and its legislation in the aftermath of joining the European Community. Despite the efforts, particularly of Conservative ministers in 1971–2, to provide reassurances on the issue of sovereignty there were many who remained unconvinced. A representative voice was that of Raphael Tuck, MP for Watford, who reminded the House on 17 February 1972 that 'We have been told how our sovereignty may be shared. Those who speak in those terms suffer from a legal squint. In fact, sovereignty knows no fellow. One is either sovereign or one is not . . . if we enter this union, we shall lose control over our whole national life as we have known it up to the present day.'[9] There were many others who shared Tuck's opinion and the issue was raised again and again. Needless to say, the federal idea was given little attention in the debates of the late sixties and early seventies while in 1976 the Secretary of State for Foreign and Commonwealth Affairs had to assure the House that the government 'would certainly resist any proposal to set up a federal state' although it was prepared to pursue cooperation 'in a pragmatic way'.[10]

The concern over British sovereignty has remained central to the debate over Europe and various British governments have tended to try and resist the loss of ultimate control over key facets of the nation's destiny. While understandable, such actions overlooked the fact that in the late twentieth century no nation was truly sovereign in any sphere whether it be economic, strategic, cultural or political. Many Britons chose to ignore that hard truth and clung to their offshore, particularistic stance.[11]

Federal propagandists have generally been given short shrift since 1945. There has been no sustained federalist campaign approximating that of Federal Union and no ongoing public debate to match those surrounding the issues of imperial federation and the Anglo-Irish relationship. Whenever individual writers have been bold enough to either explore or advocate the federal idea they have usually been taken to task for their breathless utopianism. A good example of the dismissive and uncongenial atmosphere is a review written by William Pickles in 1970 of two books with a federal theme. The first was a Penguin Special written by John Pinder and Roy Pryce entitled *Europe After de Gaulle: Towards the United States of Europe*, and the second, *Britain in a Federal Europe*, written by John Lambert. Pickles was damning in his condemnation of the 'narcotic vision' Pinder and Pryce offered up of a United States of Europe 'on federal lines'.[12] To suggest that the British would lead the way to such a vision when recent polls suggested only one fifth of the population wanted to join the Communities and even fewer wanted a federation was absurd. Pickles referred to Pinder's and Pryce's 'political unrealism', their 'panacea-loaded utopianism' and their 'utopian insanity'. As for Lambert, Pickles found his book read like 'political science fiction' full of 'the "coulds" and "woulds" that fill the federalists' dreams of how their federation will lead the world to peace'.

Pickles admitted that there was much truth in the argument that the nineteenth-century nation-state was inadequate, but to his mind the cure was 'not to be found in trying to drive whole populations along blue-printed roads to federations which, if they are ever formed and consolidated, are at least as likely to develop only larger-scale and even greedier nationalisms as to become the gently cooing distributors of good things and noble ideas that our federalists too easily paint into their dream-pictures'. It was time, argued Pickles, for all dreamers 'to wake up and face life as it is'. With so many examples of failed or stumbling federations all around, 'serious reformers, academic or journalist' should 'come down from the clouds' and deal more realistically with the pressing problems of the moment, keeping their dreams simply 'as goals'.

The scepticism at the heart of Pickles's analysis of the federal idea was representative of British opinion about Europe throughout the post-war decades. Policy has been consistently inadequate and misconceived and the public has consequently been variously suspicious or mystified by the fluctuating entreaties of its political leaders.[13] In this atmosphere, federalism and the federal idea received no sustained attention or analysis other than from the committed, and they were few in number and resources and limited in access to what was an essentially sceptical media. Federal Union had attempted to keep the flame of interest alive during the early forties but by the end of the war it had been reduced to modest circumstances, housed in genteel poverty and held together by a small band of hard-core enthusiasts. The Federal Trust was founded in 1945 in succession to the Union's research institute. Its primary aim was education but for many years it had limited activity and a marginal appeal. In fact, it was not until the mid-eighties with the resurgence of interest in the European Union that sufficient stimulus, energy and money existed to again mount a systematic publishing programme and a general campaign to enlighten the British public about the federal ideal. By the mid-nineties these activities had resulted in a series of conferences and the publication of books, pamphlets and articles all explaining and/or exploring the intricacies of the European Union, the nature of Britain's federal past and the hopes for a federal future. Much of the publication record of the associated Lothian

Foundation has concentrated on the doings and sayings of the Round Table movement and of Federal Union, but its appeal has been limited to academic specialists and committed devotees.

Scepticism is still the prevalent stance and the federal idea holds no more attraction in the United Kingdom of the 1990s than it did in the United Kingdom emerging from World War II. For most of those Britons who concern themselves with such matters the word federal conjures up a horrifying image of a centralized system of government rather than one which respects the integrity of the individual states. By the 1990s, as Donald Shell has reminded us, the word federal had became the 'F' word and consequently unacceptable.[14]

The reception given the federal idea on the domestic front was much the same, although ironically it was the perceived diversity inherent in a federal system that caused alarm rather than the centralizing features singled out by the Eurosceptics. The threat posed by a federal system to government centralized at Westminster and to the sanctity of parliamentary sovereignty was too frightening for either of the governing parties to contemplate. The majority of Britons, and certainly most English people, were Unionist in their assumptions and attitudes. In a country where a seventeenth-century concept of parliamentary authority was still readily accepted and where the nineteenth century arguments of a Freeman or a Dicey still held sway, it was not surprising that the federal idea received very little serious attention as a solution to problems bedevilling the various nations and regions of the United Kingdom in the late twentieth century.[15]

Pressure from Scotland and Wales and the remoter regions of England for changes in the governing structure of the United Kingdom had waned since the passage of the Government of Ireland Act of 1920. Without the 'Irish question' to fuel debate there was no reason for the governments of the day to devote time or energy to constitutional matters. Even the ever-present problem of congestion of business at Westminster aroused little more than occasional frustrated mutterings. Scottish and Welsh nationalists remained both divided amongst themselves and marginal within their respective nations, and before the 1960s they were never able to mount any serious challenge either to established authority or to the general acceptance of the status quo. There had been sufficient devolution of administrative powers in both Scotland and Wales since the 1880s to leave most citizens of those Celtic nations with the impression that their interests were protected. For the most part, they were content to look to the main-line political parties for action and saw no need to identify with regional or national parties.[16]

However, by mid-century there could be detected a gathering shift in attitudes in Scotland and Wales towards centralized government and the various departments and agencies it controlled. Numerous particular grievances seemed not to get the attention they deserved and Welsh, Scottish and English regional concerns appeared all too often to fall on deaf ears in

Whitehall and at Westminster. A demand for greater self-government for Scotland and Wales increasingly was heard in the fifties and early sixties. A private member's bill advocating a single-chamber parliament for Wales was briefly debated in the House of Commons in March 1955 and the case for Scottish devolution was often made both in and out of parliament.[17] The advocates of decentralized decision-making were not seeking independence, nor did a federal structure for the United Kingdom seem to interest them. Instead, the ideas that surfaced during those years bore a strong resemblance to the devolutionary proposals of the pre-1914 era and, in fact, the term home rule all round was frequently used by commentators and advocates alike. Ironically, the model to which Scottish and Welsh nationalists often referred was the Government of Ireland Act of 1920 which, though reflective of earlier federalist dreams, had left the powers and sovereignty of the Westminster parliament unimpaired.

Initially, neither the Labour nor the Conservative parties felt compelled to pay more than passing heed to the cries from the periphery for greater national or regional self-government, but with the emergence in the sixties of rejuvenated nationalist parties in Wales and Scotland as viable political forces they were obliged to respond. This was particularly so after the dramatic victory of Gwynfor Evans, the Plaid Cymru candidate, in the Carmarthen by-election in July 1966, the strong showings of Plaid Cymru candidates in by-elections in Rhondda West in March 1967 and in Caerphilly in July 1968 and the remarkable win by Winifred Ewing of the Scottish National Party in the Hamilton by-election of November 1967. Both the Labour and the Conservative parties and particularly English politicians were forced to think in a fundamental way about Celtic nationalism.

Even *The Times* bowed to the gathering evidence of the demand for changes in the constitutional make-up of the United Kingdom. It called for the establishment of a commission 'to review the constitutional arrangements for Scotland and Wales with a view to creating local parliaments for Scottish and Welsh affairs'. While acknowledging the probable need for change, *The Times* took pains to underline that the Union should be preserved: 'It is national democracy that is needed, but not the dismemberment of the United Kingdom.'[18] *The Times* urged the government not to delay, for 'the history of Ireland suggests that moderate constitutional reform can only succeed if it is presented in time'.[19]

In 1912 the Liberal Party had been responsible for introducing the third home rule bill, thereby initiating the last significant examination of a federal solution of the United Kingdom's constitutional woes. Since those heady pre-1914 days the Liberal Party had ceased to be a significant electoral force and operated as no more than a gadfly on the margins of political life. Many of its post-1945 roots, however, were still firmly embedded in the Celtic periphery and it was not surprising that it was the Liberal leader, Jeremy Thorpe, who reintroduced the 'federal' idea to his colleagues in the House of

Commons on 21 February 1968.[20] He called for the establishment of parliaments in Scotland, Wales and Northern Ireland and for a royal commission to explore the possibility of regional parliaments in England.

Thorpe pointed out that many people felt powerless to influence events given the concentration of authority in Whitehall. It was essential, he argued, 'to change the power structure in Britain'. First, the maximum number of people possible had to be involved in decision-making. That alone would go far to restore faith in democracy. And second, devolution would relieve the pressure on the Westminster parliament and allow for fuller debates and greater control over wider national and international issues. Thorpe reminded the House that 'Time and again in our constitutional history we have belatedly conceded in bitterness what could and should have been granted in logic.' He contended the demand for parliaments in Scotland and Wales was 'clear, logical and unassailable'. He asked his colleagues not to repeat the mistakes made in Ireland but to 'recognize as a mature democracy that our system of Government and parliamentary institutions are capable of improvement'.

It was clear from Thorpe's speech that the Liberal Party had a devolutionary rather than a federal system in mind, and this was underlined by a party report issued in April entitled *Power to the Provinces*.[21] The Liberals proposed parliaments for Scotland, Wales and Northern Ireland and twelve provincial assemblies in England for Northumbria, Lancastria, York, Anglia, Mercia, Trent, Severnside, Westcountry, Solent, Thames Valley, Greater London and Weald. Provincial populations would vary from 1,600,000 in Westcountry to 7,900,000 in Greater London. Each province would have a single-chamber assembly elected every three years with the membership varying between sixty and 120 depending on the population and size of the area. All existing local governments would be abolished, to be replaced by new district councils as the single tier of local government beneath the provincial assemblies. A 'federal' parliament would be established in London, representative of all the regions and provinces, with power over such national concerns as defence and foreign policy, agriculture and fisheries, customs and excise, economic and social planning, education, the nationalized industries and power, Home Office affairs and 'federal' taxation. Although the regional and provincial assemblies would have the power to raise their own taxes, the Liberals accepted that the economic inequality that existed between various parts of the country made it essential that the central government should be able to levy a balancing charge on wealthy provinces in order to subsidize the poorer ones.

This was a bold scheme but a cumbersome one. It underlined the need to relieve the Westminster parliament of an overwhelming weight of business and reinforced the case for recognizing both the increase in nationalist sentiment in Scotland and Wales and the gathering frustration in England at the remoteness and the insensitivity of central government.[22] The report did not, however, explore in any detail how power might be divided between the centre and the regions, and by appearing to allocate so much power to the central parliament the Liberals indicated their primary concern was devolutionary rather than truly federal. Jeremy Thorpe might have called for a reorganization of the governmental structure on 'federal lines' but the Liberal scheme seemed more akin to a revamping of the local government apparatus than a blueprint for a federal state on the lines either of the United States and Australia or of Canada.

By this time the general clamour for constitutional change had become irresistible. In 1966 two royal commissions were established to explore the possibility of improving local government in Scotland and England and, finally, in April 1969 the Labour government of Harold Wilson set up a Royal Commission on the Constitution. These commissions, particularly the latter, have often been seen as delaying tactics employed by politicians hoping that the need to address complex issues would evaporate by the time the commissions reported. A more generous interpretation suggests that the cumbersome and remote system of government had finally attracted the analysis it had long warranted.

Wherever the truth might lie it was clear that the federal idea had few supporters even among those prepared for major revisions in the British constitutional system. In all of the discussions in parliament, in the press, in the periodical literature and in books there was almost no support for federalism. Even J.C. Banks's *Federal Britain?*, published in 1971, was, as its subtitle made clear, 'the case for regionalism', while J.P. Mackintosh in his searching examination of the United Kingdom's centralized decision-making opted for political devolution rather than true federalism.[23] The Liberal Party continued to champion the cause and David Steel emerged as an eloquent spokesman for the federal idea, but the Liberals commanded little political support. Moreover, what the Liberals and Steel had in mind never went much further than Jeremy Thorpe's earlier proposals. Their generalizations did not suggest that they desired 'true federalism'.[24] The key here, of course, was that there was simply little public interest in the federal idea. It was alien to the British experience, involving as it did a written constitution, a supreme court and a division of sovereignty, all of which were unappetizing to most Britons who seemingly would have been happy with better local self-government or at most a restrained form of political devolution on the lines of Northern Ireland.

These attitudes were reflected in the final report of the Royal Commission on the Constitution which was published in October 1973.[25] The majority report favoured the introduction of a devolutionary system of government in the United Kingdom, and though the dissenters wanted a division of powers between the central and intermediate levels of government they too made it clear 'that an essential ingredient of such a division must be the recognition that legislative sovereignty in all matters must remain with the United Kingdom Government and Parliament'.[26] The commissioners did not ignore the federal idea but their consideration of it was relegated to a brief ten-page chapter in which they quickly dismissed it as a viable option.[27] Those ten pages contained the fullest official analysis the federal idea received in the United Kingdom in the last half of the twentieth century. That analysis resonated with Diceyan assumptions and disingenuous conclusions but it certainly reflected the contemporary mood and the prevailing state of public understanding of the federal concept.

The commissioners began by declaring, quite correctly, that there was 'very little demand for federalism in Scotland and Wales, and practically none at all in England'. Few of their witnesses had advocated it and, so they claimed, 'people who know the system well tend to advise against it'. After a very brief survey of the main elements of a federal system, the commissioners pointed out that

> It might appear from this description that a federal system would give the individual countries of the United Kingdom a large measure of autonomy. In many important domestic matters they would have sovereign powers which could not be overridden by the central government. Their entrenched position in the constitution would give them a status and influence which the central government would be bound to take into account. At the same time they could still work together in those domestic matters requiring a common policy, and would still form a single state in the eyes of the world.

These certainly were the main arguments usually proffered by promoters of the federal idea, and they looked attractive. Not so, said the commissioners. When 'federalism in action' was examined, 'the situation looks very different. . . . It then becomes clear that in practice it would not bring the advantages which it might appear to offer in theory.'

The commissioners reasoned that federal theory had largely been developed in the nineteenth century when governments played a smaller role in people's lives. Government was then concerned with only a limited range of domestic matters and its primary preoccupation was foreign affairs. 'In those circumstances,' they argued, 'it was possible to divide sovereignty neatly between federal and provincial governments. There was unlikely to be much conflict between the mainly foreign and defence responsibilities of the federal government and the mainly domestic responsibilities of the provincial governments. To all intents and purposes those matters which affected people from day to day could be fully controlled at the provincial level.' Since that time, however, there had been a large increase in the responsibilities of government. Ideas about social justice had changed and governments were now more active domestically and internationally. 'As a result of these changes,' said the commissioners,

> the federal idea of divided sovereignty is becoming difficult to sustain. Provincial governments can no longer keep *de facto* control over all matters which are constitutionally their sole responsibility. Their

sovereignty is being eroded because their electorates are demanding more than can be provided without federal help. In most federations, therefore, power is fast gravitating to the centre. The entrenchment of provincial sovereignty in federal constitutions has not prevented this. It has been overcome either by the transfer of provincial powers to the federal government through changes in the constitution or, more usually, by elaborate measures of cooperation between the provincial and federal governments which in theory leave the provinces' powers intact but which in practice put the federal government in a largely controlling position. In short, to make federalism work in modern conditions federal countries have been compelled to take steps which tend to undermine the principle of provincial sovereignty on which the system itself is based. What is actually in operation is not true federalism.

One of the reasons for increased federal involvement was a shortage of funds at the provincial level which compelled provincial governments to turn to the federal level for help. 'Not infrequently,' concluded the commissioners, 'federal help reaches them in a way which undermines their independence. One of the chief obstacles to the proper working of federalism in modern conditions is the impracticability of arranging a division of finance between the federal and provincial governments which will for any length of time satisfactorily match their respective functions under the constitution.' The interest in equalization had also tended to increase federal responsibilities as they supervised arrangements for equalizing the standard of living between the provinces.

Thus changes in the objectives and responsibilities of government were

tending to result in the by-passing of provincial sovereignty. Yet this adjustment of federalism to modern requirements is generally achieved only with difficulty. The formal division of sovereignty between the federal and provincial governments tends to slow down desirable change and may even prevent it altogether. Where sovereign rights are at stake agreement to change may not be easy to reach. Negotiations for a new allocation of functions or sources of revenue between the federation and the provinces can be long drawn out.

The commissioners seemed to be suggesting that 'true federalism' involved a rigid, unbending division of sovereign powers and that any cooperative or coordinating arrangements entered into by the two levels of government somehow made the system less than truly federal. This was a very strained interpretation of federalism. Rather than viewing the various strategies employed by the Canadians and Americans to ensure the smoothest possible functioning of their federal systems as a positive indication of the adaptive, cooperative essence of federalism, the commissioners chose to view such systems as 'awkward' and 'inflexible'. They even said by way of criticism that federalism 'depends a great deal on cooperation between governments', as if cooperation leading to stable and relatively open systems of government was a very strange idea. It reflected the inherent unwillingness in the British political elite to diminish in any way the centralized and sovereign powers of the Westminster parliament. The commissioners asserted that when cooperative and coordinating arrangements existed between federal and provincial governments the sovereignty of the provinces was intrinsically undermined. This, of course, was simply not so. The provinces or states still had their entrenched powers even if the means of exercising them or implementing them were continuously adapted to circumstance. By making the comments and assertions they did, the commissioners were revealing their dependence on literal textbook treatments of the federal idea and their personal lack of familiarity with federal states as adaptive organisms.

The commissioners went on to argue that in light of the general criticisms they had made about federalism there would need to be compelling reasons to introduce a federal system into the United Kingdom. Insofar as they were concerned, none existed. In fact, they believed a federal system would be 'particularly unsuitable for adoption in the United Kingdom'. If federalism had any merit it was for states 'coming together to form a single unit, and not for a state breaking up into smaller units'. This argument was, of course, the classic one offered time and again by Dicey and Freeman in the late nineteenth century. The fact that it was invalid did not deter the commissioners. They went on to make other equally questionable assertions such as that a federal system was most appropriate 'to the earlier stages of integration, when relations between provinces and between provincial and federal governments are inevitably characterized by a certain wariness and rivalry'. Under such circumstances, there was a necessity to have everything in writing. This in the commissioners' view would not be appropriate in the United Kingdom which 'had been governed in a spirit of unity and cooperation' for centuries. This was, at the least, an intriguing non-Celtic view of the history of the British Isles since the sixteenth century. As for the assertion that a federal system was 'intended for a much earlier stage of constitutional development', it was ironic that many of the experts who had been consulted about the adoption of federalism in the colonial setting had asserted that a federal system with its inherent acceptance of sacrificing individual or provincial interests for the common good demanded a high level of political sophistication. The commissioners were clearly unaware of those analyses.

The commissioners also noted that a federal system of government 'would require a written constitution, a special procedure for changing it and a constitutional court to interpret it'. None of these features had ever been a part of the United Kingdom's constitutional arrangements and they doubted whether they would be accepted. The commissioners then went on to make the by now standard argument about the sovereignty of parliament, not seeming to recognize that such sovereignty was at the root of much of contemporary concern. They pointed out that the United Kingdom did not have a separate body of entrenched law enshrining the basic rules of government. Parliament was sovereign and could make or alter any law by a simple majority. Its Acts were interpreted by the courts not in the light of general constitutional principles or limitations on the powers of parliament but in direct reference to the statute itself. Parliament could not be overruled by the courts; it could always change the law. In a federal system, however, the elective legislative bodies were subordinate to the judiciary in matters of dispute between federal and provincial jurisdictions. The work of judges, especially in the United States variant of federalism, tended to become political – a matter of individual judgement. 'This situation', said the commissioners, 'probably unavoidable in a federal system, is foreign to our own tradition of unitary government based upon the complete sovereignty of parliament and upon the complete dissociation of the judiciary from matters of political policy.' The commissioners concluded that 'Although there were circumstances in which benefits to be derived from federalism may outweigh those of any practicable alternative, in our view such circumstances do not exist in the United Kingdom. We believe that to most people a federal system would appear strange and artificial. It would not provide continuity with the past or sufficient flexibility for the future, and it is unlikely that it would be generally acceptable.'

The commissioners then turned to the problem of England and here they had a more telling argument. They did not believe any advocate had succeeded in producing 'a federal scheme satisfactorily tailored to fit the circumstances of England'. In their estimation,

> A federation consisting of four units – England, Scotland, Wales and Northern Ireland – would be so unbalanced as to be unworkable. It would be dominated by the overwhelming political importance and wealth of England. The English Parliament would rival the United Kingdom federal Parliament; and in the federal Parliament itself the representation of England could hardly be scaled down in such a way as to enable it to be outvoted by Scotland, Wales, and Northern Ireland, together representing less than one-fifth of the population. A United Kingdom federation of the four countries, with a federal Parliament and provincial Parliaments in the four national capitals, is therefore not a realistic proposition.

They admitted that 'the imbalance would be corrected if England were to be divided into a number of units, each having the status of a federal province'. It was clear to them, however, that such an 'artificial division into provinces with independent sovereign powers would be unacceptable to the people of England'. Also, proposals that split England into several provinces tended to overlook the fact that the province that included south-east England might itself dominate the federation. Out of a population of 55 million in 1973, 17 million lived in that region of the United Kingdom, and since it included London where the business and financial headquarters of the country were located its influence would be even greater. The commissioners concluded that there was no satisfactory way to fit England into a fully federal system.

The commissioners also regarded it as essential to maintain political and economic unity but, in their view, 'Federalism would tend to undermine that unity and make the objectives of the United Kingdom more difficult to attain.' They feared 'that provinces with sovereign powers would not always be very ready to cooperate with each other and with the central government in the wider interest'. This might lead to intergovernmental rivalry and contention to an extent that would be damaging to the interests of the United Kingdom, particularly in European Community matters. That such rivalries were rarely if ever true of federal government reflected the rather superficial examination of federalism conducted by the commissioners.

The commissioners clearly recognized that they had been highly critical of a system of government that worked reasonably well elsewhere, providing a balance of power between the centre and the provinces. They believed, however,

> that where the results are successful this is due not so much to federalism as such as to the ingenuity and common sense of those who are operating it. By and large the system is not of any great help to them in modern conditions. It tends to place difficulties in their way. They get around those difficulties in practice often by departing from the principle of provincial sovereignty on which the system itself is based. In effect what they are operating is not true federalism, and their experience suggests that division of sovereignty may no longer be fully practicable. It may be that a formal division of functions between two levels of government can be satisfactorily sustained only when one of them can if need be enforce upon the other a redistribution of those functions.

Not surprisingly the commissioners concluded

> that if government in the United Kingdom is to meet the present-day needs of the people it is necessary for the undivided sovereignty of Parliament to be maintained. We believe that only with the general ambit of one supreme elected authority is it likely that there will emerge the degree of unity, cooperation and flexibility which common sense suggests is desirable. Even if a federal system could be designed to avoid domination by England (and we do not think it could) it would endanger the essential unity which now exists and make some important tasks of government more difficult to perform. It would probably be regarded by the British people as a strange and artificial system not suited to their present stage of constitutional development, and in the end would bring the provinces very little more independence than might be achieved within a unitary system. In short, the United Kingdom is not an appropriate place for federalism and now is not an appropriate time.

This was an extraordinarily patronizing and dismissive conclusion. Apparently, the federal system was fine in less advanced countries, such as ex-colonies, but not for a 'mature' polity. What constituted maturity? A hierarchical, class-ridden state under the guise of a democratic unitary system? Or was it a state without a bill of rights and paranoid delusions about the need for secrecy? Anytime one sees 'common sense' used as a reason for anything one has to be suspicious of the ideological and cultural assumptions that constitute 'common sense'. After all, one person's 'common sense' often appears to another no more than the self-serving dictates of power. The commissioners had tended to turn a blind eye to the myriad difficulties that had been avoided by the adoption and working of a federal system. Not to have such a system in many instances would have resulted in an untold number of frictions and disputes. At least in the federal structures in place in the United States, Canada and Australia the status of the regions was recognized and respected and negotiations could begin from both a basis of equity and a desire to cooperate. Strong central government, on the other hand, could all too often result in riding roughshod over regional and minority rights and the skewing of economic activity and performance.

Having dismissed the federal idea as inappropriate for the United Kingdom, the majority of the commissioners recommended a system of legislative devolution for Scotland and Wales and the establishment of elected assemblies in those 'nations'. They agreed, however, that legislative devolution should not be applied to England or to its regions. They preferred to see the establishment of 'regional co-ordinating and advisory councils, partly indirectly elected by the local authorities and partly nominated'.[28] The recommendations were exceptionally modest, going only as far as it seemed necessary to go in Scotland and Wales and backing away almost completely from the knotty 'English question'.

In the months following the publication of the report in October 1973 the political and economic climate changed considerably. The Scottish National Party and Plaid Cymru upped their clamour for 'national' assemblies in Scotland and Wales, the economy took a downturn in the aftermath of the oil crisis of 1973 and both the Conservative and Labour governments were hard pressed to respond with positive policies. In these circumstances, the Labour government was more or less obliged to introduce the Scotland and Wales Bill in 1976. In doing so both Harold Wilson and his successor as prime minister, James Callaghan, went out of their way to reject the federal idea. Wilson thought its application to the United Kingdom would result in the division of sovereignty, a written constitution and the establishment of a constitutional court, none of which could possibly match the maturity of the existing democratic institutions and traditions of the United Kingdom. For Wilson, a federal solution would mean the insertion of 'judicial determination, theologising, legalistically-inspired findings . . . into the whole of our economic and social life'. A federal solution to the constitutional, regional and economic problems of the United Kingdom would, in Wilson's view, be at best 'totally contrived and artificial and at worst unworkable and unwanted'.[29] Later in the year James Callaghan was less acerbic but equally emphatic. The task confronting the government was 'to modernize and reinvigorate a partnership between a large historic nation and three much smaller historic nations'. Federalism was not the way to achieve that goal. While it might work well elsewhere, it was 'simply not a relevant road for the United Kingdom'. It was 'not for us'.[30]

It was clear from the debate that followed in 1977 and 1978 that Wilson and Callaghan had correctly judged the mood. There was virtually no comment on the federal idea and certainly no sustained or forceful defence of that form of government.[31] The introduction of the Scotland and Wales Bill of 1976 eventually led to the passage of the Scotland Act and the Wales Act of 1978. Neither was in the least federal and the Wales Act provided only executive devolution rather than legislative devolution. Clearly the support for any diminution of parliament's authority was now waning both at Westminster and even in the Celtic periphery. This was confirmed in March 1979 when a referendum was held on the issue of devolution in both Scotland and Wales. Neither was successful. With the advent of the Thatcher government later that year all further efforts at devolution and regionalism met with disinterest.

In the past twenty years the issue of constitutional change within the United Kingdom has continued to attract the attention of academics and of those associated with long-term commitments to structural change. In such analyses and discussions the federal idea often surfaces as an alternative to be considered alongside regionalism or some variant of devolution, but it is rare to find it advocated. One organization that did offer a thoughtful treatment was the Federal Trust for Education and Research, the offshoot of the earlier Federal Union. In 1977 it initiated a study that systematically explored the federal idea as a solution to the administrative, economic and constitutional problems besetting the United Kingdom. It reasoned that a federal structure would provide greater stability, ensure a more democratic government and provide greater protection for minorities than the current system. It opted for a number of English provinces – a balanced federal constitution – rather than the maintenance of an undivided England – an unbalanced federal constitution – but implicitly admitted that provincial or regional loyalties would have to be nurtured. It then explored the very real problems involved in fiscal federalism and the role of a federal United Kingdom in the new Europe. This was by far the best informed and most useful publication on the federal idea but it had almost no impact. It was published in 1980 at a time when there was little hope that the limited and devolutionary Scotland and Wales Acts would ever be resurrected. Since those two Acts reflected the limits the British were prepared to venture in the direction of decentralization the Federal Trust must have known its efforts would have virtually no effect. It was ably fulfilling its educational mandate but to little avail.[32]

In the 1990s discussion of constitutional reform has been primarily focused on what the Labour Party might do on achieving power. Speculation was rife on the eve of the April 1992 election but the unexpected victory of the Conservatives led by John Major shunted to one side any chance of immediate change. As Tory prospects have plummeted in the mid-to-late nineties and Tony Blair's Labour party has become the odds-on favourite to win the next election there has been a noticeable increase in the coverage accorded possible constitutional reform in both the daily press and the academic literature. Since the Labour Party is committed to no more than legislative devolution in Scotland and to only a restricted form of decentralization in Wales and the English regions these discussions have rarely touched on the federal idea and then only to dismiss it as a viable option.

At the end of the twentieth century the majority of Britons, and particularly the English, seem as wedded as ever they have been in the last two centuries to the principle of parliamentary sovereignty. This identification with and ready acceptance of the supremacy of the Westminster parliament has been sustained by the desire of the two main parties to keep off the agenda any searching discussion of parliamentary authority. Any number of administrative devices have been resorted to in order to leave the impression of a government sensitive to territorial needs and concerns, but none of these has truly rested on popular sovereignty. The British state remains highly centralized and the Westminster parliament is seen as supreme within the United Kingdom despite growing evidence that Brussels is inexorably compromising its principled sovereignty. This deep-rooted commitment to parliamentary sovereignty has not encouraged serious debate over the relationship of the citizen to the state nor 'the relationship of the various parts to the whole'.[33] The British lack a tradition of open-ended public discussion of constitutional variables, and as long as that is married to an overwhelming lack of interest in fundamental constitutional change in England, the largest of the nations of the United Kingdom, the federal idea will not receive the serious consideration it deserves as an alternative system of government. At the end of the twentieth century as at the beginning of the eighteenth, 'an incorporating union' is clearly preferred by the English.[34]

9 Conclusion

At various times over the past four centuries the British have endeavoured to preserve both the unity of the United Kingdom and the unity of their empire. During those stressful moments when the problems inherent in attempting to maintain unity while protecting diversity were most acute, the federal idea was often examined as a possible solution to the dilemma. Similarly, as the empire gradually waned and colonies aspired to independence, the British government adopted the federal idea in an attempt to ensure the post-independence viability of many of its colonial possessions. More recently, as the United Kingdom gradually turned towards Europe and closer economic and constitutional integration with its continental neighbours, the British have once more been obliged to address the federal idea and its implications.

The first intense soundings of the federal idea occurred in the early 1700s when a political union between Scotland and England was broached. Many Scots were anxious to preserve their nation's sovereignty and suggested a 'federal union' as opposed to the 'incorporating union' eventually adopted. While the schemes devised to protect Scottish political identity were often called 'federal' and in fact recommended separate Scottish and English parliaments with a central parliament for common purposes, none laid out in detail a division of powers between the two levels of government. The concept of parliamentary sovereignty had recently become widely endorsed and it was difficult for contemporary writers and lobbyists to contemplate the sharing or transferring of power let alone the division of sovereignty such a constitution would have involved. Although that division was simultaneously being established *de facto* if not *de jure* in the imperial realm, no observers in either Scotland or England made the connection to the domestic scene.

In the eighteenth century, the British were unable to accept that the sovereignty of king, lords and commons was divisible, and the majority of them have not been able to accept it to this day as a solution to the tensions between the four nations of the United Kingdom. The concentration of English power in London and its immediate area, the lack of any strong or well-defined English regional units, the subjugation of the Irish, the incorporation of Wales into the English state and the emasculation of the Scots' political identity after the Act of Union of 1707 all reaffirmed the nature of state power in the British Isles, resting as it did on the highly centralized English state in existence since the thirteenth century. When these developments were coupled with the desire for political stability in the aftermath of the upheavals of the seventeenth century it was understandable why the political elite wished to ensure that governmental control remained with a central executive operating through a single state parliament. To allow other parliaments to be established and to divide sovereignty between those regional parliaments and the centre would concede too much.

The first major challenge to the conviction that parliamentary sovereignty was indivisible occurred during the flare-up between the imperial government in London and thirteen of its North American colonies in the late eighteenth century. The American colonists asserted that British administrative and governmental practices in their empire since the early 1600s had *de facto* resulted in a division of parliamentary sovereignty. The inability or unwillingness of the British to accept that assertion led to a flurry of constitutional theorizing in the colonies about the transatlantic relationship. At the heart of many of the schemes and ideas that surfaced was a desire to retain a close connection with the mother country while allowing political discretion and constitutional and economic growth in the colonies. The failure of the British to respond to these ideas eventually led to war and the severance of the imperial tie. One can detect in the pre-war discussions the seed of the federal idea that was to be buffed and refined in *The Federalist* as well as in the debates and compromises at Philadelphia. The United States constitution devised in the 1780s was designed to do in the new nation what the British had not been prepared to do either at home or in their empire: establish a system of government that would ensure unity while allowing and protecting diversity. The new system therefore rested on the twin principles of the sovereignty of the people and the divisibility of parliamentary sovereignty and was marked by two levels of government – federal and state – both answerable directly to the people, a written constitution, a supreme court to interpret that constitution and an amendment process. The American variant of the federal idea became the model for all subsequent federations.

The British had not consciously contributed much to the theoretical discussions underpinning the United States constitution. Admittedly, many of the insights of John Locke and James Harrington had stimulated the American writers and theorists, while the British imperial system with its apparent division of powers had proved a useful launching pad for the concept of a 'federal union' which went well beyond that advocated by the Scots almost a century earlier. Nevertheless, the paucity of British commentary both before and after the American Revolution was marked. So deeply instilled had the concept of the indivisibility of sovereignty become by the late eighteenth century that no English theorist was prepared to explore the implications of the obverse, and the British, particularly the English, were so committed to the continued power and dominance of the British nation-state that anything that might undermine or emasculate it was anathema. The rapidity with which Ireland was absorbed into the Union in 1801, thereby stripping it of any countervailing authority, underscored the conviction that the strength of the United Kingdom rested on the maintenance of a strong centralized state anchored in Westminster and Whitehall. The gradual opening up of parliamentary representation to Catholics and increasingly to more men in the nineteenth century, and then to all men and women of a certain age in the twentieth century, made it seem that all regions and strata and divisions in British society were fairly represented in the central parliament, thereby undermining any suggestion of a further transfer or devolution of power. The inherent strengths of the unwritten, pragmatic British system of unitary government were uniformly praised by the British constitutional experts of the nineteenth and early twentieth centuries while the supposed rigidity and weaknesses of the alternative federal system tended to be highlighted rather than its cooperative, coordinate and adaptive qualities. It was clear that writers such as John Stuart Mill, Edward Freeman, James Bryce, Henry Sidgwick and A.V. Dicey were all thoroughly familiar with the federal idea and they provided sound expositions of its nature and operation but not one of them was prepared to push the boundaries of theoretical discussion and explore its possibilities for the British state.

Freeman and Dicey wrote more than most about the federal idea in both a United Kingdom and an imperial context but neither could accept the sundering of either the domestic or the imperial union that the divisibility of sovereignty would supposedly entail. Dicey quickly left the realm of rational thought when it came to discussing the federal idea in the context of the Anglo-Irish relationship. He was convinced that to enable the Irish to become self-governing within a federal state would lead directly to the break-up of the United Kingdom and eventually of the empire. This ran contrary to all his deep-seated veneration of British power and his concern for order. By the early twentieth century Dicey was openly a polemicist on these issues and not a constitutional theorist. Freeman never went as far as Dicey in his denunciations but he was equally convinced that to adopt a federal system for the United Kingdom would harm more than it would resolve.

Many of the points made by Dicey and Freeman were telling ones. The general lack of interest, particularly in England, and the impossibility in an increasingly complex society of devising a clean cut between federal and state powers, especially fiscal powers, were valid. These difficulties have remained and are as much a part of late twentieth-century discussions as they were in the late nineteenth, but while critical they are not insuperable if there is a desire to open up a society and allow a greater degree of involvement by the regions and the citizenry at all levels of government activity.

Dicey and Freeman did nothing to promote the emergence of a new approach to the distribution of power within British society. They were convinced the British state should be centralized or it would be weakened. Neither they nor their colleagues could be persuaded to the contrary.

When the federal idea was broached in the United Kingdom in the nineteenth and twentieth centuries it was usually by individual commentators and publicists or by non-governmental organizations and societies such as the Round Table movement and Federal Union. These advocates had no official standing, and while they were often able to gain access to powerful men and to raise the level of debate they ultimately had no impact on the major political parties. Moreover, many of those who promoted the federal idea had not grasped its true essence in the way that experts such as Freeman and Dicey had. All too often they confused federalism with devolution or home rule all round, not realizing that the primary feature of a federal system was the division of sovereign power. It quickly became clear during the protracted discussion and often heated debate over the Anglo-Irish relationship that most of those who advocated the federal idea really meant devolution while those who did identify with true federalism saw it as a means of preserving the Union and hopefully a strong central government. The confusion that underlay much of the debate surrounding the application of the federal idea to the United Kingdom was symbolized by the Government of Ireland Act of 1920 which more than any other piece of British domestic legislation owed much to the federal idea. It had been devised both to preserve the Union and give Northern and Southern Ireland their own parliaments. It was not, however, true federalism but rather 'devolution in a federal form' with all the inherent problems of such a hybrid. Its Northern Ireland variant proved a poor example of devolution and was all too easily cited by critics of the federal idea as a dysfunctional constitutional system.

While the British have never been prepared to adopt the federal idea in the United Kingdom they have often eagerly embraced it as a solution to problems in the imperial realm. Only in the colonial sphere were they ready to recognize and accept the merits of the federal system of government. No doubt this partially lay in their acceptance of the assumption that the federal idea was best suited to drawing disparate polities together – creating unity out of diversity – than in the disaggregation of an existing polity such as the United Kingdom. It was also because the sovereignty of the United Kingdom parliament did not appear to be threatened by the creation of federal states overseas, especially since the United Kingdom continued well into the twentieth century to control the key decisions affecting imperial defence and foreign policy. By the time the white settlement federations of Canada and Australia took full command of those vital matters in World War II the British government was finding it difficult to sustain its status as a first-class imperial and world power. With decolonization an accelerating necessity by mid-century, the British turned to the federal idea as a means of launching viable states into the international arena and of assuring themselves of continuing markets and stable strategic allies. The break-up of the empire that Dicey and Freeman and so many other commentators had feared was now a brute reality. Under those circumstances, the issue of parliamentary sovereignty in the imperial context was no longer a factor. The federal idea became an agreeable pragmatic device to facilitate the demission and transfer of power while preserving stability in regions often small and invariably divided by religious, ethnic and cultural differences.

What was striking about the British involvement with the federal idea in the 1950s was the expertise which could be brought to bear upon the problems connected with devising federal constitutions. By that date the British had behind them a half-century of close study and advocacy of the federal concept. The Round Table movement had provided an early stimulus and it had continued through the actions of two of its leading figures, Lionel Curtis and Philip Kerr, to promote the idea into the 1940s. The emergence of Federal Union in the late thirties had allowed the idealism and fervour that had long fuelled the Round Table organization to be channelled into the cause of European union. This led to the most intensive and searching discussion of the federal idea ever held in the British Isles, far surpassing in sophistication and depth of understanding anything generated by the debate over the Anglo-Irish relationship.

Federal Union approached the educational and intellectual dimensions of federalism with vigour, and an impressive array of experts were marshalled to explore and explain the federal idea. The contributions of Ivor Jennings and Kenneth Wheare to this discussion were particularly notable, and it was to them and their writings that the officials in the Colonial Office, the Foreign Office and the Treasury invariably turned for guidance and advice as they wrestled with the conundra associated with devising federal constitutions to suit varying complex conditions. Wheare's was the most important voice. His book *Federal Government*, published in 1946, had been immediately accepted as the classic statement. Wheare's federal construct rested heavily on the American example. Its essential underlying principle was the coordinate division of sovereignty between federal and state governments. In writing as he did, Wheare was not indulging in speculation about federalism as process but was drawing in particular on the federal experience of the Americans as well as that of the Canadians and the Australians. Moreover, the debate about the federal idea that had waxed and waned in the British Isles since the late eighteenth century had always accepted as a basic assumption that a division of sovereignty was at the heart of a 'true federalism'. Wheare was simply summarizing a century-long discussion and analysing its implications and application. He did so in lucid, cogent prose that his contemporaries in official circles in the mid-twentieth century found compelling. All the federations they devised were modelled on Wheare's analysis and guided by his insights.

Although the federal idea was attractive to British governments confronted by a bewildering number of overlapping colonial problems, it continued to be rejected by them both as a solution for metropolitan difficulties and as a safe constitutional haven for the United Kingdom in a newly constituted European union. As a consequence, the expertise surrounding the federal idea that had been built up in the Colonial Office and among a bevy of individual writers and consultants was never drawn upon for the resolution of domestic problems. During the last decades of the twentieth century the debate over both the relationship between the four nations of the United Kingdom and of the United Kingdom to Europe was conducted as if there had been no British involvement with or experience of the federal idea. There has been no sustained exploration of it as a viable constitutional alternative to the highly centralized system in place in the United Kingdom either by governments or by more disinterested constitutional experts.

It certainly suited the interests of the two major parties to have sovereign power exercised by a small executive but disarmingly presented through the medium of a representative parliament of the people. Whenever a leading politician in the Labour or Conservative governments was obliged to discuss the possible transfer of power to the regions the federal idea was always referred to as a rigid, legalistic system better suited for unsophisticated, even 'primitive', societies. The negative side of the equation was always put, especially so in major formal reviews of constitutional options. The adaptive, flexible, open processes of the federal system were left unmentioned and thus unexplored. This prevailing commitment to the idea of parliamentary sovereignty is deeply rooted. It is treated as sacrosanct and is part and parcel of the conditioning that all young citizens of the United Kingdom experience as they move through the various levels of the educational system. The lack of any open-ended public discussion of constitutional alternatives leaves little opportunity for the federal idea to receive an airing or for the citizenry to appreciate its strengths as well as its weaknesses.

British governments have also reacted unfavourably to the prospect of a federal Europe. While they have been prepared to enter into intergovernmental arrangements and to coordinate various economic and social policies with their continental neighbours, the British have generally frowned on any constitutional advance towards a federal European union. At the heart of the British argument in this setting is, intriguingly, not the *diversity* inherent in the federal idea singled out in domestic debate but the *centralizing* features of federalism. The unity that would come from drawing diverse states and peoples together under a federal umbrella is seen as a threat to the sovereignty of the British parliament and to the sovereignty of the British state. This has become the central plank of the Eurosceptics' platform. Neither they nor the various Labour and Conservative governments of recent decades have been prepared publicly to recognize or admit that much of that fabled sovereignty has already been undermined by the realities of modern international relations and will remain so even under a non-federal European union. Ironically, a federal structure might arrest the diminution of British sovereignty in that a federal constitution would define the powers and responsibilities of the states vis-à-vis the centre and ensure a coordinated approach to mutual interests and problems. But that possibility is rarely heard except in the pamphlets, writings and conferences of small educational groups such as the Federal Trust and the Lothian Foundation. Despite the sceptical atmosphere, the federal idea will undoubtedly be revisited continuously in the twenty-first century, as it has been since the seventeenth, as a potential solution to the national and regional tensions within the United Kingdom and between the United Kingdom and Europe. It offers a protection for both unity and diversity rarely found in even the most pragmatic of unitary systems.

Notes

1 INDIVISIBLE SOVEREIGNTY

1 Jenny Wormald, 'The Creation of Britain: Multiple Kingdoms or Core and Colonies?', *Transactions of the Royal Historical Society*, sixth series, II (1992), pp. 175–94. See also J.H. Elliott, *Imperial Spain 1469–1716* (London, Edward Arnold, 1963) and Mark Greengrass (ed.), *Conquest and Coalescence: The Shaping of the State in Early Modern Europe* (London, Edward Arnold, 1991). See also Jenny Wormald, 'The Union of 1603' in Roger A. Mason (ed.), *Scots and Britons: Scottish Political Thought and the Union of 1603* (Cambridge, Cambridge University Press, 1994).

2 Wormald, 'The Creation of Britain', pp. 192–3.

3 For a full treatment of this issue see Bruce Galloway, *The Union of England and Scotland* (Edinburgh, John Donald Publishers, 1985); Bruce Levack, *The Formation of the British State: England, Scotland, and the Union 1603–1707* (Oxford, Clarendon Press, 1987); and Bruce Levack, 'Conceptions of a British Polity in the Seventeenth and Eighteenth Centuries' (unpublished paper, 1990).

4 John Doddridge, 'A Breif Consideracion of the Unyon of Twoe Kingdomes in the Handes of One Kinge' in Bruce Galloway and Brian Levack (eds), *The Jacobean Union: Six Tracts of 1604* (Edinburgh, Scottish History Society, 1985), p. 146.

5 Levack, *The Formation of the British State*, p. 48.

6 See John Russell, 'A Treatise of the Happie and Blissed Unioun' in Galloway and Levack (eds), *The Jacobean Union*, pp. 75–142.

7 See Wormald, 'The Creation of Britain', p. 192; and Levack, *The Formation of the British State*, pp. 48–9.

8 See the valuable essay by David Stevenson, 'The Early Covenanters and the Federal Union of Britain' in Roger A. Mason (ed.), *Scotland and England 1286–1815* (Edinburgh, John Donald Publishers, 1987), pp. 163–81; and Paul H. Scott, *Andrew Fletcher and the Treaty of Union* (Edinburgh, John Donald Publishers, 1992), pp. 149–51. A recent work which makes a point of emphasizing the federal nature of the covenanters' proposals is Keith M. Brown, *Kingdom or Province? Scotland and the Regal Union, 1603–1715* (London, Macmillan, 1992). Valuable for the mid- and late seventeenth-century negotiations is C. Sanford Terry (ed.), *The Cromwellian Union: Papers Relating to the Negotiations for an Incorporating Union Between England and Scotland 1651–1652: With an Appendix of Papers Relating to the Negotiations: 1670* (Edinburgh 1901).

9 See here Linda Colley, *Britons: Forging the Nation 1707–1837* (New Haven and London, Yale University Press, 1992); Brown, *Kingdom or Province?* provides a useful summary of 'The British Problem, 1697–1707', pp. 177–88.

10 See George S. Pryde (ed.), *The Treaty of Union of Scotland and England 1707* (London, Thomas Nelson and Sons, 1950), pp. 36–9; and James Mackinnon, *The Union of England and Scotland: A Study of International History* (London, Longmans, 1896), pp. 211, 226–7.

11 See here William Ferguson, 'Imperial Crowns: A Neglected Facet of the Background to the Treaty of Union of 1707', *Scottish Historical Review*, vol. 53 (1974), pp. 22–44; and C.H. Firth, 'The British Empire', *Scottish Historical Review*, vol. 15, no. 59 (April 1918), pp. 185–9.

12 James Mackinnon, *The Union of England and Scotland: A Study of International History* (London, Longmans, Green and Co., 1896), pp. 211, 227.

13 William Ferguson, *Scotland's Relations with England: A Survey to 1707* (Edinburgh, John Donald Publishers, 1977), p. 234.

14 James Hodges, *The Rights and Interests of the Two British Monarchies, Inquir'd into, and Clear'd: With a Special Respect to an United or Separate State*, Treatise I and III (London 1703).

15 Ibid., p. 2.

16 Ibid., p. 3.

17 Ibid., pp. 3 and 4.

18 Ibid., pp. 6 and 7.

19 See title page of [James Hodges], *Essay Upon the Union* (1706).

20 See H.T. Dickinson, 'The Eighteenth-century Debate on the Sovereignty of Parliament', *Transactions of the Royal Historical Society*, 5S, vol. 26 (1976), pp. 189–210.

21 Ibid., p. 208.

22 John M. Gray (ed.), *Memoirs of the Life of Sir John Clerk of Penicuik, Baronet Baron of the Exchequer: Extracted by Himself from his own Journals 1676–1755* (Edinburgh 1892), vol. xiii of the Publications of the Scottish Historical Society, p. 60.

23 Daniel Defoe, *The History of the Union Between England and Scotland* (London 1786), p. 232.

24 Ibid., p. 315.

25 See Andrew Fletcher, *An Account of a Conversation Concerning a Right Regulation of Governments for the Common Good of Mankind December 1703* (Edinburgh 1704) in Andrew Fletcher, *Political Works* (London 1732), pp. 363–448. Fletcher's ideas have recently received a full and perceptive analysis by Scott, *Andrew Fletcher and the Treaty of Union*, and by John Robertson, 'Andrew Fletcher's Vision of Union' in Mason (ed.), *Scotland and England 1286–1815*, pp. 203–25. A valuable survey of Anglo-Scottish relations in the period 1660–1707 is provided by Ferguson, *Scotland's Relations with England*, pp. 142–277.

26 Fletcher, *An Account of a Conversation*, p. 447.

27 [Andrew Fletcher of Saltoun], *State of the Controversy Betwixt United and Separate Parliaments* (n.p. 1706), p. 23.

28 [Sir John Clerk of Penicuik], *A Letter to a Friend, Giving an Account How the Treaty of Union Has Been Received Here: And Wherein are Contained, Answers to the Most Material Objections Against it, with Some Remarks Upon What Has Been Written by Mr H[odges] and Mr R[idpath]* (Edinburgh 1706), pp. 10–13.

29 See a suggestive article by W.S. McKechnie, 'The Constitutional Necessity for the Union of 1707', *Scottish Historical Review*, vol. 5 (1908), pp. 52–66; and an invaluable study by F.H. Hinsley, *Sovereignty* (London, C.A. Watts and Co., 1966).

30 On the post-1707 Union see Colley, *Britons*; John M. Mackenzie, 'Essay and Reflection: On Scotland and the Empire', *International History Review*, vol. xv, no. 4 (November 1993), pp. 714–39; John Robertson, 'Union, State and Empire:

The Britain of 1707 in its European Setting' in Lawrence Stone (ed.), *An Imperial State at War: Britain from 1689 to 1815* (London, Routledge, 1994), pp. 224–57; and Daniel Szechi, 'The Hanoverians and Scotland' in Mark Greengrass (ed.), *Conquest and Coalescence*, pp. 116–33.

31 See C.S.S. Higham, 'The General Assembly of the Leeward Islands Part I', *English Historical Review*, no. clxi (April 1926), pp. 190–209, and C.S.S. Higham, 'The General Assembly of the Leeward Islands Part II', *English Historical Review*, no. clxiii (July 1926), pp. 366–88.

32 For a succinct summary of the political jobbery view see Colin Kidd, *Subverting Scotland's Past: Scottish Whig Historians and the Creation of an Anglo-British Identity, 1689–c1830* (Cambridge, Cambridge University Press, 1993), pp. 36–50.

33 William Blackstone, *Commentaries on the Laws of England* (Philadelphia, George W. Childs, 1870), Book I, chapter 2, III, p. 160.

34 On the issues of parliamentary sovereignty, custom and natural rights see John V. Jezierski, 'Parliament or People: James Wilson and Blackstone on the Nature and Location of Sovereignty', *Journal of the History of Ideas*, vol. xxxii, no. 1 (January–March 1971), pp. 95–106; Dickinson, 'The Eighteenth-century Debate on the Sovereignty of Parliament', pp. 189–210; Barbara A. Black, 'The Constitution of Empire: The Case for the Colonists', *University of Pennsylvania Law Review*, vol. 124, no. 5 (May 1976), pp. 1157–1211; John Phillip Reid, 'In Accordance with Usage: The Authority of Custom, The Stamp Act Debate, and the Coming of the American Revolution', *Fordham Law Review*, vol. xlv (1976–7), pp. 335–68; Jack P. Greene, 'From the Perspective of Law: Context and Legitimacy in the Origins of the American Revolution', *South Atlantic Quarterly*, vol. 85, no. 1 (Winter 1986), pp. 56–77; C.F. Mullett, 'Colonial Claims to Home Rule (1764–1775): An Essay in Imperial Politics', *University of Missouri Studies*, vol. ii, no. 4 [n.d.], pp. 1–31; Bernard Bailyn, 'Sovereignty' in *The Ideological Origins of the American Revolution* (Cambridge, Mass., Harvard University Press, 1967), pp. 198–229; Jack P. Greene, *Peripheries and Center: Constitutional Development in the Extended Polities of the British Empire and the United States, 1607–1788* (New York, W.W. Norton and Company, 1986); Charles M. Andrews, 'The Government of the Empire, 1660–1763' in J.H. Rose *et al.*, *The Cambridge History of the British Empire*, vol. 1 (Cambridge, Cambridge University Press, 1929), pp. 405–36; J. Ewing, 'The Constitution and the Empire: From Bacon to Blackstone', ibid., pp. 603–33; Andrew C. McLaughlin, 'The Background of American Federalism', *American Political Science Review*, vol. 12 (1918), pp. 215–40; and Robert W. Tucker and David C. Hendrickson, *The Fall of the First British Empire: Origins of the War of American Independence* (Baltimore, Md, Johns Hopkins University Press, 1982), pp. 172–86.

35 McLaughlin, 'The Background of American Federalism'.

36 Fred J. Hinkhouse, *The Preliminaries of the American Revolution as Seen in the English Press 1763–1775* (New York, Columbia University Press, 1926), p. 118.

37 Tucker and Hendrickson, *The Fall of the First British Empire*; the following quotations are from pp. 172–85.

38 Charles F. Mullett, 'English Imperial Thinking, 1764–1783', *Political Science Quarterly*, vol. 45, no. 4 (December 1930), pp. 548–79.

39 A.L. Burt, *Imperial Architects* (Toronto 1913).

40 Dickinson, 'The Eighteenth-century Debate on the Sovereignty of Parliament', pp. 189–210.

41 See here the invaluable study by Samuel H. Beer, *To Make a Nation: The Rediscovery of American Federalism* (Cambridge, Mass., Harvard University Press, 1993).

42 Dickinson, 'The Eighteenth-century Debate on the Sovereignty of Parliament', p. 208.
43 Akhil Reed Amar, 'Of Sovereignty and Federalism', *Yale Law Journal*, vol. 96, no. 7 (June 1987), pp. 1425–1520. This article provides a valuable synopsis of British and colonial thinking in the 1760s and 1770s.
44 Ibid., p. 1444.
45 Ibid., p. 1450.
46 Greene, *Peripheries and Center*, chapter 9, covers the ground explored above by Amar.

2 NINETEENTH-CENTURY PRACTICE AND THEORY

1 For a summary of the various schemes see L.F.S. Upton, 'The Idea of Confederation: 1754–1858' in W.L. Morton (ed.), *The Shield of Achilles: Aspects of Canada in the Victorian Age* (Toronto/Montreal, McClelland and Stewart, 1968), pp. 184–207; and W.H. Nelson, 'The Last Hopes of the American Loyalists', *Canadian Historical Review*, vol. 32, no. 1 (March 1951), pp. 22–42. Another scheme for 'perpetual union' of the British North American colonies was submitted to the Colonial Office in 1826 by Richard John Uniacke, the Attorney-General of Nova Scotia. Uniacke wanted to preserve the attachment between the colonies and the mother country – 'home', as he called it – and he thought union would facilitate that. As further reasons for union, Uniacke also emphasized the need to improve communications and the American threat to British interests. His ideas died on the desk of Lord Bathurst and apparently had no influence on British thinking about the colonies. His son did make the scheme available to Lord Durham but with what affect is unclear. See Reginald G. Trotter, 'An Early Proposal for the Federation of British North America', *Canadian Historical Review*, vol. 6, no. 2 (June 1925), pp. 142–54.
2 R.G. Trotter, 'Durham and the Idea of a Federal Union of British North America', *Canadian Historical Association Annual Report* (1925), pp. 54–65; also Upton, 'The Idea of Confederation', pp. 191–3. For a recent analysis of the genesis of Canada Confederation see Ged Martin, *Britain and the Origins of Canadian Confederation, 1837–67* (Vancouver, UBC Press, 1995). The quotations in the following paragraph are from Trotter, 'Durham and the Idea of a Federal Union'.
3 The quotations in this paragraph are from Ged Martin, 'Confederation Rejected: The British Debate on Canada, 1837–1840', *Journal of Imperial and Commonwealth History*, vol. 11, no. 1 (October 1982), pp. 33–57, which is an excellent analysis of the schemes and ideas of Stephen and Howick.
4 See John M. Ward, 'The Third Earl Grey and Federalism, 1846–1852', *Australian Journal of Politics and History*, vol. iii (1957), pp. 18–32; John M. Ward, *Earl Grey and the Australian Colonies 1846–1857: A Study of Self-government and Self-interest* (Melbourne, Melbourne University Press, 1958); Bruce A. Knox, 'The Rise of Colonial Federation as an Object of British Policy, 1850–1870', *Journal of British Studies*, vol. 11, no. 1 (November 1971), pp. 92–112; Ged Martin, 'Britain and the Future of British North America 1841–1850', *British Journal of Canadian Studies*, vol. 2, no. 1 (June 1987), pp. 74–96; and Ged Martin, 'An Imperial Idea and its Friends: Canadian Confederation and the British' in Gordon Martel (ed.), *Essays in Honour of A.P. Thornton* (London, Macmillan, 1986), pp. 49–94.
5 Confidential 'Minute by James Stephen on Canadian Affairs', 30 April 1836, CO 537/137, ff. 29–49.

6 Memorandum on 'Canada' by Lord John Russell, 28 March 1839, PRO 30/20/3C, ff. 233–6. For Grey's views re free trade and federation see Grey to Elgin (draft), no. 10, 31 December 1846, C0 42/534, ff. 369–79. For Elgin's scepticism see Elgin to Grey, 7 May 1847 in A.G. Doughty (ed.), *The Elgin–Grey Papers 1846–1852*, vol. 1 (Ottawa, The King's Printer, 1937), pp. 34–5. Also Grey to Russell, 8 August 1849, PRO 31/22/8A.

7 Elgin to Grey, 2 June 1847, quoted in Martin, 'Britain and the Future of British North America', p. 80.

8 See here the comments of P.S. Hamilton in 1855 in Upton, 'The Idea of Confederation', p. 199.

9 Ibid., p. 187.

10 For Head's ideas and for a general and perceptive overview see among others Martin, 'An Imperial Idea and its Friends'; Knox, 'The Rise of Colonial Federation'; Chester Martin, 'Sir Edmund Head's First Project of Federation, 1851', *Canadian Historical Association Annual Report* (1928), pp. 14–26; Chester Martin, 'Sir Edmund Head and Canadian Confederation, 1851–1858', *Canadian Historical Association Annual Report* (1929), pp. 5–14; Alice R. Stewart, 'Sir Edmund Head's Memorandum of 1857 on Maritime Union: A Lost Confederation Document', *Canadian Historical Review*, vol. 26, no. 4 (December 1945), pp. 406–19; Reginald G. Trotter, 'The British Government and the Proposal of Federation in 1858', *Canadian Historical Review*, vol. 14, no. 3 (September 1933), pp. 285–92; Bruce Knox, 'The British Government, Sir Edmund Head, and British North American Confederation, 1858', *Journal of Imperial and Commonwealth History*, vol. 4 no. 2 (January 1976), pp. 206–17.

11 Quoted in James A. Gibson, 'The Colonial Office View of Canadian Federation, 1856–1868', *Canadian Historical Review*, vol. 35, no. 4 (December 1954), pp. 279–313.

12 Ibid., p. 292.

13 'Minute on a Federal Government for the Australian Colonies' by R.L. of the Board of Trade, 8 May 1857, CO 201/500, ff. 289–94. His opinion was shared by Sir W. Denison, the Governor of New South Wales, who thought, 'No nations have ever except under pressure of common danger consented to a federation.' Its machinery was 'cumbrous' and 'ineffective' and would probably cause irritation between the colonies, especially if the colonies did not give the federal government adequate powers and strength to use the powers. See Sir W. Denison to Colonel Gore Brown [1858], Carnarvon Papers, PRO 30/6/132, f. 126.

14 See Carnarvon's speech introducing the British North America bill: 3 Hansard (H of L), vol. 185, 19 February 1867, cols 557–75. See also Bowen to Carnarvon, 14 December 1866, Carnarvon Papers, PRO 30/6/135, ff. 149–56.

15 For Austin's treatment of the issue of sovereignty in a federal system see John Austin, *The Province of Jurisprudence Determined* (London, Weidenfeld and Nicolson, 1954), pp. 245–53.

16 Ibid., p. 8.

17 See Walter Bagehot, *The English Constitution* (London, Thomas Nelson and Sons, n.d.), chapter 7, pp. 304–41, especially p. 315.

18 E.A. Freeman, *History of Federal Government from the Foundation of the Achaian League to the Disruption of the United States* (London 1863), pp. 9, 10, 15, 16, 90–91.

19 *The Federalist* was the title given to the eighty-five essays by Alexander Hamilton, John Jay and James Madison in 1787–8 in support of the constitution of the United States. See A. Hamilton, J. Jay and J. Madison, *The Federalist: A Commentary on the Constitution of the United States* (New York, The Modern Library, 1937).

20   See John Stuart Mill, *On Liberty; Representative Government; The Subjection of Women: Three Essays* (London, Oxford University Press, 1954), pp. 380–401.

21   For a useful survey of the ideas of British theorists on federalism see John Pinder, 'The Federal Idea and the British Liberal Tradition' in Andrea Bosco (ed.), *The Federal Idea*, vol. 1 *The History of Federalism from Enlightenment to 1945* (London, Lothian Foundation Press, 1991), pp. 99–118.

22   A.V. Dicey, 'Home Rule from an English Point of View', *Contemporary Review* (July 1882), pp. 66–86.

23   Baron Acton, 'Nationality' in *The History of Freedom and Other Essays* (London, Macmillan and Co. Ltd., 1909), pp. 270–300.

24   See A.V. Dicey, *Lectures Introductory to the Study of the Law of the Constitution*, 2nd edn (London, Macmillan, 1886). A particularly critical and telling comment on Dicey's views is Ferdinand Mount, *The British Constitution Now* (London, Heinemann, 1992), pp. 47–65.

25   A.V. Dicey, 'Parliamentary Sovereignty and Federalism' in *Lectures Introductory to the Study of the Law of the Constitution*, 2nd edn (London, Macmillan, 1886), pp. 128–30.

26   James Bryce, *The American Commonwealth*, 2 vols, 2nd edn (London, Macmillan, 1891).

27   James Bryce, 'Flexible and Rigid Constitutions' in *Studies in History and Jurisprudence*, vol. 1 (Oxford, Clarendon Press, 1901), pp. 145–254; Bryce also closely examined the creation of the Australian federation by comparing it to the American and Canadian precedents: 'The Constitution of the Commonwealth of Australia', ibid., pp. 468–553.

28   Henry Sidgwick, 'Modern Federalism' in *The Elements of Politics*, 4th edn (London, Macmillan and Co., 1919), pp. 426–39.

29   Henry Sidgwick, 'Federal and Other Component States', ibid., pp. 530–50.

3   'FEDERATION' OF THE EMPIRE

1   Two important articles on this issue are Ged Martin, 'Empire Federalism and Imperial Parliamentary Union, 1820–1870', *Historical Journal*, vol. 16, no. 1 (1973), pp. 65–92; and Ged Martin 'The Idea of "Imperial Federation"' in Ronald Hyam and Ged Martin, *Reappraisals in British Imperial History* (London, Macmillan, 1975), pp. 121–38. See also M.D. Burgess, 'Imperial Federation: Edward Freeman and the Intellectual Debate on the Consolidation of the British Empire in the Nineteenth Century', *Trivium 13* (1978), pp. 77–94.

2   [Anon.], 'Our Colonial Empire', *Westminster Review*, vol. 58, no. 114 (October 1852), pp. 214–34.

3   [Anon.], 'Our Australian Possessions', *London Quarterly Review*, vol. 1 (December 1853), pp. 517–57. The author of this article was probably the Reverend William Arthur. See W.A. Forbes, 'Imperial Federation', *London Quarterly Review*, vol. 64 (July 1885), pp. 320–35.

4   Edward A. Freeman, 'The Proposed Revision of the Swiss Federal Constitution', *Fortnightly Review*, vol. 2 (October 1865), pp. 533–48.

5   Auberon Herbert, 'The Canadian Confederation', *Fortnightly Review*, vol. 7 (April 1876), pp. 480–90.

6   Arthur Mills, 'Our Colonial Policy', *Contemporary Review*, vol. 11 (June 1869), pp. 216–39.

7   J.A. Froude, 'England and Her Colonies', *Fraser's Magazine (January 1870), pp. 1–16.*

8   Herman Merivale, 'The Colonial Question in 1870', *Fortnightly Review*, vol. 13 (February 1870), pp. 152–75.

9 Edward Jenkins, 'Imperial Federalism', *Contemporary Review*, vol. 16 (January 1871), pp. 165–88; and Edward Jenkins, 'An Imperial Confederation', *Contemporary Review*, vol. 17 (April 1871), pp. 60–79.

10 The Westminster Palace Conference held in July 1871 ranged over a variety of topics associated with closer union, and 'federation' was touched on by a number of participants, but there were no explicit schemes outlined and almost no exploration of philosophic principles; simply assertions that the empire should be drawn closer together in a more formal way. Some speakers did suggest that successful federations resulted from steady growth and were not framed suddenly, which would have surprised the devisors of the United States Constitution. See Edward Jenkins (ed.), *Discussions on Colonial Questions: Report of the Proceedings of a Conference held at Westminster Palace Hotel on July 19, 20, and 21, 1871* (London 1872).

11 Edward A. Freeman, 'The Growth of Commonwealths', *Fortnightly Review*, vol. 20 (October 1873), pp. 434–56.

12 Lord Blachford, 'The Integrity of the British Empire', *Nineteenth Century*, vol. 2 (October 1877), pp. 355–65.

13 [Anon.], 'The Federation of the English Empire', *Westminster Review*, no. ccxx (April 1879), pp. 147–53; no. ccxxi (July 1879), pp. 22–9; and no. ccxxii (October 1879), pp. 153–62. Another anonymous author also emphasized the need to relieve the congestion in parliament and to separate local, national and imperial affairs. He wanted to see an 'imperial federated democracy' which would result in the preservation of British power but observe imperial obligations. For this writer the 'questions of empire and citizenship are one and indivisible. If we want to maintain our empire, we must maintain and advance our citizenship; if we want to maintain and advance our citizenship, we must maintain our empire. Within, we must adjust our constitution to the preparedness of the people for power; without, we must adjust our empire according to the preparedness of the races whom we rule, to rise from subjects into citizens. Our colonists and colonies everywhere must be regarded as the complement of citizenship and empire.' See [Anon.], 'Imperium et Libertas', *Westminster Review*, no. ccxxiii (January 1880), pp. 43–52.

14 See A.V. Dicey, 'Home Rule From an English Point of View', *Contemporary Review*, vol. 42 (July 1882), pp. 66–86.

15 One writer was clearly aware of the rising national consciousness in at least Scotland and was convinced that 'the maintenance of [Scottish] nationality will not only be just to Scotland but will also strengthen the Empire, of which Scotland forms an integral part'. See W. Scott Dalgleish, 'Scotland's Version of Home Rule', *Nineteenth Century*, vol. 13 (January 1883), pp. 14–26.

16 Labilliere made this remark while commenting on a paper given by George Baden-Powell at the Royal Colonial Institute on 9 December 1884. See *Proceedings of the Royal Colonial Institute*, vol. 16 (1884–5), p. 81.

17 J.N. Dalton, 'The Federal States of the World', *Nineteenth Century*, vol. 16 (July 1884), pp. 96–117.

18 George Baden-Powell, 'National Unity', *Proceedings of the Royal Colonial Institute*, vol. 16 (1884–5), pp. 43–94.

19 Edward A. Freeman, 'Imperial Federation', *Macmillan's Magazine*, vol. 51 (April 1885), pp. 430–45. See also Burgess, 'Imperial Federation'.

20 See for example Samuel Wilson, 'A Scheme for Imperial Federation', *Nineteenth Century*, vol. 17 (April 1885), pp. 590–98. Another writer, W.A. Forbes, had read and absorbed Freeman but his profound belief that only imperial union would ensure strength and that only federation would ensure union overcame his understanding. He finally admitted he had not the skill to devise an

appropriate scheme. See W.A. Forbes, 'Imperial Federation', *London Quarterly Review*, vol. 64 (July 1885), pp. 320–35.

21 Henry Thring, 'The Fallacy of "Imperial Federation"', *Nineteenth Century*, vol. 19 (January 1886), pp. 22–34.

22 F.P. de Labilliere, 'Imperial Federation', *Proceedings of the Royal Colonial Institute*, vol. 17 (1885–6), pp. 319–42.

23 For Sir Frederick Young's comments see ibid., pp. 327–9.

24 A similar sentimental appeal was made by Sir George Ferguson Bowen in June 1886 but he at least had read *The Federalist* and John Stuart Mill and recognized that if federation was to succeed it had to 'proceed primarily from the Colonies; and that no change should be made in the existing system without their previous and full consent'. See Sir George Ferguson Bowen, 'The Federation of the British Empire', *Proceedings of the Royal Colonial Institute*, vol. 17 (1885–6), pp. 282–315. In responding to a paper by Sir Graham Berry entitled 'The Colonies in Relation to the Empire', R.G. Haliburton judged Blackstone's dictum that the British parliament was omnipotent with respect to the colonies as 'utterly baseless' and was critical of the degree to which it was 'tacitly acquiesced in by both British and Colonial statesmen'. He was the only commentator to do so in the late nineteenth century. Despite his strong views, Haliburton argued that imperial federation could be a means of protecting colonial rights. See the comment by R.G. Haliburton on Sir Graham Berry, 'The Colonies in Relation to the Empire', *Proceedings of the Royal Colonial Institute*, vol. 18 (1886–7), pp. 3–43.

25 See particularly Henry Parkes, 'Our Growing Australian Empire', *Nineteenth Century*, vol. 15 (January 1884), pp. 138–49; Henry Parkes, 'Australia and the Imperial Connection', *Nineteenth Century*, vol. 15 (May 1884), pp. 867–72; Robert Stout, 'A Colonial View of Imperial Federation', *Nineteenth Century*, vol. 21 (March 1887), pp. 351–61; John Merriman, 'The Closer Union of the Empire', *Nineteenth Century*, vol. 21 (April 1887), pp. 507–16; Goldwin Smith, 'The Canadian Constitution', *Contemporary Review*, vol. 52 (July 1887), pp. 1–20; C.R. Lowell, 'English and American Federalism', *Fortnightly Review*, vol. 49 (February 1888), pp. 189–95; E.J. Phelps, 'The Constitution of the United States', *Nineteenth Century*, vol. 23 (February–March 1888), pp. 297–316, 441–57; [Anon.], 'The Swiss Constitution', *Westminster Review*, vol. 129 (February 1888), pp. 133–51. See also Luke Trainor, *British Imperialism and Australian Nationalism: Manipulation, Conflict and Compromise in the Late Nineteenth Century* (Cambridge, Cambridge University Press, 1994).

26 C.B. Roylance-Kent, 'Federal Government', *Westminster Review*, vol. 129 (May 1888), pp. 573–86.

27 To some degree, the wider issue was kept alive. For example, the *Scottish Geographical Magazine* ran a series of articles in 1891 on the subject of 'Britannic Confederation'. However, by choosing Edward Freeman to write on 'The Physical and Political Basis of National Unity', the editors opened the door for another trenchant critique of the federal system similar to those Freeman had launched in the eighties. See Edward A. Freeman, 'Britannic Confederation II: The Physical and Political Basis of National Unity', *Scottish Geographical Magazine*, vol. 7, no. 7 (July 1891), pp. 345–57.

28 These issues are fully addressed in Martin, 'Empire Federalism and Imperial Parliamentary Union'; and Martin, 'The Idea of "Imperial Federation"'.

29 These various arguments are succinctly outlined in Seymour Ching-Yuan Cheng, *Schemes for the Federation of the British Empire* (New York, Columbia University Press, 1931), pp. 227–49.

30 See George R. Parkin, *Imperial Federation: The Problem of National Unity* (London, Macmillan and Co., 1892); and F.P. de Labilliere, *Federal Britain: or,*

Unity and Federation of the Empire (London, Sampson Low, Marston and Company, 1894).

31 The arguments favouring federation are summarized in Ching-Yuan Cheng, *Schemes for the Federation of the British Empire*, pp. 182–226.

4 'FEDERATION' OF THE UNITED KINGDOM

1 David Thornley, *Isaac Butt and Home Rule* (London, MacGibbon and Kee, 1964), pp. 98–9. For Butt's full federal proposal see Isaac Butt, *Home Government for Ireland, Irish Federalism: Its Meaning, its Objectives and its Hopes*, 3rd edn (Dublin 1871). Sharmon Crawford recommended a 'federal' resolution of the Anglo-Irish relationship in the 1840s. See B.A. Kennedy, 'Sharmon Crawford's Federal Scheme for Ireland' in H.A. Cronne, T.W. Moody and D.B. Quinn (eds), *Essays in British and Irish History in Honour of James Eadie Todd* (London, Macmillan, 1949), pp. 235–54. For the general context in which these proposals surfaced see John Kendle, *Ireland and the Federal Solution: The Debate over the United Kingdom Constitution, 1870–1921* (Kingston and Montreal, McGill-Queen's University Press, 1989), chapter 1.

2 Chamberlain to Labouchere, 26 December 1885, quoted in A. Thorold, *The Life of Henry Labouchere* (London, Constable, 1913), p. 272. For a fuller treatment of Chamberlain's reasoning at this time see Kendle, *Ireland and the Federal Solution*, pp. 24–31 and 39–40; Richard Jay, *Joseph Chamberlain: A Political Study* (Oxford, Clarendon Press, 1981); and Richard Jay, 'Nationalism, Federalism and Ireland' in Murray Forsyth (ed.), *Federalism and Nationalism* (St Martin's Press, New York, 1989), pp. 209–49.

3 Gladstone clearly stated his attitude towards parliamentary sovereignty in a speech at Dalkeith on 26 November 1879: 'Nothing can be done . . . by any wise statesman or right-minded Briton to weaken or compromise the authority of the Imperial Parliament, because the Imperial Parliament must be supreme in these three Kingdoms. And nothing that creates a doubt upon that supremacy can be tolerated by any intelligent and patriotic man.' And in his election address of 17 September 1885, Gladstone again asserted, 'To maintain the supremacy of the Crown, the unity of the Empire, and all the authority of Parliament necessary for the conservation of that unity, is the first duty of every representative of the people. Subject to this governing principle every grant to portions of the country of enlarged powers for the management of their own affairs is . . . not a source of danger but a means of averting it, and is in the nature of a new guarantee for increased cohesion, happiness, and strength.' See Sir Wemyss Reid (ed.), *The Life of William Ewart Gladstone* (London 1899), pp. 634 and 689.

4 See W. Scott Dalgleish, 'Scotland's Version of Home Rule', *Nineteenth Century* (January 1883), pp. 14–26; Arthur D. Elliot, 'Home Rule for Scotland', *Nineteenth Century* (March 1886), pp. 466–75; [Anon.], 'Home Rule for Scotland', *Scottish Review*, vol. 8 (July 1886), pp. 1–20; W. Mitchell, 'Scotland and Home Rule', *Scottish Review*, vol. 11 (1888), pp. 323–46; W. Wallace, 'Nationality and Home Rule, Irish and Scottish', *Scottish Review*, vol. 12 (July 1888), pp. 171–87; B.D. MacKenzie, 'Home Rule for Scotland', *Westminster Review*, vol. 132 (1889), pp. 553–65. For full coverage of the writing and thinking on Scottish home rule in the late 1880s and throughout the 1890s see Kendle, *Ireland and the Federal Solution*, p. 57–85.

5 G. Osborne Morgan, 'Welsh Nationality', *Contemporary Review* (January 1888), pp. 84–93; G. Osborne Morgan *et al.*, 'The New Round Table: Home Rule for Wales', *Westminster Review*, vol. 133 (1890), pp. 394–416;

and D. Lloyd George, 'National Self-government for Wales', *Young Wales*, I (January–December 1895), pp. 231–40.

6   G.B. Lancaster Woodburne, 'Imperial Federation and Home Rule', *National Review*, vol. 5 (1885), pp. 606–15.

7   Thring, 'Home Rule and Imperial Unity', *Contemporary Review*, vol. 51 (March 1887), pp. 305–26. See also [Anon.], 'Home Rule and Imperial Federation', *Westminster Review*, vol. 132 (September 1889), pp. 225–30.

8   A forceful argument for 'the adoption of some form of federal government in the place of the present unitarian system' was offered by Thomas Alfred Spalding in his *Federation and Empire: A Study in Politics* (London 1896). He believed the 'paralysis of Parliament' was owing to the fact that 'we are endeavouring to conduct a federal government under the guise of unity'. He concluded that 'a federal rather than an incorporating union is demanded by circumstances'. See especially, ibid., pp. 1, 8, 19–20, 125 and 224.

9   J.A. Murray Macdonald, 'The Liberal Party and Imperial Federation', *Contemporary Review*, vol. 7 (May 1900), pp. 644–55.

10 For Brassey's ideas at the turn of the century see T.A. Brassey, 'Imperial Government' in *Problems of Empire: Papers and Addresses of the Hon. T.A. Brassey* (London, Longmans and Co., 1904), pp. 1–13; and T.A. Brassey, 'Federal Government for the United Kingdom and the Empire', *Nineteenth Century* (August 1901), pp. 190–201. For a summary of the fortunes of imperial federation in 1900 see Edward Salmon, 'Imperial Federation: The Condition of Progress', *Fortnightly Review*, vol. 74 (December 1900), pp. 1009–19.

11 J.A. Murray Macdonald to the editor, *The Times*, 19 September 1904.

12 Another writer who meant 'devolution' when he wrote 'federal' was Godfrey R. Benson, 'Federal Government for the United Kingdom', *Contemporary Review* (February 1902), pp. 214–20.

13 See J.E. Kendle, 'The Round Table Movement and "Home Rule All Round"', *Historical Journal*, vol. 11, no. 2 (1968), pp. 332–53.

14 J.A. Murray Macdonald, 'The Constitutional Controversy and Federal Home Rule', *Nineteenth Century* (July 1911), pp. 33–43.

15 Dunraven, 'The Need for a Re-creation of Our Constitution', *Nineteenth Century* (September 1911), pp. 404–16.

16 Dunraven, 'The Need for a Constitutional Party', *Nineteenth Century* (November 1911), pp. 981–92.

17 J.A.R. Marriott, 'The Key of the Empire', *Nineteenth Century* (November 1911), pp. 805–19. Marriott's view was given unsolicited but firm backing by *The Spectator*. The anonymous writer asserted that all talk about federalism was 'cant'. The real root of the home rule proposed for Ireland was nationalism not federalism, for 'it is clear that no movement to divide a united kingdom or a united republic could arise unless it were inspired by a distinct national feeling'. Moreover, it implied 'a binding together of previously separate units, not disintegration of a previous whole'. See 'Federalism True and False', *The Spectator*, 20 April 1912, pp. 611–12. See also J.A. Marriott, *English Political Institutions* (Oxford, Clarendon Press, 1910).

18 The manoeuvrings and the debates surrounding both home rule and the federal idea during the years 1912–14 can be followed in Kendle, *Ireland and the Federal Solution*, pp. 128–76.

19 For Morgan's views see J.H. Morgan, 'Home Rule and Federalism', *Nineteenth Century* (June 1912), pp. 1230–42; and J. H. Morgan, 'The Constitution: A Commentary' in J.H. Morgan (ed.), *The New Irish Constitution: An Exposition and Some Arguments* (London 1912), pp. 3–49.

20 For Churchill's speech see *The Times*, 13 September 1912.

21 'Mr Churchill's Latest Escapade', *The Spectator*, 21 September 1912, pp. 396–7.

See also A.G. Gardiner, 'Mr Churchill and Federalism', *Fortnightly Review* (November 1912), pp. 803–12.

22 Herbert Samuel, 'Federal Government', *Nineteenth Century* (October 1912), pp. 676–86.

23 Dunraven, 'A Last Plea for Federation', *Nineteenth Century* (December 1913), pp. 1125–42.

24 See Charnwood, 'Federal Home Rule and the Government of Ireland Bill', *Nineteenth Century* (April 1913), pp. 834–45.

25 F.S. Oliver, as the author of *Alexander Hamilton*, was certainly familiar with 'true federalism' but even he was guilty of mixing his terms and leaving the impression that he was not as clear as he might have been. For instance, he liked to use the recently approved constitution of South Africa as a federal example when that constitution was patently not federal but unitary with devolutionary features. See F.S. Oliver, *What Federalism is NOT* (London, John Murray, 1914).

26 For a detailed analysis of the discussion and promotion of the federal idea in 1918 both outside and inside government circles see Kendle, *Ireland and the Federal Solution*, chapter 8; and John Kendle, *Walter Long, Ireland and the Union, 1905–1920* (Montreal and Kingston, McGill-Queen's University Press, 1992), chapter 5.

27 Harold Cox, 'The Government of England', *Edinburgh Review* (July 1918), pp. 190–208. Another writer who recognized that home rule was not federalism and that the force behind home rule was nationalism was Joseph R. Fisher, 'The Federal Panacea for Ireland', *Nineteenth Century and After* (July 1918), pp. 59–67.

28 See J.A.R. Marriott, 'The Problem of Federalism', *Nineteenth Century* (June 1918), pp. 1291–1302.

29 For a full analysis of the motivation lying behind the drafting of the Government of Ireland Act of 1920 see Richard Murphy, 'Walter Long and the Making of the Government of Ireland Act, 1919–20', *Irish Historical Studies*, vol. 25, no. 97 (May 1986), pp. 82–96; and Kendle, *Walter Long*, chapter 6.

30 A valuable overview of these issues can be found in George Boyce, 'Federalism and the Irish Question' in Andrea Bosco (ed.), *The Federal Idea*, vol. 1, *The History of Federalism from the Enlightenment to 1945* (London, Lothian Foundation Press, 1991), pp. 119–38.

5 THE ROUND TABLE MOVEMENT, THE EMPIRE AND WORLD ORDER

1 For the founding of both the 'kindergarten' and the Round Table movement, and for their activities, see Walter Nimocks, *Milner's Young Men: The 'Kindergarten' in Edwardian Imperial Affairs* (Durham, N.C., Duke University Press, 1968) and John Kendle, *The Round Table Movement and Imperial Union* (Toronto, University of Toronto Press, 1975). For an excellent appraisal of Lionel Curtis see Deborah Lavin, *From Empire to International Commonwealth: A Biography of Lionel Curtis* (Oxford, Clarendon Press, 1995).

2 Milner to George Parkin, 24 July 1905, File Box A1: Letters 1905–6, Milner Papers, Bodleian Library.

3 Curtis to R. Jebb, 19 November and 31 December [1906], Jebb Papers, Institute of Commonwealth Studies (ICS), London.

4 Curtis to R. Brand, 16 March 1908, Jebb Papers, ICS.

5 Curtis to R. Jebb, 21 December 1908, ibid.

6 [Philip Kerr], 'The Month', *The State* (January 1909), p. 13.

7   Amery to Deakin, 2 November 1909, copy, File Box: Imperial Union, Milner Papers, Bodleian Library.
8   Quoted without reference in J.R.M. Butler, *Lord Lothian (Philip Kerr) 1882–1940* (London, Macmillan and Co. Ltd, 1960), p. 37.
9   Kerr to Brand, 1 November 1909, Box 16, Lothian Papers, Scottish Record Office (SRO).
10 Kerr's sensitivity to Canadian, and thus dominion, nationalist opinion and to the near impossibility of imperial federation is clear from his article 'The Month: Overseas Affairs', *The State* (January 1910), pp. 14–22, written in Canada in November 1909.
11 Minutes of a meeting held at Ledbury, 15/18 January 1910, Box 16, Lothian Papers, SRO.
12 Curtis to Kerr, 19 September 1910, GD 40/17/12, Lothian Papers, SRO.
13 Kerr to Curtis, 30 September 1910, GD 40/17/2, ibid.
14 [Lionel Curtis], *Round Table Studies* (London 1910), pp. 250–351.
15 [Lionel Curtis], *The Project of a Commonwealth* (London, Macmillan and Co., 1915), p. 153.
16 Ibid., p. 290.
17 Ibid., pp. 290–91.
18 Ibid., p. 291.
19 Ibid., p. 295.
20 Lionel Curtis, *The Problem of the Commonwealth* (Toronto, Macmillan Company of Canada, 1916).
21 For Molony's ideas see E. Molony to L. Curtis, 3 June 1912, Round Table Papers, Bodleian Library. For the 1912 discussions see S.R. Mehrotra, *India and the Commonwealth 1885–1929* (London, George Allen and Unwin Ltd, 1965), pp. 79–83; DeWitt C. Ellinwood, 'The Future of India in the British Empire: The Round Table Group Discussions, 1912', *Nanyang University Journal*, vol. 3 (1969), pp. 196–204; DeWitt C. Ellinwood, 'The Round Table Movement and India, 1909–1920', *Journal of Commonwealth Political Studies* (November 1971), pp. 183–209; and Kendle, *The Round Table Movement and Imperial Union*, pp. 224–9.
22 For the Round Table movement's role in the acceptance of 'dyarchy' by the British government see Kendle, *The Round Table Movement and Imperial Union*, pp. 229–47; and Lionel Curtis, *Dyarchy* (Oxford, Oxford University Press, 1920). For an analysis of Curtis's role see Deborah Lavin, 'Lionel Curtis and Indian Dyarchy' in Andrea Bosco (ed.), *The Federal Idea*, vol. 1, *The History of Federalism from Enlightenment to 1945* (London, Lothian Foundation Press, 1991), pp. 193–209.
23 See Kerr to Simon, 13 September 1928, 245/731–8, Lothian Papers, SRO. An excellent study of the genesis of the federal basis of the India Act of 1935 is R.J. Moore, *The Crisis of Indian Unity 1917–1940* (Oxford, Clarendon Press, 1974).
24 Lothian to Ramsay MacDonald, 9 November 1931, quoted in Butler, *Lord Lothian*, p. 179. For more detailed treatments of Kerr's (Lothian's) role in Anglo-Indian affairs in the 1930s see Gerard Douds, 'Lothian and the Indian Federation' in John Turner (ed.), *The Larger Idea: Lord Lothian and the Problem of National Sovereignty* (London, The Historians' Press, 1988), pp. 62–76; and Andrea Bosco, 'Lord Lothian, Lionel Curtis and the Making of the Indian Federation' in Andrea Bosco and Julian Bavetta (eds), *Annals of the Lothian Foundation*, vol. 1 (London, Lothian Foundation Press, 1992), pp. 123–56. For a valuable overview see T.G. Fraser, 'Federal Solutions to the Problems of Indian Unity, 1930–1946' in Preston King and Andrea Bosco (eds), *A Constitution for Europe: A Comparative Study of Federal Constitutions*

and Plans for the United States of Europe (London, Lothian Foundation Press, 1991), pp. 267–83.

25 Professor Herbert A. Smith, 'Federalism and Legalism' in E.M. Handley to Lothian, 18 December 1930, GD 40/17/252, Lothian Papers, SRO.

26 For Churchill's speech see 5 Hansard (H of C), vol. 260, 3 December 1931, col. 1289.

27 See Bluebook re Indian Round Table Conference 12 November 1930–19 January 1931. Proceedings of Sub-Committees (Part I) [Sub-Committee no. 1 (Federal Structures)] (London, HMSO, 1931), Mss. Eng. Hist. C585, J.C.C. Davidson Papers, Bodleian Library.

28 For Lothian's speech see 5 Hansard (H of L), vol. 83, 8 December 1931, cols 307–8.

29 See the Nizam of Hyderabad to Willingdon, 1 August 1931, copy, GD 40/17/149, Lothian Papers, SRO.

30 For Hoare's speech see 5 Hansard (H of C), vol. 276, 27 March 1933, col. 705.

31 For Wolmer's speech see 5 Hansard (H of C), vol. 296, 10 December 1934, cols 94–8.

32 For Amery's speech see ibid., 11 December 1932, cols 326–7. There is a valuable anonymous memorandum in the Lothian Papers that underlines that the 'essence of a federation is that sovereignty is divided' and that 'no federal Government will work which depends upon the voluntary cooperation of the Princes'. See 'The Indian Constitution' [n.d.], GD 40/17/155, ff. 610–29, Lothian Papers, SRO.

33 For Wolmer's speech see 5 Hansard (H of C), vol. 301, 30 April 1935, col. 286.

34 For Brentford's speech see 5 Hansard (H of L), vol. 83, 9 December 1931, col. 390.

35 For Lloyd's speech see ibid., vol. 97, 18 June 1935, cols 447–9.

36 For Phillimore's speech see ibid., 19 June 1935, cols 569–70.

37 Lothian's lectures and speeches on this theme have been conveniently brought together by John Pinder and Andrea Bosco (eds), *Pacifism is not Enough: Collected Lectures and Speeches of Lord Lothian (Philip Kerr)* (London, Lothian Foundation Press, 1990). See also Turner (ed.), *The Larger Idea*.

38 Lothian's 'The Ending of Armageddon' was reprinted in Patrick Ransome (ed.), *Studies in Federal Planning* (London, Macmillan and Co. Ltd, 1945), pp. 1–15.

39 See particularly Harold J. Laski, *Studies in the Problem of Sovereignty* (New Haven, Yale University Press, 1917); Harold J. Laski, *The Foundations of Sovereignty and Other Essays* (London, Allen and Unwin, 1921); Harold J. Laski, *A Grammar of Politics* (London, Allen and Unwin, 1925); Lionel Robbins, *Economic Planning and International Order* (London, Macmillan and Co. Ltd, 1937); and Lionel Robbins, *The Economic Causes of War* (London, Jonathan Cape, 1939).

6 FEDERAL UNION

1 These were brought together along with other articles and lectures on the federal idea in Patrick Ransome (ed.), *Studies in Federal Planning* (London, Macmillan, 1943).

2 This volume was reissued by the Lothian Foundation Press in 1991.

3 These reports have now been published. See Patrick Ransome (ed.), *Towards the United States of Europe* (London, Lothian Foundation Press, 1991).

4 Clarence Streit, *Union Now: A Proposal for a Federal Union of the Democracies of the North Atlantic* (London, Jonathan Cape, 1939).

5 For the early history of Federal Union see Andrea Bosco, 'Lothian, Curtis, Kimber and the Federal Union Movement (1938–40)', *Journal of Contemporary History*, vol. 23 (1988), pp. 465–502; Richard Mayne, John Pinder and John C. de V. Roberts, *Federal Union: The Pioneers: A History of Federal Union* (London, Macmillan, 1990); Sir Charles Kimber, 'Foreword', and Andrea Bosco, 'Introduction' to Ransome (ed.), *Towards the United States of Europe*; and Andrea Bosco, *Federal Union and the Origins of the 'Churchill Proposal': The Federalist Debate in the United Kingdom from Munich to the Fall of France 1938–1940* (London, Lothian Foundation Press, 1992).

6 W.B. Curry, *The Case for Federal Union* (Harmondsworth, Penguin Books Ltd, 1939).

7 For these statements of purpose see ibid., pp. 9–11 and the front cover of the 'Penguin Special'.

8 Ibid., pp. 19–20.

9 Ibid., p. 62.

10 Ibid., p. 133.

11 Sir William Beveridge, 'Peace by Federation' in Sydney E. Hooper (ed.), *The Deeper Causes of the War and its Issues* (London, George Allen and Unwin Ltd, 1940), pp. 156–206. Beveridge did not want this essay, written in the winter of 1939, to be included in Patrick Ransome's 1945 edited collection *Studies in Federal Planning* because he thought the political scene had shifted dramatically.

12 See J. Middleton Murry, 'Pre-conditions of Federal Union' in Melville Channing-Pearce (ed.), *Federal Union: A Symposium* (London, Lothian Foundation Press, 1991), pp. 155–63.

13 Lionel Robbins, a leading supporter of Federal Union, would not necessarily have disagreed with the analysis but he believed the central authority should be wielded by the federal as opposed to the national government. See Lionel Robbins, *Economic Planning and International Order* (London, Macmillan, 1937), pp. 244–6; Lionel Robbins, *The Economic Causes of War* (London, Jonathan Cape, 1939), pp. 104–9; and, particularly, Robbins's Federal Union pamphlet 'Economic Aspects of Federation' in Ransome (ed.), *Studies in Federal Planning*, pp. 77–106.

14 For Federal Union involvement with a possible Anglo-French union see Andrea Bosco, 'Federal Union, Chatham House, the Foreign Office and Anglo-French Union in Spring 1940' in Andrea Bosco (ed.), *The Federal Idea*, vol. 1, *The History of Federalism from Enlightenment to 1945* (London, Lothian Foundation Press, 1991), pp. 291–325; and Bosco, *Federal Union and the Origins of the 'Churchill Proposal'*.

15 For the memorandum and the accompanying minutes on it see FO 371/24364, ff. 356–71, PRO. This was not the first time that the Foreign Office had been obliged to consider a federal plan. In 1929–30 Aristide Briand, the French foreign minister, had proposed a European federal union. Briand's scheme had involved no loss of sovereignty by participating nations and was therefore confederal rather than federal in nature. It was also a vague scheme lacking in detail. While the Foreign Office had been supportive of the general notion of cooperation, it was relatively easy for it to brush the idea aside. Briand's proposal had not provided an opportunity to grapple with 'true federalism' but the general comments within the Office and at cabinet level revealed a marked caution towards any enveloping European ties outside the embrace of the League of Nations. This episode has been fully explored by P.J.V. Rolo, *Britain and the Briand Plan: The Common Market That Never Was: An Inaugural Lecture* (University of Keele, 6 December 1972); Robert W.D. Boyce, 'Britain's First "No" to Europe: Britain and the Briand Plan, 1929–30', *European Studies*

Review, vol. 10 (1980), pp. 17–45; and Carl H. Pegg, *Evolution of the European Idea, 1914–1932* (Chapel Hill and London, University of North Carolina Press, 1983). A valuable collection of essays is Peter M.R. Stirk (ed.), *European Unity in Context: The Interwar Period* (London and New York, Pinter Publishers, 1989).

16 See Orme Sargent to Sir A. Cadogan, 28 February 1940, FO 371/24298, ff. 185–6, PRO.

17 FO 371/24364, ff. 365–71, PRO.

18 Ransome (ed.), *Towards the United States of Europe*, p. 47.

19 In March 1940 the research department was reconstituted as the Federal Union Research Institute. Its committee was comprised of Sir William Beveridge, Dr Ivor Jennings, Professor Lionel Robbins, Sir Drummond Shields, C.D. Kimber, Professor F. A. Hayek, Professor G.W. Keeton, Harry Ross, Barbara Wootton and Patrick Ransome.

20 Edward Mousley, 'The Meaning of Federalism' in Channing-Pearce (ed.), *Federal Union*, pp. 21–38.

21 See Duncan Wilson, 'The History of Federalism' in ibid., pp. 39–56; and Ivor Jennings, 'Federal Constitutions' in ibid., pp. 57–71.

22 See K.C. Wheare, 'What Federal Government Is' in Ransome (ed.), *Studies in Federal Planning*, pp. 17–38.

23 The constitutional research committee was composed of Sir William Beveridge, Lionel Curtis, Professor A.L. Goodhart, Patrick Ransome, Professor J. Chamberlain, F. Gahan, Dr Ivor Jennings and K.C. Wheare.

24 See W. Ivor Jennings, *A Federation for Western Europe* (Cambridge, Cambridge University Press, 1940). For the minutes of the three constitutional conferences and the two draft constitutions see Ransome (ed.), *Towards the United States of Europe*, pp. 117–66. A young Harold Wilson attended the first of the constitutional conferences.

25 Jennings, *A Federation for Western Europe*, pp. vii–viii and 1–3.

26 The economists' committee was composed of Sir William Beveridge, E.F.M. Durbin, Professor F.A. Hayek, Professor L.C. Robbins, H.D. Dickinson, J.M. Fleming, J.E. Meade and Barbara Wootton. Again, Harold Wilson attended the key meetings of this sub-committee and, in fact, prepared a paper for its consideration entitled 'Economic Aspects of Federation' which was critical of Hayek's liberal, anti-collectivist approach to the allocation of powers in a federation. See Ransome (ed.), *Towards the United States of Europe*, pp. 205–14.

27 See Barbara Wootton, 'Economic Aspects of Federal Union' in ibid., pp. 53–4.

28 For the detailed discussions of the economists' committee see Lionel Robbins, 'Interim Report on Economic Aspects of the Federal Constitution' in ibid., pp. 91–7.

29 See particularly 'Report of a Conference on the Relations of the Dominions to a Possible Federation of Western Europe', 5–6 April 1941, in ibid., pp. 265–9. For an analysis of the impact of a federation of western Europe on the British Commonwealth of Nations see Jennings, *A Federation for Western Europe*, chapter 3.

30 See G.W. Keeton, 'Federation and India' in Channing-Pearce (ed.), *Federal Union*, pp. 187–94.

31 See Georg Schwarzenberger, 'Federation and the Colonial Problem' in ibid., pp. 195–206.

32 Others attending the meetings of the colonial research committee were Professor Norman Bentwich, S. Caine, Dr M. Fortes, Arthur Lewis, Professor Arnold Plant, R.V. Vernon, Professor Reginald Coupland, E.E. Evans-Pritchard, G.E. Harvey, Dr W.B. Mumford and Dr Audrey Richards. A particular lucid and thoughtful essay on the topic was written by Norman Bentwich,

'The Colonial Problem and the Federal Solution' in Ransome (ed.), *Studies in Federal Planning*, pp. 107–36.

33 For the minutes of the meetings of the colonial research committee and for Lugard's two memoranda – 'The Relation of Federal Union to the Colonies' and 'Memorandum on the Relations of a Federal Union with the Non Self-governing Dependencies' – see Ransome (ed.), *Towards the United States of Europe*, pp. 167–92.

7 FEDERALISM AND DECOLONIZATION

1 See Max Beloff, 'The "Federal Solution" in its Application to Europe, Asia, and Africa', *Political Studies*, vol. 1, no. 2 (1953), pp. 114–31; F.G. Carnell, 'Political Implications of Federalism in New States' in Ursula Hicks (ed.), *Federalism and Economic Growth in Under-developed Countries: A Symposium* (London, George Allen and Unwin Ltd, 1961), pp. 16–59; and Walter Lipgens, *A History of European Integration*, vol. 1, *1945–1947: The Formation of the European Unity Movement* (Oxford, Clarendon Press, 1982).

2 Arthur Creech Jones (Secretary of State for the Colonies), 'Constitutional Development in Smaller Colonial Territories', 8 December 1948, Cabinet. Commonwealth Affairs Committee. C.A. (48) 19, Cab. 134/55, PRO.

3 Ibid.

4 Minutes of meeting, 19 January 1949, Cabinet. Commonwealth Affairs Committee, Cab. (49) 1st meeting, Cab. 134/56, PRO.

5 See CO 1032/144, PRO, for Macmillan's request of 28 January 1957 and Watts's draft response of 1 February 1957.

6 See P.R. Odgers, 'Draft Report of the Official Committee on Colonial Policy', 12 July 1957, CO 1032/146, PRO.

7 See H.B. [Hilary Blood], 'The Smaller Territories', 15 October 1957, CO 1032/131, PRO. This memorandum was published in February 1958 by the Conservative Political Centre on behalf of the Conservative Commonwealth Council as *The Smaller Territories: Problems and Future*. For a recent analysis of this issue see W. David McIntyre, 'The Admission of Small States to the Commonwealth', *Journal of Imperial and Commonwealth History*, vol. 24, no. 2 (May 1996), pp. 244–77.

8 Lord Hailey, *The Position of Colonies in a British Commonwealth of Nations* (London, Oxford University Press, 1941), pp. 33–4.

9 Lord Hailey, *World Thought on the Colonial Question* (Johannesburg, Witwatersrand University Press, 1946), pp. 6–7, 11.

10 For an excellent discussion of the background to the federation of the British West Indies see Elisabeth Wallace, *The British Caribbean: From the Decline of Colonialism to the End of Federation* (Toronto and Buffalo, University of Toronto Press, 1977). Also, Sir John Mordecai, *Federation of the West Indies* (Evanston, Northwestern University Press, 1968), chapter 1; David Lowenthal (ed.), *The West Indian Federation* (New York, Columbia University Press, 1961); and Hugh W. Springer, *Reflections on the Failure of the First West Indian Federation* (Cambridge, Mass., Centre for International Affairs: Harvard University, 1962).

11 See 5 Hansard (H of C), vol. 156, 4 July 1922, cols 235–6.

12 Ibid., cols 260, 274–5.

13 Ibid., vol. 167, 25 July 1923, col. 491. See also Sir Henry W. Thornton to L.S. Amery, 25 February 1929, with memorandum attached entitled 'Confederation of the British West Indies', and T.R. St Johnston (Governor of Antigua) to Lord Passfield, 3 December 1929, CO 318/395/6, PRO; and 'Notes of a

Meeting Between Sir John Campbell, Colonel St Johnston and J.B. Sidebotham on 25 July 1930' plus a separate note by Campbell dated 29/7/30, ibid. Discussions in the Colonial Office about a possible federation in the West Indies intensified in late 1930 and early 1931 under the Labour government. For the relevant minutes and memoranda see CO 318/402/2, PRO.

14 One observer, a Captain Gammons, speaking in the House of Commons on 15 April 1943, believed the Colonial Office should take the initiative. If it was waiting for federation to happen spontaneously it would never happen: 'History tells us that it is very seldom that people sit down in cold blood and decide to federate. This only happens either as a result of war or by the influence of some outside power.' See 5 Hansard (H of C), vol. 388, 15 April 1943, col. 1437.

15 For the response in the West Indies to Oliver Stanley's despatch of 14 March 1945 see CO 1042/91, PRO.

16 This memorandum became Cmd. 7120, *Closer Association of the British West Indian Colonies* (May 1947).

17 See on this Angus MacKintosh to D.R. Serpell, 7 January 1947, enclosing a draft of the memorandum 'Closer Association of the British West Indian Colonies', T 220/347, PRO. The appendices to the final version outlined the division of powers in Australia, Canada and India.

18 In addition, papers were prepared on financial arrangements including the revenue of the new federal government and the organization of the federal public services, a customs union, the judiciary, communications and penal administration. Separate files were opened on each subject and can be found at CO 318/484/2–8 and CO 318/485/1, PRO.

19 See Minute by Angus MacKintosh, 30 May 1947, CO 318/484/1, PRO.

20 McPetrie's draft, the revisions to it and the discussions of it are all in CO 318/484/1, PRO.

21 See memorandum entitled 'Federation: Discussions with Sir George Seel', 21 January 1952, CO 1042/107.

22 Treasury opinion generally and the preparation for the 1953 Conference can be followed in T 220/358 and 359, PRO.

23 See 'Financial Assistance to Federation from HMG', March 1953, T 220/360, PRO.

24 See 'Conference on West Indian Federation', 19 March 1953, ibid.

25 See 'UK Policy in its Caribbean Territories – II', May 1955, CO 1031/1700, PRO.

26 5 Hansard (H of C), vol. 555, 29 June 1956, cols 871–931.

27 Ibid., vol. 556, 11 July 1956, cols 532–4.

28 See 'Memorandum by the Secretary of State for the Colonies', 25 November 1959, CPC (59) 26. Cabinet Colonial Policy Committee, Cab. 134/1558, PRO; also CO 1031/2370–1, PRO.

29 The British had by the 1950s, however, finally given up any real hope of achieving the East African federation so ardently pushed by Leo Amery and Edward Grigg in the twenties. There had been some interest in the early forties: see A.J. Dawe, 'A Federal Solution for East Africa', July 1942, CO 967/57, PRO; and a Kenyan federation was briefly considered in the early 1960s but the idea was not pursued: see Minutes of the third meeting of the Colonial Policy Committee, 2 February 1962, Cab. 134/1561, PRO.

30 For the recommendations of the Bledisloe Commission see Cmnd. 5949 (1939), *Report of the Rhodesia and Nyasaland Royal Commission*; for the history of federal initiatives in Central Africa see the Monckton Commission report of 1960: Cmnd. 1148, *Report of the Advisory Commission on the Review of the Constitution of Rhodesia and Nyasaland* (October 1960), a draft of which is in the Monckton Papers at the Bodleian Library, Oxford. Also helpful is J.R.T.

Wood, *The Welensky Papers: A History of the Federation of Rhodesia and Nyasaland* (Durban, Graham Publishing, 1983).

31 Wood, *The Welensky Papers*, pp. 119–22.

32 Ibid., p. 21.

33 See 'Note of a Meeting Held in the House of Commons, 3 April 1950 Between Secretary of State for the Colonies, Prime Minister of Southern Rhodesia, the Secretary of State for Commonwealth Relations, and the High Commissioner for Southern Rhodesia', DO 35/3590, PRO.

34 The acquiring of Wheare as an advisor to constitutional discussions can be followed in DO 35/3591 and 3593, PRO.

35 See 'Note of a Meeting Held in Mr Baxter's Room, Commonwealth Relations Office at 11 am on Wednesday, 20 December 1950', DO 35/3591, PRO.

36 Ibid.

37 See memorandum entitled 'Closer Association in Central Africa', 16 February 1951, *Confidential*, DO 35/3591, PRO.

38 The Colonial Office acquired material from Chatham House on contemporary cooperative developments in Europe, and on 31 January 1951 the Research Department of the Foreign Office prepared a memo for the Colonial Office on 'Closer Union in Africa: The European Pattern' which was highly revealing and critical of federation. See DO 35/3592, PRO.

39 See 'Minutes of Meetings and Conference Papers March 1951', DO 35/3596, PRO.

40 See Confidential Report on the 'Conference on Closer Association in Central Africa' [1951], CO 35/3594, PRO.

41 See J.J.S. Garner to G.H. Baxter, 17 April 1951, and Baxter to Garner, 19 April 1951, DO 121/137, PRO.

42 See 'Note of a Meeting held in the Secretary of State's Room at 11:00 Wednesday 18 April 1951', ibid.

43 Hastings Banda to James Griffiths, 18 July 1951, DO 35/3597, PRO. Late in 1951, A.B. Cohen confirmed that Central African federation was both essential and urgent because of the Afrikaner menace. He and others, such as David Stirling and the Capricorn Society, saw a federation in Central Africa as a step towards a large federation of Central and East Africa numbering eight territories in all – Kenya, Tanganyika, Uganda, Zanzibar, Northern Rhodesia, Southern Rhodesia, Nyasaland and Bechuanaland north of the 22nd parallel. Cohen was of the opinion that such a federation would come in time 'with substantial local agreement if we play our cards properly'. See A.B. Cohen to G.H. Baxter, 6 November 1951, DO 35/3603, PRO.

44 See 5 Hansard (H of C), vol. 497, 4 March 1952, cols 210–19.

45 See 'Preparations for Closer Association Conference in April 1952: Note of a Meeting Held in the CRO at 3:40 pm, Tuesday, 12 February 1952, to Discuss Preliminary Drafting of Conference Documents', DO 35/3607, PRO.

46 For the comments on Wheare see G.H. Baxter to the Permanent Under Secretary of State, 4 April 1951, DO 35/3596, PRO.

47 See 'Note of a Meeting Held in the CRO at 2:30 on Tuesday 15 April 1952', DO 35/3607, PRO. Close attention was also given by the civil servants to taxation schemes in a federation. The need for a federal authority to have both the power to make policy and the power to raise finances for its requirements was made very clear. The constitutions of Australia, Canada, India and South Africa were studied to see how income tax responsibilities were divided and what was or was not on the concurrent lists. See 'Note on Federal Income Tax Systems' circulated on 25 April 1952 by the United Kingdom delegates, DO 35/3610, PRO.

48 See Cmd. 8573 'Southern Rhodesia, Northern Rhodesia and Nyasaland: Draft

Federal Scheme Prepared by a Conference Held in London in April and May, 1952'. For comparison of the White Paper on Central Africa with the Standing Closer Association Committee Report on the West Indies see a lengthy Minute by Geoffrey Eastern dated 26 July 1952, CO 1031/754, PRO.

49 See 'Copy of a Minute Dated the 21st January 1944 by R.S. Champion, Chief Secretary to the Government, Aden', CO 725/89/2, PRO. For a valuable secondary treatment see Glen Balfour-Paul, *The End of Empire in the Middle East: Britain's Relinquishment of Power in her Last Three Arab Dependencies* (Cambridge, Cambridge University Press, 1991).

50 Governor J. Hathorn Hall to Oliver Stanley, 9 March 1944, CO 725/89/2, PRO.

51 T. Hickinbotham to Oliver Lyttelton, 25 October 1952, enclosing a memo entitled 'A Proposal to Establish a Federation of the States of the Western Aden Protectorate', CO 1015/166, PRO.

52 See Sir Bernard Reilly to Hickinbotham, 8 January 1953 (draft); A.R. Thomas, 'Confidential Memorandum [c. January 1953]'; 'Note on the Proposal for the Federation of the Western Aden Protectorate', 4 March 1953; and Vile to Marnham, 6 March 1953, ibid.

53 Minute by J.E. Marnham, 6 February 1953, ibid.

54 See Minute by Kennedy, 29 July 1953, and by Edmunds, 31 July 1953, T 220/257, PRO. For Lyttelton's despatch in response to Hickinbotham's ideas plus various useful Treasury minutes see T 220/256, PRO.

55 See Minutes of the 10th meeting of the cabinet's Colonial Policy Committee (CPC), 19 June 1958, Cab. 134/1557, PRO.

56 For a 1956 discussion in this context see 'Conclusions of the Cabinet' on Tuesday, 13 March 1956, CM 56, Cab. 128/30, PRO; and for a similar 1958 discussion see CO 1015/1669, PRO.

57 For the previous two paragraphs and other useful comments re the nature of the proposed federation see CO 1015/1671, PRO.

58 For this paragraph see CO 1015/1672, PRO.

59 See 'Closer Association Between United Kingdom Territories in South East Asia', CO 1022/61, PRO.

60 For the deliberations of the Federation of Malaya Constitutional Commission see CO 889/1, PRO.

61 For the British analysis of the merits of a wider federation in South-east Asia see 'Proposed Federation of Malaysia: Commission of Enquiry: Introduction' [1962], CO 947/2, PRO.

62 See draft report of the Cobbold Commission of Inquiry, May 1962, CO 947/7, PRO.

63 See T.B. Williamson to R.F.A. Grey, 1 December 1955, CO 554/856, PRO. For a valuable insight into both Colonial Office attitudes and the realities on the ground, see Sir Bryan Sharwood Smith, *Recollections of British Administration in the Cameroons and Northern Nigeria 1921–1957: 'But Always as Friends'* (Durham, N.C., Duke University Press, 1969).

64 Discussions in the Colonial Office about Nigerian federation occupy dozens of files but the essence of the internal debate can be followed in: CO 554/259, 260, 261, 262, 263, 277, 840, 846 and 856; and CO 1521.

8 'THE FEDERAL SOLUTION IS NOT POSSIBLE FOR US'

1 Anthony Eden in a speech at Columbia University, 11 January 1952, in reference to a possible federated Europe. Cited by A Correspondent [probably Max Beloff], 'Britain and European Federation', *The Round Table* (June 1952), p. 213.

2 There is a valuable discussion of post-1945 European federalist activities and the British part in them in Richard Mayne and John Pinder, *Federal Union: The Pioneers: A History of Federal Union* (London, Macmillan, 1990). See also Clemens A. Wurm, 'Great Britain: Political Parties and Pressure Groups in the Discussion on European Union' in Walter Lipgens and Wilfried Loth (eds)*Documents on the History of European Integration*, vol. 3 (Berlin, Walter de Gruyter, 1988), pp. 628–762; Michael Burgess (ed.), *Federalism and Federation in Western Europe* (London, Croom Helm, 1986); Stephen George, *An Awkward Partner: Britain in the European Community* (Oxford, Oxford University Press, 1990); Hugh Thomas, *Ever Closer Union: Britain's Destiny in Europe* (London, Hutchinson, 1991); Andrew Geddes, *Britain in the European Community* (Manchester, Baseline Books, 1993); and Brian Brivati and Harriet Jones (eds), *From Reconstruction to Integration: Britain and Europe Since 1945* (Leicester, Leicester University Press, 1993). For a volume full of pungent opinion and stimulation see Giles Radice, *Offshore Britain and the European Idea* (London, I.B. Tauris and Co. Ltd, 1992). A recent and useful appraisal of the British involvement with federalism has been provided by Michael Burgess, *The British Tradition of Federalism* (Leicester, Leicester University Press, 1995).

3 See [Lionel Curtis], 'Untempered Mortar: The Case for Organic Union', *The Round Table* (March 1948), pp. 524–34. For the authorship of this and the following article see John Kendle, *The Round Table Movement and Imperial Union* (Toronto, University of Toronto Press, 1975), pp. 297–300.

4 See [Lord Altrincham], 'Britain's Role in the World Today: A Criticism of the Federal Case', *The Round Table* (March 1948), pp. 535–44.

5 The debate over the federal idea continued in the next two issues of *The Round Table*. See 'British Commonwealth and Western Union', *The Round Table* (June 1948), pp. 633–42; and [Lionel Curtis], 'A Debate Continued', *The Round Table* (September 1948), pp. 749–61.

6 See *The Times*, 4 May 1950.

7 See 'Closer Union in Africa: The European Pattern', 31/1/51, DO 35/3592.

8 Kenneth C. Wheare, 'Federalism and the Making of Nations' in Arthur W. Macmahan (ed.), *Federalism: Mature and Emergent* (Garden City, New York, Doubleday and Company, Inc., 1955), pp. 28–43.

9 Membership in the European Communities was debated in 1967 on 8, 9 and 10 May. See 5 Hansard (H of C), vol. 746, 8 May 1967, cols 1061–1184; 9 May 1967, cols 1281–1414; 10 May, cols 1504–1655. A debate was held in October 1971 on the government's decision of principle to join the European Communities. See 5 Hansard (H of C), vol. 823, 21 October 1971, cols 912 ff. for the start of the debate. The European Communities Bill was presented and given first reading on 21 January 1972; second reading began on 15 February 1972 and ended 5 July 1972; third reading took place on 13 July 1972 and royal assent was granted on 17 October 1972. For Raphael Tuck's comment see 5 Hansard (H of C), vol. 831, 17 February 1972, col. 721.

10 See 5 Hansard (H of C), vol. 905, 18 February 1976, col. 739.

11 For an early comment on the assertion that 'interdependence today is a much commoner experience than independence' see Max Beloff, 'International Integration and the Modern State', *Journal of Common Market Studies*, vol. 2, no. 1 (October 1963), pp. 52–62. For Beloff's arguments regarding Europe and federalism generally see Max Beloff, *An Historian in the Twentieth Century: Chapters in Intellectual Autobiography* (New Haven and London, Yale University Press, 1992). For valuable discussions of the United Kingdom's relationship with Europe since World War II see A.J. Nicholls, 'Britain and the EC: The Historical Background' in Simon Bulmer, Stephen George and Andrew Scott (eds), *The United Kingdom and EC Membership Evaluated* (New York, St

Martin's Press, 1992), pp. 3–9; Christopher Lord, 'Sovereign or Confused? The "Great Debate" about British Entry to the European Community 20 Years On', *Journal of Common Market Studies*, vol. 30, no. 4 (December 1992), pp. 419–36; and Derek Hearl, 'Britain and Europe Since 1945', *Parliamentary Affairs*, vol. 47, no. 4 (October 1994), pp. 515–29.

12 See John Pinder and Roy Pryce, *Europe After de Gaulle: Towards the United States of Europe* (London, Penguin Books, 1969); John Lambert, *Britain in a Federal Europe* (London, Chatto and Windus, 1968); and William Pickles, 'The Bourbons of Europe', *Journal of Common Market Studies*, vol. 9, no. 2 (December 1970), pp. 175–83.

13 For an excellent elaboration of these points see Philip Allott, 'Britain and Europe: A Political Analysis', *Journal of Common Market Studies*, vol. 13, no. 3 (March 1975), pp. 203–23.

14 See Donald Shell, 'The British Constitution 1991–2', *Parliamentary Affairs*, vol. 46, no. 1 (January 1993), pp. 1–16. There has been much academic and journalistic comment in recent years as the United Kingdom government has struggled with the implications of the Maastricht treaty and as John Major has had to deal with the Eurosceptics in his party. For a flavour of the varying commentary see Andrew Phillips, 'Britain Sleepwalks into the New Europe', *The Times*, 9 December 1990; Robin Smyth and Dick Leonard, 'Hello Major, Goodbye Euro-ghost', *The Times*, 9 December 1990; 'A Blueprint for Europe: When the Dreaming has to Stop', *The Economist*, 15 December 1990; Conor Cruise O'Brien, 'Pursuing a Chimera: Nationalism at Odds with the Idea of a Federal Europe', *Times Literary Supplement*, 13 March 1992; Lord Beloff, 'A Country Stuck on a Continental Shelf', *The Times*, 4 July 1994; 'Tory Rebels Form European Alliance against Federalism', *The Times*, 7 September 1994; Andrew Roberts, '1945 and All That', *The Spectator*, 11 February 1995; David Baker, Imogen Fountain, Andrew Gamble and Steve Ludlam, 'Backbench Conservative Attitudes to European Integration', *Political Quarterly*, vol. 66, no. 2 (April–June 1995), pp. 221–33. The January–March 1995 issue of *Political Quarterly* is devoted to reviewing and assessing Britain's relationship to Europe on the eve of the 1996 Inter-governmental Conference (IGC). For John Pinder's continuing affirmation of both a federal and a larger European Community see John Pinder, *The Federal Case* (London, European Movement, 1991); John Pinder, *European Community: The Building of a Union* (Oxford, Oxford University Press, 1991); John Pinder, 'The Future of the European Community: A Strategy for Enlargement', *Government and Opposition*, vol. 27, no. 4 (Autumn 1992), pp. 414–32; and John Pinder, 'The New European Federalism: The Idea and the Achievements' in Michael Burgess and Alain-G. Gagnon (eds), *Comparative Federalism and Federation: Competing Traditions and Future Directions* (Toronto, University of Toronto Press, 1993), pp. 45–66.

15 See Michael Keating and Barry Jones, 'Scotland and Wales: Peripheral Assertion and European Integration', *Parliamentary Affairs*, vol. 44, no. 3 (July 1991), pp. 311–24. In an earlier article, Keating had pointed out that 'The most radical form of regionalizing the state would be federalism and, while this was advocated by the Liberal Party, *The Scotsman* and, for a time, *The Economist*, the proposals were vague, particularly on responsibility for economic policy and finance. The main problem with federalism, however, is that it would strike at the heart of the Westminster regime, since federalism implies limits on the power of central government and an abridgment of parliamentary sovereignty. No government and neither of the main parties was prepared to countenance this and there was, in any case, no popular constituency, except perhaps in Scotland, for such radical change.' See Michael Keating, 'Regionalism, Devolution and the State 1969–1989' in Patricia L. Garside and Michael

Hibbert (eds), *British Regionalism 1900–2000* (London, Mansell, 1989), pp. 158–72. Bernard Crick offers some perceptive comments on the theory of parliamentary sovereignty in 'The English and the British' in Bernard Crick (ed.), *National Identities: The Constitution of the United Kingdom* (Oxford, Blackwell Publishers, 1991), pp. 90–104; as does David Marquand in 'The Twilight of the British State? Henry Dubb Versus Sceptred Awe', *Political Quarterly*, vol. 64, no. 2 (April–June 1993), pp. 210–21.

16 There are a number of articles and books now available on the development of nationalist institutions and attitudes in Wales and Scotland. The following are both useful and representative: Vernon Bogdanor, *Devolution* (Oxford, Oxford University Press, 1979); Jack Brand, *The National Movement in Scotland* (London, Routledge and Kegan Paul, 1978); Andrew Marr, *The Battle for Scotland* (London, Penguin Books, 1992); David McCrone, *Understanding Scotland: The Sociology of a Stateless Nation* (London, Routledge, 1992); Robert McCreadie, 'Scottish Identity and the Constitution' in Crick (ed.), *National Identities*, pp. 38–56; Richard J. Finlay, 'Pressure Group or Political Party? The Nationalist Impact on Scottish Politics, 1928–1945', *Twentieth Century British History*, vol. 3, no. 3 (1992), pp. 274–97; J. Graham Jones, 'Early Campaigns to Secure a Secretary of State for Wales 1890–1939', *Transactions of the Honourable Society of Cymmrodorion* (1988), pp. 153–75; J. Graham Jones, 'Socialism, Devolution and a Secretary of State for Wales, 1940–65', ibid. (1989), pp. 135–59; J. Graham Jones, 'The Parliament for Wales Campaign, 1950–1956', *Welsh History Review*, vol. 16, no. 2 (December 1992), pp. 207–36; and Dafydd Elis Thomas, 'The Constitution of Wales' in Crick (ed.), *National Identities*, pp. 57–67.

17 See 'Scotland's Case for Devolution', *The Times*, 30 December 1952. For the brief debate on the Government of Wales Bill see 5 Hansard (H of C), vol. 537, 4 March 1955, cols 2439–538.

18 See *The Times*, 4 November 1967.

19 See 'A Celtic Dawn', *The Times*, 24 November 1967. Professor Thomas Wilson of the Department of Political Economy, University of Glasgow, pointed out that to respond effectively to Scottish and Welsh nationalism, to relieve the parliamentary burden and to make responsible government more effective would mean the adoption of home rule all round. See Thomas Wilson, 'Constitutional Implications of Home Rule All Round', *The Times*, 16 November 1967. By February 1968 *The Times* was underlining the need for an assessment of the financial implications of a 'federal' solution whether in the form of devolution or greater home rule. It was particularly concerned about possible variations in social services among the various parts of the 'federation'. See 'The Case for Home Rule', *The Times*, 7 February 1968.

20 See 5 Hansard (H of C), vol. 759, 21 February 1968, cols 432–5. Also *The Times*, 22 February 1968.

21 For a synopsis of the report see *The Times*, 19 April 1968.

22 See 'Regions and Nations', *The Times*, 19 April 1968.

23 See J.C. Banks, *Federal Britain? The Case for Regionalism* (London, George C. Harrap and Co. Ltd, 1971); and J.P. Mackintosh, *The Devolution of Power: Local Democracy, Regionalism and Nationalism* (Harmondsworth, Penguin Books Ltd, 1968).

24 For an example of Steel's thinking see David Steel, 'Federalism' in Neil MacCormick (ed.), *The Scottish Debate: Essays in Scottish Nationalism* (London, Oxford University Press, 1970), pp. 80–88.

25 See Cmnd. 5460, *Royal Commission on the Constitution 1969–1973*, vol. 1, *Report* (London, HMSO, 1973).

26 Cmnd. 5460–I, *Royal Commission on the Constitution 1969–1973*, vol. 2,

Memorandum of Dissent by Lord Crowther-Hunt and Professor A.T. Peacock (London, HMSO, 1973), p. 132.

27 See *Royal Commission on the Constitution*, vol. 1, chapter 13, pp. 152–61.

28 Ibid., pp. 486–7. The royal commission was often referred to as the Kilbrandon Commission after its chair, Lord Kilbrandon. For the critical reception accorded the Kilbrandon Commission report see John P. Macintosh, 'The Report of the Royal Commission on the Constitution 1969–1973', *Political Quarterly* (January–March 1974), pp. 115–23; Nevil Johnson, 'Editorial: The Royal Commission on the Constitution', *Public Administration*, vol. 52 (Spring 1974), pp. 1–12; Eric M. Barendt, 'The British Constitution: The Kilbrandon Report', *The Round Table* (April 1974), pp. 173–84; Brian Smith, 'Confusions in Regionalism', *Political Quarterly*, vol. 48, no. 1 (January–March 1977), pp. 14–29. For an intriguing but questionable comparison of Kilbrandon and Dicey see D.G. Boyce, 'Dicey, Kilbrandon and Devolution', *Political Quarterly*, vol. 46, no. 3 (July–August 1975), pp. 280–92.

29 For Wilson's remarks see 5 Hansard (H of C), vol. 903, 3 January 1976, cols 214–17.

30 For Callaghan's remarks see 5 Hansard (H of C), vol. 922, 13 December 1976, col. 985.

31 Richard Wainwright (Colne Valley) did point out in the House of Commons on 16 December 1976 that 'the federal solution has been dismissed only by unsupported assertion and has been brushed aside in the same assertive way as Kilbrandon brushed it aside, without arguing the case and without facing up particularly to the manifest success of a federal structure in West Germany', but Wainwright's was a lone unheeded voice. See 5 Hansard (H of C), vol. 922, 16 December 1976, col. 1797.

32 See Bernard Burrows and Geoffrey Denton, *Devolution or Federalism? Options for the United Kingdom* (London, The Macmillan Press Ltd, 1980).

33 See Michael Keating and Barry Jones, 'Scotland and Wales: Peripheral Assertion and European Integration', *Parliamentary Affairs*, vol. 44, no. 3 (July 1991), pp. 311–24; also Vernon Bogdanor, 'The English Constitution and Devolution', *Political Quarterly*, vol. 50, no. 1 (January–March 1979), pp. 36–49.

34 One writer, Bernard Crick, seemed prepared to consider the federal idea as a solution to pressing United Kingdom problems and as a step away from a time-worn, outdated constitutional system. See Bernard Crick, 'The English and the British' in Crick (ed.), *National Identities*, pp. 90–104. For some examples of the most recent academic discussions see Chris Moore, 'Regional Government in the United Kingdom: Proposal and Prospects', *Regional Politics and Policy*, vol. 1, no. 3 (Autumn 1991), pp. 223–41; James Cornford, 'On Writing a Constitution', *Parliamentary Affairs*, vol. 44, no. 4 (October 1991), pp. 558–71; Ian Loveland, 'Labour and the Constitution: The "Right" Approach to Reform?', *Parliamentary Affairs*, vol. 45, no. 2 (April 1992), pp. 173–87; Martin Burch and Ian Holliday, 'The Conservative Party and Constitutional Reform: The Case of Devolution', *Parliamentary Affairs*, vol. 45, no. 3 (July 1992), pp. 386–98; and Jack Brand, 'Scotland and the Politics of Devolution: A Patchy Past and Hazy Future', *Parliamentary Affairs*, vol. 46, no. 1 (January 1993), pp. 38–48. For the various party proposals re Scottish devolution see Arthur Leathley, 'Battle of Britain Begins over Rival Plans for Scotland', *The Times*, 1 December 1995.

Index